GROWING IN CHARACTER

Carl Simmons

Group

Loveland, Colorado

group.com

Group resources actually work!

This Group resource incorporates our R.E.A.L. approach to ministry. It reinforces a growing friendship with Jesus, encourages long-term learning, and results in life transformation, because it's

Relational
Learner-to-learner interaction enhances learning and builds Christian friendships.

Experiential
What learners experience through discussion and action sticks with them up to 9 times longer than what they simply hear or read.

Applicable
The aim of Christian education is to equip learners to be both hearers and doers of God's Word.

Learner-based
Learners understand and retain more when the learning process takes into consideration how they learn best.

SEASON TWO

Growing Out: From Disciples To Disciplers

GROWING IN CHARACTER

Visit our website: **group.com**

Credits

Senior Editor: Candace McMahan
Executive Editor: Rebecca L. Manni
Chief Creative Officer: Joani Schultz
Copy Editor: Nancy Friscia
Art Director: Paul Povolni

Cover Designer: Holly Voget
Book Designer: Jean Bruns
Illustrator: Wes Comer
Print Production: Paragon Prepress
Production Manager: Peggy Naylor

Unless otherwise indicated, all Scripture quotations are taken from the *Holy Bible,* New Living Translation, copyright © 1996, 2004. Used by permission of Tyndale House Publishers, Inc., Carol Stream, Illinois 60188. All rights reserved.

ISBN 978-0-7644-3923-0

10 9 8 7 6 5 4 3 2 1   19 18 17 16 15 14 13 12 11 10

Printed in the United States of America.

Contents

What *Growing Out* Looks Like 5

Why R.E.A.L Discipleship Works. 7

About the Sessions 11

Choose Your Environment 15

Getting Connected 18

SESSION 1: Following Jesus Where You Already Are 19

SESSION 2: Loving and Honoring Your Spouse 29

SESSION 3: Loving and Growing Your Children 41

SESSION 4: How to Lead Without Being the Boss 55

SESSION 5: Temper, Temper 67

SESSION 6: Address Your Stress 81

SESSION 7: For the Love of Money 93

SESSION 8: Following Jesus to Work 105

SESSION 9: The Heart of Hospitality 117

SESSION 10: Loving What's *Really* Good 131

SESSION 11: The D-Word *(Discipline)* 143

SESSION 12: Standing in the Truth 157

SESSION 13: Merge With Care 169

Leader Notes 179

What *Growing Out* Looks Like

Growing Out is more than a series of Bible studies—it's a progression that will take you and your group from becoming disciples of Jesus to becoming discipl*ers* of *others* in Jesus. As you move through each season, you'll grow from the inside out—and as you grow, your life in Jesus will naturally expand and branch out to others in your world.

And here's the best part: As you grow out together, you'll realize how much you're *already* discipling others—starting with those in your group!

Growing Out is designed to allow you to jump in at the most appropriate place for you and your group. To help you discover your entry point, take a look at these descriptions of each season:

Season 1: Growing in Jesus focuses on developing your relationship with Jesus. Because, let's face it, the first person you have to disciple is *yourself.* More to the point, you need to learn how to let Jesus *show* you how to be his disciple. So in this season, we focus on your relationship with Jesus and how to deepen it through spiritual disciplines such as prayer, worship, Bible study…and, not least of all, through your relationships with other Christians (such as the ones you're sitting with).

After you've been grounded in your relationship with Jesus, how does that shine into the rest of your life? That's where *Season 2: Growing in Character* comes in. This season focuses on how you can invite Jesus into your most important relationships—with your family, your friends, and the people you work with—and how to keep Jesus at the center of all of them.

Season 3: Growing in Your Gifts focuses on discovering the gifts, talents, and passions God has given you and how God might want to use them to serve others—whether that's inside or outside your church walls. After this season, you'll have a better sense of who God has created you to be, and why.

And with that, you're ready for *Season 4: Growing Others.* If you've gotten this far, you've developed and deepened your walk with Jesus, you've learned how to actually live it out among those people you most care about, and you've begun to discover how God has uniquely built you. Now…how do you take what God has shown you and help *others* walk through the same process?

If you've completed Seasons 1 through 3, you already know the answer because that's *exactly* what you've been doing with your group. Season 4 will help you reach out to even more people. Call it mentoring, discipling, or just being a good Christian friend to someone who needs it, after Season 4 you'll be ready to come along-side anyone who's ready to have a deeper relationship with Jesus. Just as you were in Season 1.

In the final two seasons, you'll explore what it takes to lead others where God wants you *and* them to go next. Because as you've walked through the first four seasons, guess what? You've been growing. Others know it. And God is honoring it. So whether you see yourself that way or not, God has matured you to the point where you're ready to lead. And we're going to help you get *more* ready.

Season 5: Growing in Leadership focuses on how to stay functional even as you learn how to lead. You'll walk together through the challenges of leadership—communication, conflict resolution, building consensus, learning how to adjust your ministry, and learning to stay focused on God instead of *"your* ministry."

And as you keep growing out, God may well put things on your heart that you'll need to be the one to initiate. That brings us, at last, to *Season 6: Growing in Your Mission.* God has given you a specific vision for ministry, and now you literally need to make the dream real. We'll help walk you through the issues that come with a God-given vision. Things like, first of all, how do you know it really *is* God and not just you? How do you get others on board (and praying—a *lot*)? And how will *you* keep growing, even as the vision continues to grow and take shape?

Because, no matter where you are, you never stop *Growing Out*. God will always see to that.

Enjoy *Growing Out,* and may God bless you as you grow out together!

Why R.E.A.L. Discipleship Works

Before we go any further, go back and take one more look at the copyright page of this book (it's page 2—the one with all the credits). Go to the top of the page where it declares, "Group resources actually work!" Take a minute or two to read that entire section describing Group's R.E.A.L. guarantee, and then come back to this introduction. I'll wait for you here...

Now that we're literally back on the same page, let's explore R.E.A.L. a little more deeply. Your desire to go deeper is the reason you're reading this book, and it's not only our goal but also our *passion* to help you accomplish that desire. When it comes right down to it, there's nothing more R.E.A.L. than discipleship. Think about it:

Relational

At the heart of it, discipleship *is* relationship. First and foremost, it's about developing the most important relationship you'll ever have— your relationship with Jesus. And as your relationship with Jesus grows, it becomes far more than anything you've ever imagined.

Like any great relationship, it doesn't develop on its own. It's intentional. It's work. But it's way more than that. What we get back is far more than what we put in. How could it *not* be? It's a relationship with *Jesus.* And as that relationship grows, we'll want to bring Jesus into every other relationship we have.

So we've kept that in mind as we've designed these sessions. You'll gain a deeper understanding of God's Word, but even more important, you'll discover how to share what you've learned with those around you. And that discovery *has* to happen in community. We've made these sessions very relational because, after all, you're learning how to become discipl*ers*. By definition, that means learning how to speak God into others' lives. As you do that, you'll get as much back as you give, if not more. Because that's what happens in great relationships.

You'll notice that we often suggest getting into pairs or smaller groups. That's because participation—and learning, not to mention life change—increases when everyone's involved. It's more challenging, sure, but it's also more rewarding. Be sure to take advantage of the times we suggest it.

All this is a long way of saying that by the time you've finished this season, you'll not only have a deeper relationship with Jesus, but your spiritual relationships with others will be richer and deeper than you had ever anticipated. And when that happens, be sure to thank us; a little affirmation goes a long way toward helping us to keep doing what we do here.

Experiential

Experiences? Yeah, we've got experiences. And as you discover together where God wants to take you next, you'll have experiences of your own long after you've completed these sessions.

Research has proven again and again that the more senses we engage in the learning process, the more likely a session is to stick and truly become woven into our daily lives. Jesus knew that, too. That's why he used everyday items to make his message more real. Not only that, but he invited people out of their comfort zones to conquer their fear of the unknown. We like to do that, too. A lot.

And because it's so different from what we're used to when studying God's Word, this is often the hardest part of R.E.A.L. learning for people to embrace. Is it *really* OK to have fun when we're studying the Bible? Does it truly honor God? Wouldn't it distract us from focusing on God?

First, let's make it clear that these are legitimate concerns. I've wrestled with all of them as I've developed these sessions. We want to honor Jesus. Discipleship isn't a joke. It's serious business. It's about the rest of your life and how you'll glorify God with it. There's nothing more serious than that.

Nonetheless, sometimes the best way to get serious is to set aside our expectations first, so we're able to open up and get down to what we're *really* wrestling with, rather than just come up with the right answers, go home, and never really deal with the things God wants us to deal with. The experiences in this book go a long way toward accomplishing that. Here are just a few of the ways people "got R.E.A.L." as we field-tested this curriculum:

- A church elder in our group declared from the beginning, in no uncertain terms and with a bit of a growl, "I don't *do* games." A few weeks in, he shared, "This is exactly what [my wife and I] needed right now." Several weeks later, this same game-hating elder proclaimed, "I really *liked* that activity! It worked *perfectly!*"

- One of our hosts, who also prepared the session's snack, suggested, "I'll make sure I pull it out of the oven just when everyone gets here." She understood that not only the look and taste of the snack but also the smell would help people experience the session more acutely.

- A pastor in our group enjoyed one particular activity so much that he went ahead and used it in his own church's small-group training class.

- Another woman shared how her husband had been initially skeptical about R.E.A.L. learning and about small groups in general. (Anyone else detecting a pattern among the men, by the way?) Several sessions later, she was positively glowing as she shared how we'd "broken through" and how much he'd opened up as we'd gone along—and for that matter, how he was still talking about the session the next morning.

Discipleship *is* a lifelong adventure. And we're here to help you embrace that adventure. Together. That's why we've not only built in activities to get you thinking about your faith (and expressing it) in brand-new ways, but...well, let's just move on to...

Applicable

This is pretty straightforward. You're here not only to learn but also to grow. And that means taking what you've learned and using it.

We give you opportunities in every session to do that—to give you a safe place to experiment, if you will. We also provide opportunities at the end of each session for you to take what you've learned and "Walk It Out" in the rest of your life—so that your faith *becomes* your life, and you can take practical steps toward sharing your life in Jesus so others can see and respond to it as well.

Learner-Based

For some of you, the Bible passages and ideas you're studying may be familiar. But as you explore them in fresh ways in these sessions, you'll experience and understand God's Word in ways you've never considered before. We're studying God's living Word, after all. So we want to help you not only learn brand-new things but also find new significance and meaning in familiar and taken-for-granted ideas.

Therefore, we've been very deliberate about choosing the right approaches for the right sessions. When an activity works, let's get up and do it. If a movie clip brings out the meaning of what you're learning, throw in the DVD and let's talk. If a snack not only works as an icebreaker but also as a discussion starter about a much deeper subject, let's serve it up and dig in. And when it's time to just open up God's Word and really wrap our minds around what God wants us to understand about a given subject—or to be reminded of what God has already shown us (because we forget that all too easily, too)—then we'll bust out our Bibles and read as many passages as it takes to begin to grasp (or re-grasp) that.

You're also here to discover who *you* are in Jesus. The body of Christ is made of millions of unique parts. You're one of them. We *know* one size doesn't fit all, and we've built *Growing Out* to reflect that. So whatever reaches you best—the Bible study, the activities, the questions, the take-home pieces, whatever—use them to their fullest extent. I'll give you some more ideas of how to do this in the next two sections.

However you approach these sessions—and whether you do that as a leader or as a participant—be sure to help others in your group approach things in the ways God can best reach them. And as God works in all of you, celebrate it. A lot.

May God bless you as you begin your journey together. And as God takes each of you to the places and experiences he has prepared for you, never forget: You're all in this together. You, God, and everyone he puts in your path. And *that's* discipleship.

—*Carl Simmons*

About the Sessions

Now that you know why we do what we do, let's talk about *how* we do it—and more important—how *you* can do it.

You may already understand this, but just so we're clear: Discipleship is *not* about completing a curriculum. It's about developing and deepening the most important spiritual relationships you have—first with God, then with those God brings you in contact with— because *none* of those relationships is an accident. They're all intentional, and we need to be intentional as well.

In fact, that's why we refer to each study as a season, rather than as a study, book, or quarter. Each of us grows at our own pace. Your season of growth might be longer or shorter than someone else's, and that's OK. God will take as long as you need to get you where he wants you. So spend as much time in each season as you need to. But stay committed to moving forward.

Also, each season has been built so that whether you're a participant or a leader, you can get the most out of each session. And that starts with the layout of each lesson. Keep a finger here, flip over to one of the sessions, and let's look at why this is so different.

This isn't just a leader guide. It's not just a guide for group members. It's *both!* And the way we've set up the sessions reflects that.

Leaders: The left-hand pages contain *your* instructions, so you're constantly on track and know what's happening next. What you do, what you say—all the basics are there. You'll also want to be sure to check out the "Leader Notes" beginning on page 179—they'll give you specific prep instructions for each session as well as great tips to make each session the best it can be.

Group Members: You don't care about all that leader stuff, do you? Didn't think so. Now you don't need to. The right-hand pages are just for you. Write your answers, journal whatever else God is saying to you, record insights from your group discussions, doodle while you listen—you've got plenty of room for all of it. All the questions and Bible passages you'll be using are right there. Use your pages to get the most out of what God is showing you each week.

Got all that? Good. Now let's talk about what each session looks like.

Come and See

In this (usually) brief opening section, you'll take time to unwind and transition from wherever you're coming from—a hectic drive to church on a Sunday morning or the end of a busy day—into the theme of the session. You and your group might enjoy a snack or a movie clip together; maybe it'll be an activity; maybe you'll just talk with someone else. Then you'll be ready to dig in deep. And maybe—because you were too busy having such a good time doing it—you won't even realize that you've already gotten down to business.

Seek and Find

This is the heart of each session, and usually the longest section. You'll spend roughly a half-hour digging into God's Word and discovering its meaning in a way you hadn't realized before. You think you understand these things now? Just *wait*. Through a variety of experiences and powerful questions that take a fresh look both at Scripture and at what's going on in your own head and heart, you'll discover how God's Word *really* applies to your life.

Go

Now you'll move from understanding how what you've been studying applies to your life to considering ways to act on it. Again, through meaningful experiences and questions, you'll discover what you can do with what God has shown you through today's session. Which will take you directly into...

Walk It Out

This is the take-home part of the session. With a partner or partners, you'll each choose a weekly challenge to apply this session to your life in practical ways in the coming week and beyond.

We've broken out the challenges very specifically, to meet you wherever you are:

know it Some of you are visual learners—you get it by reading it. Others of you just don't feel comfortable being "outward" in your faith yet. This section's for you. We'll give you ways to reflect on God's Word, internalize it, and ultimately start sharing it in ways you might not have considered before.

live it This suggestion is usually for the more reflective among you. You want to share what God is doing, but you need to process what God is doing in *you* before you can share it with anyone else. The ideas here will help you do just that.

share it You're already a relational person, and God built you that way. Therefore, you're ready to share Jesus with someone else in a meaningful way. So here's a way to do it. Now go make it happen!

go for it You're probably a more creative or kinesthetic type. You not only want to share your faith, but you also want to do something a little more out-of-the-box. We've got just the thing for you. And here's where you'll find it.

do it together Here's something you can do together as a group. It might be an outreach event, a retreat suggestion, or just a great idea for a get-together outside of your session time. Every so often, try one of these as a group, and see what God does with it.

By the way, if God has really spoken to you about something else during a session and you know you need to do whatever he's urging you to do, don't feel you have to choose from the ideas we've provided. Be obedient. Share what God is showing you with your group so they can pray for you and encourage you.

There's one more section to tell you about. It appears at the very end. It's not even part of the session per se, but it could end up meaning a lot to you.

Go Deeper

I can't emphasize this enough, so I'm repeating it: Discipleship is *not* about completing a curriculum. It's about developing and deepening the most important spiritual relationships you have—first with God, then with those God has brought you in contact with—because *none* of those relationships is an accident.

Therefore, it's possible you'll work through this season and think, Before I go any further, I *really* need a deeper understanding of... That's why I've provided a list of resources at the end of each session to help you do just that. At Group, we're not shy about recommending other publishers—and if a resource applies to more than one area of spiritual growth, we'll recommend it more than once. This isn't about selling Group products (although there's always much more dancing in the halls here when that happens). It's about your growing relationship with Jesus, and about being willing to invite God into whatever you're still wrestling with.

And that painful thing you're feeling when you do that? That's called growth. But the good news is: We're in this together. So pull over whenever you need to! Or jump right into the next season. We're here for you either way.

Which brings us to a little reminder at the very end of each session: If there's an area in which you'd like to see *us* dig deeper and create more resources to help *you,* tell us! Write to us at Group Publishing, Inc., P.O. Box 481, Loveland, CO 80539; or contact us via e-mail at smallgroupministry.com. We'd love to hear what you're thinking. (Yes—*really!*)

Choose Your Environment

Growing Out works well in a variety of venues. We want to help you wherever you are. Don't be shy about trying any of them! Here are some additional ideas, depending on your venue.

Sunday School

First, you may have noticed that I've chosen the word *group* instead of *class* throughout. Not every group is a class, but every class is a group. You're not here just to study and learn facts—you're also here to learn how to live out what you've learned. Together. As a group. We hope that becomes even truer as you work through these sessions.

We've constructed these sessions to run an hour at a brisk pace, but we understand the limitations a Sunday school program can put on the amount of time you spend on a session. So if a great question has started a great discussion and you don't want to cut it off, feel free to trim back elsewhere as needed. For example, since much of our field test group was made up of couples who could talk on the way home, we discovered that making "Walk It Out" a take-home instead of an in-class piece was one good way to buy back time without losing impact.

Try not to be one of those groups that say, "Great—we can skip that experience now!" Remember, the more senses and learning styles you engage, the more these sessions will stick. So play with these activities. Give yourself permission to fail—but go in expecting God to do the unexpected.

And if you don't have specific time limitations, read on.

Small Groups

If you need more than an hour for a session—and you're not tied to a clock or a calendar—take it! Again, taking the time to understand what God wants to tell your group is *way* more important than "covering the material" or staying within the one-hour or 13-week parameters. This happened repeatedly while field-testing—a great discussion ensued, people got down to things they were really wrestling with, and we decided we'd explore the session further the following week.

Learn to recognize rabbit trails—and get off them sooner rather than later—but don't short-circuit those occasions when the Holy Spirit is really working in people's lives. Those occasions will happen often in these sessions. If you're having a rich discussion and are really digging in, take an extra week and dig even deeper. Give the full meaning of the session time to sink in.

One-on-One Discipleship

Although this curriculum is designed for a larger group setting, we absolutely don't want to discourage you from using it in a more traditional, one-on-one discipleship setting. True, some of the activities might not work in a setting this small, and if that's the case, feel free to bypass them and go directly into the Bible passages and questions—there are plenty left to work with. The important thing is that you work together through the issues themselves, and at the pace you need to move forward.

But don't take this as an opportunity to entirely excuse yourselves from experiences—have a little fun together, and see what God does. Allow yourselves to be surprised.

Also—and it's probably obvious for this and the next scenario—all those recommendations we make to form smaller groups or twosomes? You can skip those and jump right into the discussion or activity.

Smaller Groups or Accountability Groups

One more thing: We don't want to discourage you from doing one-on-one discipleship, especially if you've already got a good thing going. There are some great and healthy mentoring relationships out there, and if you're already involved in one, keep at it! That said, research has shown repeatedly that learning can happen at a more accelerated rate—and more profoundly—in settings other than the traditional teacher-student relationship. So if you're just starting out, consider gathering in groups of three or four.

- It's an environment that allows everyone to learn from one another. While there's often still a clear leader, the playing field feels more level, and the conversations often become more open and honest.

- If one person leaves for any reason—and there are plenty of legiti-mate ones—the group or accountability relationship isn't finished. Everyone else presses forward. No one is left hanging.

- The dynamics of a group of three or four are simpler than those of larger groups. And a group of three or four can be the best of both worlds, offering the rich discussions of a large group and the intimacy and accountability of one-on-one relationships.

- Again, we're about creating disciplers, and a smaller group allows growing disciplers to test-drive their own instructions, struggles, and transparency in an environment in which they can be both honestly critiqued and wholeheartedly encouraged. And when that happens, growth happens—for everyone.

If you'd like to delve into this further, Greg Ogden's *Transforming Discipleship* (InterVarsity) is a great resource to get you started, as are any number of materials from ChurchSmart Resources (churchsmart.com).

Whatever setting or environment you use for *Growing Out,* use it to its fullest. May God bless your efforts and those of the people with whom you share life!

Getting Connected

Pass your books around the room, and have people write their names, phone numbers, e-mail addresses, and birthdays in the spaces provided. Then make it a point to stay in touch during the week.

name	phone	e-mail	birthday

Following Jesus Where You Already Are

"An elder must live a blameless life" (TITUS 1:6A).

"You are the salt of the earth. But what good is salt if it has lost its flavor? Can you make it salty again? It will be thrown out and trampled underfoot as worthless. You are the light of the world—like a city on a hilltop that cannot be hidden. No one lights a lamp and then puts it under a basket. Instead, a lamp is placed on a stand, where it gives light to everyone in the house. In the same way, let your good deeds shine out for all to see, so that everyone will praise your heavenly Father" (MATTHEW 5:13-16).

In this session, we'll journey...

Salt loses a flavor, light must shine!

from ⟶ **to**
examining our current roles in life... | discovering how we can live a "blameless" and "flavorful" life wherever we are.

Before gathering, make sure you have...

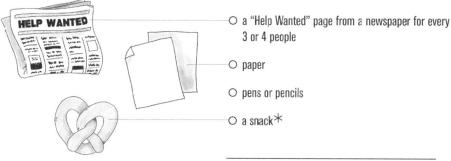

HELP WANTED

○ a "Help Wanted" page from a newspaper for every 3 or 4 people

○ paper

○ pens or pencils

○ a snack⁎

⁎See **Leader Notes**, page 181, for details.

Come and See

(about 15 minutes)

Before starting this first session, have people pass their books around the room, and have each person write his or her name, phone number, and e-mail address in the space provided on page 18.

Form groups of three or four. Encourage people to get with others they don't know well. If this is the group's first time together, have people take a few moments to introduce themselves.

Give each group a page from the "Help Wanted" section. Then look through the ads together, and discuss these questions: ———→

Give groups about five minutes to share, and then call everyone back together. Share highlights and insights from your group discussion.

We must learn of [Jesus'] positive interactions and involvements with us in the concrete occasions of our day-to-day activities. When we act 'in his name,' we act on his behalf, and he always involves himself in the process.

—Dallas Willard, The Great Omission

》 Our focus this season is going to be on our job descriptions as Christians. We come from different walks of life and play a variety of roles, but there's a certain character Jesus wants to develop in each of us. This character shows the rest of the world that we have a living relationship with Jesus that affects every part of our lives.

Jesus has already changed our lives—and he wants us to become even more like him. He wants to start in the places we already occupy: in our homes, in our workplaces, and in our relationships. So let's begin to dig deeper into how Jesus can change us where we are right now.

◉ What are some of the more interesting jobs advertised? For which jobs do you meet some or all of the requirements?

◉ What's the most interesting or unique job you've ever had? Explain.

Seek and Find

(about 25 minutes)

Give everyone a sheet of paper and a pen or pencil.

» **Before we can talk about where we're headed, we need to understand where we already are. Write down some of the roles you play in life. For example, you're playing the role of a student or group member right now. You also play roles in your family, at work, and with your friends. List at least five roles you play, but no more than 10.**

Allow two minutes for everyone to write, and then regain their attention. Discuss this question:

» **Let's take a look at God's Word and at a different kind of job description. This passage, by the way, is going to be the framework for our entire study.**

Ask for a volunteer to read Titus 1:5-9.

» **OK, truthfully: How many of you just thought, What does this have to do with me? This passage is about *leaders*? Raise your hands if that's what you were thinking.**

After people have responded, discuss these questions:

» **Some of the qualities listed in this passage may come easily to us. About others we can honestly say, "God has dealt with me in this area, and I'm doing better." Still others might be a continuing struggle. But it's important to come to terms with where we are right now—even if it's not where we'd like to be—and how God wants to inject his grace into our situation, whatever it is.**

Here's the good news: The fact that we're together right now, desiring to learn more about what God wants, proves that God is already helping us become the kind of people God wants us to be. And God is not going to give up on us, even if we sometimes give up on ourselves. We'll be spending the next few months discovering the great things God has in store for each of us.

Seek and Find

◎ Review your lists. How can some of these roles sometimes feel like just roles—something you're just acting out—instead of something that reflects who you really are?

† **Titus 1:5-9**

◎ Is there anything in this passage that doesn't seem relevant to every follower of Jesus? If so, what?

◎ Which of the qualities listed in this passage has God already helped you with? Talk a little about that.

◎ Are there any qualities in this passage that seem impossible for you to attain? Explain.

Go

(about 15 minutes)

>> **We're almost finished with this first session, so let's share a snack as we continue our discussion. Take a handful, and pass the snack to the next person.**

Pass the snack around, and as it's going around the room, have a volunteer read Matthew 5:13-16. Discuss these questions: ⟶

> 'Ye are the salt.'
> Jesus does not
> say: 'You must
> be the salt.'
> —Dietrich Bonhoeffer,
> The Cost of
> Discipleship

◎ What's wrong with this snack?

 Matthew 5:13–16

◎ In what ways do we Christians sometimes seem bland or unappealing to others, rather than as people who have been "salted" by Jesus?

The looks on our faces, no reflection of joy.

(a salty)

◎ Who's the "saltiest" Christian you know? How do you see that person's life affecting those around him or her?

minister Asharge. She always have a pleasantness (smile) with her. She always is always ready to pray w/ you. I see her dispensing love to her brothers & sisters, encouraging words willing to spending a few moment w/ people.

◎ Jesus says that we're already salt and light. How have you found that to be true in some of your other relationships?

The relationships of people (Christians) God has placed me in a close & personal. These are people who are committed to the word of God. and doing it.

◎ What parts of your life need to be salted more by the life you have in Jesus? What would help you become more "seasoned"?

Taking a bold step towards relatives That I don't have a lot of contact with, going to them to talk about Jesus. especially when I know that are sick. To do it. w/ wisdom!

Walk It Out

(about 5 minutes)

> **》 The following options are here to help you put what you've learned into practice. But if God has prompted you to do something else through this session, then by all means do that!**

choose 1:

know it

Dig into the book of Titus this week. It's only three chapters—read a chapter a day twice over, so it sinks in! As you read, ask God to remind you of what he's already done in your life and what he wants to do next. As God reveals it, start walking it out!

live it

Write down all the ways God has shown—and continues to show—his love to you. As you see examples during the week, write them down, and take time to thank God right then and there for each gift. At the end of the week, read everything you've written, and thank God again. Share what you've learned with someone else.

share it

If you have a friend who's spiritually curious (or at least open), invite him or her to read one of the gospels with you. Ask him or her to record observations and questions as they come up. Use your conversations to point out Jesus' claims and the teachings that make Christianity unique.

Form pairs, select the option you'd like to take on this week, and share your choice with your partner. Write what you plan to do in the space provided, and make plans to connect with your partner before the next session to check in and encourage each other. Take five minutes to do that now.

go for it

Share God's love with someone you don't know. Find a practical way to show compassion to someone in need. Fill a gas tank, buy a hot meal, or just provide a listening ear. Commit to doing something meaningful that requires your intentional time and effort.

✓ do it together

Use real seasoning in your relationships with others—as you share a meal together. Build an entire dinner and setting around the cuisine of your choice. Find music and decorations from the country or region whose food you're enjoying. Then extend invitations, in person when possible, to people both inside and outside your group. Have fun and—more important—grow relationships.

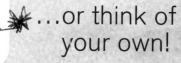 ...or think of your own!

Because I want God to help me in every facet of my life, I'll "Walk It Out" by:

_____

_____

_____

_____

_____

Walk It Out continued

prayer⊙

Come back together. Ask God to give you a deeper appreciation for what he has already done in your lives. Also ask God to reveal how he wants to salt all the people in the group so they'll be able to season others in their households, their friendships, and their places of work.

To dig deeper into understanding Christian character and how to be saltier, check out some great resources:

Quiet Strength Men's Bible Study: Discovering God's Game Plan for a Winning Life by Tony Dungy and Karl Leuthauser (Group)

Christian Character: 12 Studies for Individuals or Groups by Andrea Sterk and Peter Scazzero (InterVarsity)

The Pillars of Christian Character: The Basic Essentials of a Living Faith by John MacArthur (Crossway)

Conjectures of a Guilty Bystander by Thomas Merton (Image)

Salt and Light: Living the Sermon on the Mount by Eberhard Arnold (Plough Publishing House)

Loving and Honoring Your Spouse

"He must be faithful to his wife" (TITUS 1:6).

"As the Scriptures say, 'A man leaves his father and mother and is joined to his wife, and the two are united into one.' This is a great mystery, but it is an illustration of the way Christ and the church are one. So again I say, each man must love his wife as he loves himself, and the wife must respect her husband" (EPHESIANS 5:31-33).

In this session, we'll journey...

from ⟶ **to**

exploring how we do—and don't—give priority to our spouses...

identifying how we can meet our spouses' needs in ways Jesus wants us to.

Before gathering, make sure you have...

○ the same translation of the Bible, for a choral reading you'll do. It might be easier, in fact, to print out an online translation of Ephesians 5:21-33 and hand it out to everyone (The particular translation, of course, is your call.)

○ newsprint tablet, blackboard, or white board (If you're in a small-group setting, a notepad is OK.)

○ 5 coins for each person ✻

○ 1 towel for every 8 to 10 people

✻See **Leader Notes**, page 182, for details.

Come and See

(about 10 minutes)

》 **Let's jump right into the deep end today. Find a partner—someone you're not related to—and discuss these questions together:** ⟶

Allow five minutes, and then get everyone's attention. Ask for volunteers to share highlights from their discussions.

》 **This season we're focusing on how a living relation-ship with Jesus affects every part of our lives. We're going to start with the most important human relation-ship in our lives right now. For many of us, that person is a spouse, and because of the Titus thread that runs through this season, this session will assume that.**

For others of us, though, that's not the case. No matter what your current situation is, the bigger question remains: How do you show the love of Christ to the most important person or people in your life? As we learn to share our lives in Jesus with those people, we begin to understand how to share it with others as well—and our most important relationships become deeper and more intimate as a result. Loving those closest to us the way Jesus loves them is a topic we all need to learn more about.

◎ Who's the most important person in your life, and why? ("Because he or she's my *husband*" isn't an acceptable answer. Share something specific about *why* he or she's so important to you.)

because this is the person God has joint me up in marriage. He's my sefector, He provides, He does many things when I am on this thought when He moving about. He's often telling me He saw something that I may like or want. tells me me to go check it out) He always key to have his family 1st and all circumstances.

◎ As best you can remember, when did you realize that something had changed in your relationship? Was it a dramatic change or did it happen more gradually?

Seek and Find

(about 30 minutes)

Have everyone turn to Ephesians 5:21–33; if you've printed out a specific translation for everyone, pass it out now. Then read the passage aloud as a choral reading, without any breaks between sections, as follows:

> **Everyone:** Read verse 21 together.
>
> **Women only:** Read verses 22–24.
>
> **Men only:** Read verses 25–31.
>
> **Everyone:** Read verses 32–33 together.

Then discuss these questions: ————————————————→

>> **You're going to get a chance to do some submitting right now. For some of you this activity might be very easy; for others, maybe not so much.**
>
> **Pair off again—only this time, partner with your spouse if he or she's here. If not, try to find someone you're comfortable talking to.**

Allow a few moments for everyone to pair up.

>> **The younger person in your pair will go first. Take three minutes to share something you're currently struggling with outside of your marriage. It might be a work situation, a problem with a family member or neighbor, or something you've really been wrestling with God over. Tell your partner what you really think about the situation and, if possible, how he or she could help. If your partner is your spouse or someone**

Seek and Find

 Ephesians 5:21-33

◎ Some form of the word *submit* is used four times in the first four verses. What's your reaction to that word? What personal experiences— positive or negative—does it bring to mind?

◎ Describe a time you submitted to your spouse (or another important person in your life). Why did you choose to do it? How did it affect your relationship?

◎ What's the connection between *submitting* to someone and *loving* someone? How are they different? How does submitting show the other person how important he or she is to you?

Seek and Find continued

you're close to, be sure not to direct any criticism or blame as you describe your situation.

Those of you listening: Do nothing but listen. Don't suggest. Don't commiserate. Don't get defensive. Don't do anything but *listen*.

After three minutes, we'll switch roles. And again, as your partner shares, be quiet and don't interrupt! Even if your partner is not your spouse, this is a good opportunity to talk about something you've been wrestling with—and to practice your listening skills!

Try to give 30 seconds' notice before it's time for each partner to stop talking. Let pairs know when three minutes are up and it's time to switch. After another three minutes, call everyone back together to discuss these questions: ⟶

Write down everyone's suggestions to this third question where all can see. Make a point of acknowledging each person's contribution as you do so.

> " For a marriage relationship to flourish, there must be intimacy. It takes an enormous amount of courage to say to your spouse, 'This is me. I'm not proud of it—in fact, I'm a little embarrassed by it—but this is who I am.'
>
> —Bill Hybels

◎ Which was easier for you: talking or listening? Why?

◎ How do you feel honored when you know someone is really listening to you?

◎ What are some other ways we can honor our spouses or others?

Go

(about 15 minutes)

Give everyone five coins. Gather in a circle, and put a towel in the middle. If you have a large group, form smaller groups of six to eight, and ask someone to lead each smaller group.

>> **Close your eyes and listen as I read the following questions. Don't answer out loud, but for every question to which you answer yes, toss one coin into the center of the circle. Try not to notice how others around you respond. For those of you without a spouse, reflect on the most important person in your life right now as I ask these questions.** (Pause.)

- **Within the past month, was there a time you let your day get so full that you barely had time for your spouse?** (Pause.)

- **Have you recently ignored your spouse—even for a minute— because you were watching television, doing something on the computer, using a cell phone, or texting?** (Pause.)

- **Within the past year, have you let work get in the way of a time the two of you had planned to be together?** (Pause.)

- **Within the past six months, have you let a dispute over children, friends, or activities come between you?** (Pause.)

- **Have you ever let a hobby or other interest consume so much of your time that your spouse felt neglected?** (Pause.)

Open your eyes. And let's talk. ⟶

We're going to do Walk It Out a little differently today. Get back with your spouse (or the person you've partnered with today), and discuss the following options. Those of you talking with your spouses may very well come up with something you can do together. Even if it's not exactly one of the suggested options, that's fine—in fact, it's probably better to come up with something completely specific to your situation. In any case, commit to doing it this week and to keeping each other accountable.

Let's come back together in five minutes for prayer.

◎ What things can you assume from the number of coins in the middle of the circle?

◎ What's one way your spouse (or other important person in your life) *has* shown that you take priority in his or her life? How has that helped you to "return the favor"?

◎ What's your biggest challenge in giving priority to your spouse (or to others)? What's one practical change you could make to overcome that?

Walk It Out

(about 5 minutes)

>> **The following options are here to help you put what you've learned into practice. But if God has prompted you to do something else through this session, then by all means do that!**

choose 1:

☐ **know it**

Reread Ephesians 5:21–33 this week. Also check out 1 Peter 3:1–7. Consider how to honor your spouse (or the person who is most important to you right now) in the ways described in these passages. Ask God to help you turn those ideas into realities.

☐ **live it** Do the following as a couple: Individually, throughout the week, keep a running list of ways your spouse has been there for you. Has he or she helped you do something around the house? done something nice for you? encouraged you or told you he or she loved you? Write it all down. At the end of the week, exchange lists. Thank your spouse for his or her love for you. Together thank God for each other.

☐ **share it** Been married awhile? Take a younger couple under your wing. Listen to their joys, their questions, and their struggles. When it's appropriate, tell them how God has helped you through the challenges you've faced as a couple. Talk about what you wish you'd known a little earlier. Start by sharing a meal together, and consider making a longer-term commitment to helping this couple grow in their marriage and in Jesus.

Form pairs, select the option you'd like to take on this week, and share your choice with your partner. Write what you plan to do in the space provided, and make plans to connect with your partner before the next session to check in and encourage each other. Take five minutes to do that now.

go for it

One of the great tragedies is that not everyone follows the Bible's advice in caring for family. Contact a domestic-abuse organization to see what you can do to support its efforts to fight abuse or to assist a child, teen, or spouse in an abusive situation.

do it together

Men, get together with the other men in the group as women do the same. Take another look at the list you made as a group, and brainstorm ways to do something special for your spouses this week. For example, you might choose to give up your normal Saturday activities to do something that gives priority to your spouse. Or throw a party for your spouses at which you do all the work. After your groups have come up with several ideas, select one to do this week. (Don't tell your spouses what you're planning to do—let it be a surprise!)

...or think of your own!

Because Jesus wants me to give priority to my most important relationships, I'll "Walk It Out" by:

_____

_____

_____

Walk It Out continued

prayer⊙

Get back into your circle(s) from "Go," and have each person take back one coin. Let them keep their coins as reminders to give priority to their spouses this week.

Have everyone reflect silently on their commitments for a minute, and then close in prayer, asking for God's help to make those commitments a reality.

Go Deeper

Find more ways to bring Jesus deeper into your marriage by checking out these great resources:

HomeBuilders Couples Series® (Family Life)

The Five Love Languages: How to Express Heartfelt Commitment to Your Mate by Gary Chapman (Northfield Publishing)

His Needs, Her Needs: Building an Affair-Proof Marriage by Willard F. Harley Jr. (Revell)

Sacred Marriage by Gary Thomas (Zondervan)

Loving and Growing Your Children

...And his children must be believers who don't have a reputation for being wild or rebellious" (TITUS 1:6).

"Fathers, do not provoke your children to anger by the way you treat them. Rather, bring them up with the discipline and instruction that comes from the Lord" (EPHESIANS 6:4).

In this session, we'll journey...

from ⟶ **to**
exploring our relationships with our children...

identifying ways we can truly model Jesus to them.

Before gathering, make sure you have...

Optional activities (choose one or both):

Option A:

○ a variety of items that could have symbolic meaning for group members–such as rocks, leaves, CDs or DVDs, spice jars, stuffed animals, or candles✶

○ modeling clay or modeling dough (see page 44)

Option B:

○ DVD of *The Incredibles* (see page 53)✶

✶See **Leader Notes**, page 183, for details.

Come and See

(about 10 minutes)

Have everyone turn to a partner and discuss these questions: ⟶

Allow five minutes, and then bring people back together to share highlights and insights from their discussions.

》 **We're continuing to explore how to bring Jesus further into our deepest relationships, and this week we'll be focusing on our relationships with our children. For some of us, these might be the deepest relationships we have.**

But unlike our relationships with our spouses and our friends, this role carries a much broader set of responsibilities. We have to do more than love our children—we're charged with bringing them up in the faith. Teaching them. Disciplining them. *Modeling Jesus to them*. This responsibility can be both scary and overwhelming. But as we let Jesus work through our relationships with our children, he can accomplish far more than we'd hoped—and the results might look very different from what we had in mind.

Not all of you might have children, but we all need to learn to love those closest to us the way Jesus loves them and help them to grow the way Jesus wants them to grow. You may well be in a relationship where you can help another person do that—where you're a spiritual parent. So stay with us; there's something in this session for you, too.

Let's all find out together how God wants us to model Jesus to others.

Come and See

◎ What's one phrase or habit that always reminds you of your mother or father?

◎ How have you tried to emulate or avoid your parents' behaviors in your own life?

Seek and Find

(about 30 minutes)

》 Let's begin by looking at a general example that can work wherever we are.

Ask for a volunteer to read 1 Thessalonians 2:7–13, and then discuss these questions: ⟶

》 Let's get a little more specific about parenting now. Would someone read Ephesians 6:1-4? Then discuss this question: ⟶

If you've chosen **Option A,** *read on.*
If you're doing **Option B,** *go to page 53.*

Form groups of four or five. Give each group a selection of the symbolic items you've collected, and make sure each person gets a stick of modeling clay or a can of modeling dough.

1 Thessalonians 2:7-13

◎ How does Paul describe his behavior toward the Thessalonians? What did he model for them?

◎ How do you see that model being passed on to others here?

◎ What are some positive traits that your parents, or other adults, modeled for you? How has that modeling affected your walk with Jesus? How have you been able to pass those traits on to others?

 Ephesians 6:1-4

◎ Why do you think the command to honor our parents is the first one God attached a promise to?

Seek and Find continued

》 We're going to try some parent-honoring right now. If you could construct a trophy for your parents, or someone who was like a parent to you, what would it look like? What qualities or acts would it honor? If you had a tough relationship with your parents, don't get wrapped up in that right now—either find something about them you can honor, or choose someone who was a surrogate parent instead.

Using the items I've supplied—or other items you have with you—create a simple trophy that conveys what you want to honor about this person. For example, you might use a rock to honor a parent who was a "solid influence" in your life or a coin to honor that person's generosity. You can also use the modeling clay to sculpt something else or to attach items to each other.

The children will follow the example, instead of following the advice.

—Lord Palmerston

Take five minutes to create your trophies. When you've finished, show off your trophies to one another. Then discuss these questions: ⟶

Allow 15 minutes, and then bring everyone back together. Share highlights from the discussions.

◎ What's one thing your trophy says about the person you're honoring? What other things came to mind while you were making your trophy?

◎ Reread Ephesians 6:4. What character traits do you believe you model well for your children? Which traits does your spouse or do others model that you wish you shared?

◎ What's a specific situation you're currently facing in which you have an opportunity to model Jesus to your children? How will you do that?

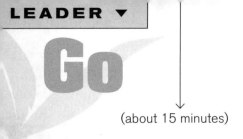

(about 15 minutes)

Read Psalm 127:3-4. Then discuss: ⟶

Psalm 127:3-4

◎ If you could point your children (or those whose lives you're invested in) like an arrow in a specific direction, where would you "shoot" them? Why?

◎ What's difficult about letting go of that arrow?

◎ What's the next major release point you anticipate for each of your "children"? What can you do to help prepare them—and yourself—for that time?

Walk It Out

(about 5 minutes)

>> **The following options are here to help you put what you've learned into practice. But if God has prompted you to do something else through this session, then by all means do that!**

GROUP ▼

choose 1:

live it What's one way you could honor your kids more? Consider how God wants to change you in that area—and change your children in the process. As you model behavior, your kids will catch it. Ask God to help you to know what your next steps are.

know it Spend some time reading the book of Proverbs. It's chock-full of wisdom and offers practical ways to pass that wisdom on to our children. If you're ambitious, read five chapters a day and finish the entire book in a week. Or read a chapter a day and spend the entire month working through all 31 chapters. After each day's reading, ask God how he wants you to use what you've studied.

share it Who's going through the same child-raising struggles you've already experienced? Get together with that parent or couple. Don't brag about your expertise—just let them know they're not alone, they're not bad parents, and they're not going crazy. (You remember feeling that way, right?) Share how God helped you through your own struggles. Start with a meal or a cup of coffee, and consider a longer-term commitment.

Form pairs, select the option you'd like to take on this week, and share your choice with your partner. Write what you plan to do in the space provided, and make plans to connect with your partner before the next session to check in and encourage each other. Take five minutes to do that now.

☐ ## go for it
Many kids grow up in single-parent homes. Even when both parents are present, other responsibilities often prevent parents from giving kids the time and attention they crave. Use your children's existing friendships as an opportunity to reach out to kids who could use a caring adult in their lives. This will mean getting involved in your children's activities. Most children don't want to just sit around and talk, but you should have plenty of time to talk "on the fly." All of you will benefit from the time together.

☐ ## do it together
As a group, treat neighborhood kids to a fun day of activities. Take them to a ballgame, an amusement park, the mall—whatever is most appropriate and enjoyable. Be sure to get parents' permission first. Be very specific in letting parents know where you'll be and what times you expect to be there—and stick to that itinerary. As much as possible, let kids choose the activities, but provide necessary adult guidance. And bring plenty of healthy snacks—you're all going to need some extra energy!

...or think of your own!

Because discipling my children requires me to model Jesus to them, I'll "Walk It Out" by:

_____

_____

_____

_____

Walk It Out continued

Come back together. Ask someone to read Hebrews 11:17-19.

》 Every child, regardless of age, is a promise from God—and God wants to fulfill his promise in each of our children's lives. Sometimes we get so wrapped up in a given situation with our children—or so wrapped up in ourselves—that we forget that. So let's slow down for a moment.

What's one area in which you know you could honor your children more? Maybe it's quality time; maybe it's any amount of time at all; maybe you need to ask your child's forgiveness for something and let God's grace work through that process. Let's silently reflect on that now and begin handing it over to God. Afterward, I'll lead us in prayer, and when I pause, you'll mention the one way you want to be more honoring of your children. If you're not comfortable saying it out loud, add it silently to our prayer.

Allow a minute for everyone to reflect, and then close your prayer time.

prayer⊙　**》 Lord, we want our children to become the people you want them to be. Help us to release them into your hands so you can do what you want to do. And use us to reveal yourself to them. We also thank you for all the ways you've used us to speak into our kids' lives, even when we weren't aware of it.**

At the same time, we acknowledge that we've failed sometimes—maybe lots of times—and we ask that you help us become better parents. Right now we confess our need for you in...[say your word here].

We know you honor our prayers, and we ask for your Spirit to work through us to become the parents you want us to be, even as you help our kids become the people you want them to be. In Jesus' name, amen.

SEEING IT DIFFERENTLY
Seek and Find–Option B

LEADER To prompt your group to think about a session in a fresh way, we'll occasionally recommend video clips that your group can enjoy instead of (or in addition to) another part of the session. You'll be surprised by how effectively movies can portray eternal truths, or at least point toward them.

Instead of the trophy activity and discussion, watch a scene from *The Incredibles*, an animated movie about a family discovering and using their superpowers for good. Cue the movie to 1:13:39 (DVD Chapter 19), as the entrance to the cave is being shown. Before starting the clip, encourage everyone to especially follow Violet, the daughter, during this scene. Stop the clip at 1:15:39, after Violet puts her mask on.

After viewing the clip, discuss these questions:

GROUP

◎ Think about the quote "Your identity is your most valuable possession." In what ways do you think that's true (or not)?

◎ How do you see Violet's identity change during the course of this scene? What things enabled or forced her to change?

◎ Reread Ephesians 6:4. What character traits do you believe you model well for your children? Which traits does your spouse or do others model that you wish you shared?

Pick up at Go on page 48.

Go Deeper

Learn how to better disciple your children by checking out these great resources:

HomeBuilders Parenting Series® (Family Life)

Shift: What It Takes to Finally Reach Today's Families by Brian Haynes (Group)

Revolutionary Parenting: What the Research Shows Really Works by George Barna (Barna Books)

Family Driven Faith: Doing What It Takes to Raise Sons and Daughters Who Walk With God by Voddie T. Baucham Jr. (Crossway Books)

Age of Opportunity: A Biblical Guide to Parenting Teens by Paul David Tripp (P & R Publishing)

How to Lead Without Being the Boss

For an elder must live a blameless life" (TITUS 1:7a).

"Don't lord it over the people assigned to your care, but lead them by your own good example. And when the Great Shepherd appears, you will receive a crown of never-ending glory and honor" (1 PETER 5:3-4).

In this session, we'll journey...

from ────────────→ **to**
exploring roles in which we're
already leading in some way...

discovering how to set a
Christ-like tone in those roles.

Before gathering, make sure you have...

○ a newsprint tablet, blackboard, or white board (If you're in a small-group setting, a notepad is OK.)

○ 2 sheets of paper for everyone

○ pens or pencils

Optional activities (choose one or both):

○ **Option A:** Discussion at the end of Come and See (see page 56)

○ **Option B:** DVD of *The Lord of the Rings: The Fellowship of the Ring* (see page 65)

See **Leader Notes**, page 184.

Come and See

(about 15 minutes)

>> **Let's begin. Form groups of three or four. Decide who your leader is. Once you've done that, I'll tell you what to do next.**

Give groups up to a minute to assemble and decide on a leader. Once groups look settled in, get everyone's attention.

>> **Now it can be revealed: Choosing a leader *was* the activity. So let's talk about the decisions you've just made.** ⟶

Write down everyone's answers to this last question for all to see. Make a point of acknowledging each person's contribution as you do so.

If you've chosen **Option A,** *read on.*
If you're doing **Option B,** *go to page 65.*

Discuss the following question: ⟶

Write down everyone's suggestions to this question as well, keeping the list from the previous question available. Circle any similarities, and add to either list as new things are suggested. Again, acknowledge each person's contribution as you do so. Then continue your discussion.

>> **We know a gifted leader when we see one. We recognize that God has given that person certain abilities or character traits that make him or her the obvious (or at least easiest) choice to lead others. What we may miss, though, is that God has given all of us leadership qualities and abilities and has placed each of us where we can set the tone for those around us.**

This isn't meant to dismiss obvious gifts of leadership. We've already recognized those gifts today. But let's expand our vision to realize that each of us, at some point, will be given the opportunity to set an example for others. We do this as spouses and parents, as we've already seen, but this week we're going to see how God might want to use each one of us to lead—or maybe how he's *already* using us, without our even realizing it.

> *The authority by which the Christian leader leads is not power but love, not force but example, not coercion but reasoned persuasion. Leaders have power, but power is safe only in the hands of those who humble themselves to serve.*
>
> —John Stott

Come and See

◎ Who's the leader in each of your groups? Why did you pick him or her?

◎ How is this like how we decide on leaders in other parts of our lives (when we have the choice)?

◎ What qualities do you normally look for in a leader?

◎ Now let's look at this from a different angle. What qualities do you look for in a friend?

◎ Why do you think our two lists differ?

◎ Who do you think really influences you more: your leaders or your friends? Explain.

Seek and Find

(about 30 minutes)

Ask for volunteers to read Philippians 3:12–17 and 1 Thessalonians 1:2–10, and discuss: ⟶

Ask everyone to find a partner and sit back to back, either in chairs or on the floor. Give everyone two sheets of paper, and make sure everyone has a writing surface, such as a book.

》 Now let's try a different kind of imitation. First, use one of the sheets of paper I've given you to draw any kind of picture you want. Do include some detail in your pictures. And don't show them to your partner. You'll have just one minute.

Give everyone one minute to draw.

》 Now you're going to help your partner forge the picture you just drew. There's just one catch: You can't let your partner see your drawing. Your partner must listen as you tell him or her what to draw—and try to duplicate it based on the description you're giving. The person whose birthday comes earliest in the year will be the first "forger." After two minutes, we'll switch roles. Remember, no peeking!

After two minutes, have partners switch roles. Allow two more minutes; then give partners the opportunity to compare pictures to see how close they came to the originals. Bring everyone back together, and discuss these questions: ⟶

Philippians 3:12-17; 1 Thessalonians 1:2-10

◎ In what ways do people lead by example in these passages? What things are "imitated" or passed on here?

◎ What good results do you see from these churches "imitating both us and the Lord"?

◎ How close did you come to reproducing the original artwork? What, if anything, made it easier for you to visualize what you needed to draw?

◎ What are some ways we model, and help to "reproduce," Jesus in others?

◎ Who models Jesus to you? What's one thing you've learned about Jesus from them?

◎ What's one thing God has shown you that you wish everyone else could see as clearly? How might God use you to help others see or even imitate that?

(about 10 minutes)

Read 1 Peter 5:1-7, and answer these questions: ⟶

1 Peter 5:1-7

◎ Who's your "flock" right now? In other words: Who has God put in your care or your sphere of influence—regardless of the official authority you have (or don't have) over them? (And for our purposes, a flock can be one person.)

◎ Where else do you think God might be calling you to be more of a leader, whether it's by example or in a more official role? What do you feel you need in order to take the next step?

◎ Who can you rely on for support—and as an example for *you*—as you move forward?

Walk It Out

(about 5 minutes)

GROUP ▼

choose 1:

☐ live it

Reflect on your answers during "Go." In what situation is God calling you to be more of a leader right now? What or who could help you move forward? Contact those who can either equip you with the tools you need, guide you through the next steps, or be your encouragers or prayer partners.

☐ know it

Spend time reading about people in the Bible who led by example, whether it was their choice or not. Read the stories of Joseph, Ruth, or Daniel and his friends. Or read passages that show how God took a "natural" leader like Peter and turned him into the leader God intended him to be. (Start with Matthew 26:31-35, 69-75; John 21:15-19; and Acts 2–4, and go from there).

☐ share it

During this session, you may have thought of someone you're leading right now, if only by example. Think of a practical way to put your words and actions together this week. Make it evident to this person that you're not only leading; you're also *following* the greatest Leader of all.

Form pairs, select the option you'd like to take on this week, and share your choice with your partner. Write what you plan to do in the space provided, and make plans to connect with your partner before the next session to check in and encourage each other. Take five minutes to do that now.

☐ go for it *and* do it together

Is there a need in your neighborhood or community that isn't being addressed? Take it on as a group. Put together a plan, looking for ways that your natural leaders and leaders-by-example can work together, using all the gifts God gave them. Be sure to get permission from the people directly involved or local officials who might need to OK such a project.

...or think of your own!

Because God has put me where he wants me and wants to use me there, I'll "Walk It Out" by:

_____

_____

_____

_____

_____

_____

_____

Walk It Out continued

prayer↻

Have groups stay in their pairs and share ways God is working in their lives right now. Or they can confess their doubts that God knows what he's doing in their circumstances. Or both. Ask pairs to pray for each other after sharing.

Allow five minutes. Close your prayer time together by thanking God for each person's situation, even if it's *not* making sense at this time. Ask God to reveal how he wants to use each of you where he's put you and for the strength to walk that out.

SEEING IT DIFFERENTLY
Come and See—Option B

LEADER   Instead of the discussion at the end of Come and See, watch a scene from *The Lord of the Rings: The Fellowship of the Ring.* Cue the movie to 1:29:21 (DVD Chapter 23), where Elrond says, "The ring cannot be destroyed…" Stop at 1:32:34, where Boromir says, "Then Gondor will see it done." Then discuss these questions:

GROUP

◎ What motivated Frodo to act? How did it differ from what motivated the other leaders?

◎ How did Frodo's willingness make him a leader, despite his stature (in more ways than one)?

◎ When have you said, "I do not know the way," but were willing to do what it took to get something done? How did others respond initially? later on?

If time's not an issue, go ahead with the discussion in Option A. Otherwise, pick up at the leader statement at the end of Come and See that begins with **We know a gifted leader when we see one.**

Dig deeper into developing as a leader—of *any* kind—and setting the tone wherever God has put you by checking out these resources:

Outflow: Outward-Focused Living in a Self-Focused World by Steve Sjogren and Dave Ping (Group)

You Don't Need a Title to Be a Leader: How Anyone, Anywhere, Can Make a Positive Difference by Mark Sanborn (WaterBrook)

The Radical Reformission: Reaching Out Without Selling Out by Mark Driscoll (Zondervan)

The Irresistible Revolution: Living as an Ordinary Radical by Shane Claiborne (Zondervan)

Outreach Ministry in the 21st Century: The Encyclopedia of Practical Ideas (Group)

Temper, Temper

"...He must not be arrogant or quick-tempered" (TITUS 1:7).

"And 'don't sin by letting anger control you.' Don't let the sun go down while you are still angry, for anger gives a foothold to the devil" (EPHESIANS 4:26-27).

In this session, we'll journey...

from ⟶ **to**
identifying how our bad reactions affect ourselves and others...
discovering how to respond to others in a more Christ-like manner.

Before gathering, make sure you have...

○ a pitcher of salt water and enough cups to serve everyone✶

○ a newsprint tablet, blackboard, or white board (If you're in a small-group setting. a notepad is OK.)

○ 1 bowl or bucket filled with water for every 4 people

○ 1 sponge or rag for every 4 people

○ 1 small cup of dirt for each person(You're going to need a lot of cups this week!)

○ extra rags or hand towels for cleaning and drying hands

Optional activities (choose one or both):

○ **Option A:** opening discussion in Come and See (see page 68)

○ **Option B:** DVD of *Fried Green Tomatoes* (see page 79)

✶See **Leader Notes**, page 184, for details.

Come and See

(about 15 minutes)

If you've chosen **Option A**, *read on.*
If you're doing **Option B**, *go to page 79.*

If you have more than eight people in your group, form smaller groups to discuss these questions: ————————————→

》 We've discussed things that irritate us. Now let's take things up a notch.

Discuss these questions: ————————————————→

We all have our hot buttons—things that annoy, upset, or anger us. They might be trivial, or they might be so serious that we feel justified in our anger and maybe even in the things we say and do as a result. The Bible has a lot to say about our anger and our reactions to it. It points us to the deeper causes of our anger, and it tells us how anger affects not only us but also those around us. Anger is usually not pretty, but it's something we all need to address. So let's begin.

◎ What irritates you to no end (even if it's not a big deal to anyone else)?

◎ How do you normally react when you're irritated? How long do you hold on to your reactions afterward?

◎ What would you say is the one circumstance or behavior that truly angers you the most? How do you react?

◎ Why do you think that particular circumstance or behavior sets you off?

Seek and Find

(about 30 minutes)

》 Since we've probably already gotten a little worked up just thinking about the things that anger or irritate us, we should stop here and have a drink of water before moving on.

Serve salt water, but ask everyone to wait to drink until the whole group has been served. After everyone has had a taste—and reacted—discuss this question: ⟶

Ask for a volunteer to read James 3:2-12, and then discuss: ⟶

》 Before we move forward in James, let's take 30 seconds to look again at our opening quote from Titus, reprinted on your group page. Also read the dictionary entry next to it.

After everyone has read the information on the next page, discuss these questions: ⟶

James 3:2-12

◎ What are some ways the tongue is described here? Which description resonates with you the most, and why?

◎ How was your reaction to the salt water like some of the reactions to anger you described earlier?

◎ Think again about the salt water you just tasted. What are some ways we leave a bitter taste in the mouths of others by the things we say to them or by our reactions to them?

"...He must not be arrogant or quick-tempered."
—*Titus 1:7*

"ar·ro·gant: exaggerating or disposed to exaggerate one's own worth or importance often by an overbearing manner.
—Merriam-Webster Online Dictionary"

◎ What's the connection between being arrogant and being quick-tempered? When have you seen this connection in your own life?

◎ You may not let loose on others or be overbearing; then again, you *might*. In any case, what are some ways your temper—and arrogance—*do* come through?

Seek and Find continued

Read James 3:13-18, and then discuss: ————————————→

Write down everyone's responses for all to see, and thank them for their contributions.

After discussing the last question, form groups of four. Give each group a bucket or bowl of water with a sponge or rag already in it and a clean towel or rag. Also give each person a cup of dirt.

>> **We've just listed a variety of reasons that can cause us to lose our tempers. Now we're going to dig a little deeper. Well, we won't literally dig, but there will be some dirt involved.**

Decide who in your group will go first. That person will dump a cup of dirt into the water while saying one of the reasons we've listed—or another that comes to mind. Then that person will reach into the bowl and wring out the sponge [or rag] **that's inside.**

Once everyone has had a turn, take 10 minutes to discuss these questions: ————————————→

Allow 10 minutes for discussion, and then bring everyone back together to share highlights and insights.

James 3:13-18

◎ What reasons are given in this passage for the negative or hurtful things that come out of our mouths? What are some others you can think of?

◎ Think about those times you feel "squeezed" or "wrung out." What "dirt" tends to come out of you that you wish you could take back?

◎ Reread James 3:13-14, 17-18. What alternatives to anger and speaking badly about others does James give us here? How would you do each of these things?

◎ What things can we put into ourselves—instead of dirt—that would help us to respond better under pressure or stress?

Go

(about 10 minutes)

Ask for a volunteer to read Ephesians 4:26–5:2. Then discuss these questions: ⟶

Ephesians 4:26–5:2

◎ Think about a time when anger controlled your relationship with someone else and gave a foothold to the devil. How did you finally get past it—or did you? Explain.

◎ How would you like to see God change your communication so it becomes more "good and helpful"—so it builds people up rather than tears them down?

Walk It Out

(about 5 minutes)

》 **The following options are here to help you put what you've learned into practice. But if God has prompted you to do something else through this session, then by all means do that!**

choose 1:

☐ know it

Read and pray over this week's Scriptures. Ask God to reveal how you've let bad attitudes come through in your words and actions. Then ask God for forgiveness and direction. What good words and actions can you substitute so you can respond with grace when "squeezed"? How can you build others up instead of tearing them down?

☐ live it

If you've hurt others with your words—or others have hurt you with theirs—seek them out, and set things right this week. Be sure to prepare your heart beforehand. Consider whether you need help seeing the other side of the argument or creative solutions to the problem. Do you need to own up to a part of the disagreement and receive forgiveness as well? Pray about these things as you prepare to meet.

☐ share it

Do you know someone who's taken a beating from others recently? Seek that person out this week, and encourage him or her. Set aside time to listen and let him express some of the hurt and anger he's been feeling. And if that happens, don't react—pray. Invite God into the situation.

Form pairs, select the option you'd like to take on this week, and share your choice with your partner. Write what you plan to do in the space provided, and make plans to connect with your partner before the next session to check in and encourage each other. Take five minutes to do that now.

☐ **go for it** Get formal training to be a peacemaker in your church, workplace, or neighborhood. Perhaps your church, your job, or another organization in the area offers this kind of training. One such organization is Peacemaker Ministries (HisPeace.org). You may know others. In any case, make it happen!

☐ **do it together**
Is there a divisive situation in your town, neighborhood, or church right now? As a group plan an event that will help people on both sides to look past their differences and focus on their commonalities. It could be as uncomplicated as a block party or something formal that gets both sides to sit down and talk through their differences.

...or think of your own!

Because I need Jesus, rather than my own anger, to dictate my responses to others, I'll "Walk It Out" by:

_____

_____

_____

_____

Walk It Out continued

prayer⊙

Take extra time to pray today. Use Ephesians 4:26–32 as a prompt to confess those times when anger and bitterness have crept into your lives. Let pairs stay together to pray if people are not comfortable doing this as a group.

Close your prayer time by asking God to forgive you for times in which anger has overtaken your group members. Ask God for the ability to show grace to those people or situations that push our buttons.

SEEING IT DIFFERENTLY
Come and See—Option B

LEADER Instead of the opening discussion, watch a scene from *Fried Green Tomatoes*. Cue the movie to 1:21:02 (DVD Chapter 27), where Evelyn—a woman who's slowly discovering how to stand up for herself after being walked on all her life—is cruising into the parking lot. Stop at 1:23:08, where the two young women are left dumb-founded and crying. Then discuss these questions:

GROUP

◎ How do you normally react when you're irritated? How long do you hold on to your reactions afterward?

◎ What is the one circumstance or behavior that truly angers you the most? How do you react?

◎ Why do you think that particular circumstance or behavior sets you off?

Pick up at the beginning of Seek and Find on page 70.

To dig deeper into effective ways to deal with anger, check out these great resources:

The Other Side of Love: Handling Anger in a Godly Way by Gary Chapman (Moody)

Getting Rid of the Gorilla: Confessions on the Struggle to Forgive by Brian Jones (Standard)

Good and Angry: Exchanging Frustration for Character in You and Your Kids! by Scott Turansky and Joanne Miller (Shaw Books)

The Anger Workbook: A 13-Step Interactive Plan to Help You... by Les Carter and Frank Minirth (Thomas Nelson)

Address Your Stress

"*He must not be a heavy drinker, violent, or dishonest with money.*" (TITUS 1:7B).

"*Then Jesus said, 'Come to me, all of you who are weary and carry heavy burdens, and I will give you rest. Take my yoke upon you. Let me teach you, because I am humble and gentle at heart, and you will find rest for your souls. For my yoke is easy to bear, and the burden I give you is light*'" (MATTHEW 11:28-30).

In this session, we'll journey...

from ⟶ **to**

identifying how stress drives us from Jesus (and into lesser things)...

understanding how we can allow Jesus to carry our burdens.

Before gathering, make sure you have...

○ beanbags, stress balls, or other soft items that can be tossed around–2 for every group of 4 to 5

○ books∗–at least 3 or 4 per person

○ a newsprint tablet, blackboard, or white board (If you're in a small-group setting, a notepad is OK.)

∗See **Leader Notes**, page 185, for details.

Come and See

(about 10 minutes)

Have people form groups of four to five. Give each group two beanbags.

》 **Everyone here has probably already experienced a certain amount of tension today, so let's de-stress a bit. Some of you are holding beanbags. Take a few moments to squeeze them.** (Pause.) **Let out some of that stress. That's it.**

Now toss your beanbag to someone else so he or she can squeeze it. But don't give any clue who you're going to toss it to. Keep squeezing and tossing for the next minute, and when you've finished, discuss these questions: ————————————→

After five minutes, bring everyone back together, and share highlights from the group discussions.

》 **Last week we discussed one particular reaction to stress: anger and negative talk. But there are plenty of other poor ways to respond to stress. We're going to touch on some of them today, as well as learn what we really need to do to have the kind of perspective God desires us to have.**

> *The visible world daily bludgeons us with its things and events. They pinch and pull and hammer away at our bodies. Few people arise in the morning as hungry for God as they are for cornflakes or toast and eggs.*
>
> —Dallas Willard,
>   Hearing God

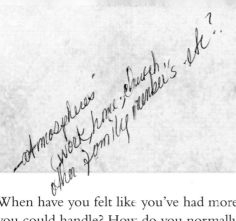
atmosphere (work/home: church members' at? other family members etc.)

◎ When have you felt like you've had more things thrown at you than you could handle? How do you normally respond when that happens?

I usually go somewhere alone and talk w/ God.

◎ Is all stress bad? Why or why not? No

it may promote you to move — in a positive direction — for your life, things happen and you may find yourself freaking out but — it may make you move into the blessings of God. (where otherwise you still ~~would~~) in a stay still ~~

Seek and Find

(about 35 minutes)

If you have more than 12 in your group, have them return to their earlier groups, and ask someone from each group to help you.

>> **First, I'd like to ask everyone to stand with your arms straight in front of you, palms up. How long do you think you could stand like this before your arms get tired?**

Allow time for people to respond.

>> **Let's see if *this* changes things.**

Place a book in each person's hands. Allow about 10 seconds for everyone to adjust to the extra weight, and then give everyone another book. Then another.

After giving everyone a third book, say: **Some of you may be getting a little tired by now. Others of you are probably determined to see how long you'll last. Those of you who are getting tired, feel free to give your books to someone else—or to more than one person, if you like. As the rest of you get tired, you're also welcome to hand off your books to someone else.**

Allow up to another minute for group members to give away their books. If people are still holding books after a minute, give them a round of applause, and let them put their books down. Then discuss these questions: ————————

Have everyone read the quotation from Richard Swenson, and then discuss these questions: ————————

Write down everyone's responses to that last question where all can see, and thank them for their contributions. Pointing to the list, ask everyone to answer this question: ————————→

◎ When you're overwhelmed in real life, do you normally unload everything on one person, "share the wealth" with as many people as possible, or try to grin and bear it? Explain.

◎ Think about a time you've experienced the truth of this quote. What part did you play in that overloading? What parts were out of your control?

◎ When is it OK to share your struggles with others, and when is it not OK? Give specific examples of each, if you can.

When we have consulted God and knowing that they are praying people, and not

◎ When is it appropriate to take on extra burdens? When isn't it?

I don't believe we should never take on extra burdens. - God says His burdens are light. - He won't add on (heavy)

> People do not operate on the principle of overloading. Instead they operate on the basis of 'one more thing won't hurt.' Yet this is only true if it is true. Once we are maximally loaded down, adding one more thing will hurt. The pain of overload is real pain.
>
> —Richard Swenson,
> Margin

◎ What are some unhealthy ways that people try to deal with their stresses and burdens when they become too much?

They hook themself up with people doing carnal minded things. Act eating disorders,

◎ When have you been guilty of one of these?

Seek and Find continued

Have people rejoin their earlier groups, read Matthew 11:28–30, and discuss: ⟶

Allow 15 minutes for discussion, and then bring everyone back together. Share highlights and insights from the small-group discussions.

In the normal yoking the load is equally distributed between the two that are yoked together, but when we are yoked with Jesus Christ, He bears the load and we who are yoked to Him share in the joy and the accomplishment of the labor but without the burden of the yoke.

—Dwight Pentecost, Design for Discipleship

Matthew 11:28-30

◎ Be honest: In what ways does taking Jesus' yoke and letting him teach you just sound like one more thing you can't deal with right now? What would you say to someone who gave *you* that excuse?

◎ How can we learn *of* Jesus, instead of just facts *about* him? What clues does Jesus give us in this passage, and what would those things look like in your life?

◎ How would doing these things help us with our own burdens?

Go

(about 10 minutes)

》 **Let's reflect one more time on this passage. Everyone, close your eyes and remain silent.**

Read Matthew 11:28–30 aloud.

》 **"All of you who are weary and carry heavy burdens." Apply that phrase to yourself. It might mean: All of you who are tired. All of you who are stressed out. All of you who are burned out. All of you who feel you don't have it in you anymore. All of you who are tired of living this way. All of you who are tired of living— period. "Come to me," Jesus says," and I will give you rest."** (Pause.)

Take one more minute to reflect quietly on what this promise of Jesus means to you and where you are in relation to that promise right now. When you've finished, find a partner, share your reflections, and then discuss these next two questions. When you've finished discussing, work through the "Walk It Out" section together. ⎯⎯⎯⎯⎯⎯⎯⎯⟶

Allow 10 minutes for partners to discuss the questions and "Walk It Out" options, and then call everyone back together for your prayer time.

◎ If we really *can* find our rest in Jesus, what's holding you back from trusting him and finding that rest right now?

◎ What can you do about it? More to the point, what burden do you need to give to Jesus?

Walk It Out

(about 5 minutes)

>> **The following options are here to help you put what you've learned into practice. But if God has prompted you to do something else through this session, then by all means do that!**

choose 1:

live it Do you feel totally overextended? Address it. Make a list of areas in your life in which you need to establish breathing room. Plan how to better balance your finances, emotions, body, and time. Commit this plan to God, and ask for his power to live it out.

know it

Reread Matthew 11:28-30. But don't just read a handful of words and shut your Bible. Spend half an hour taking this passage to heart. Ask Jesus what you still need to give to him, what he wants to teach you about his life, and what it means to share his yoke. Push past your need to *do* something, and just spend time *being* before Jesus.

share it Is there a family in your group, church, neighborhood, or at work that is overwhelmed right now? Reach out to them. Invite them to dinner, and give them a chance to relax. Help meet a need they're struggling with. Or just sit and listen, and when it's appropriate, share how God has helped you through similar times.

Form pairs, select the option you'd like to take on this week, and share your choice with your partner. Write what you plan to do in the space provided, and make plans to connect with your partner before the next session to check in and encourage each other. Take five minutes to do that now.

go for it
People all around you are facing crises. Some struggle with addictions or other destructive habits; others are overwhelmed by financial or family circumstances; some may be depressed and may even have thoughts of suicide. Find a support group or hotline you can contribute to. The issue doesn't have to be one you've struggled with personally, but it's also possible that God wants to use your experiences to speak to others who are in desperate need.

do it together
Plan a weekend or all-day retreat. Make it far enough from home for group members to mentally separate from their daily stresses. Plan times to eat, play, pray, and worship together. It's also important to plan at least one extended time (an hour or more) for individuals to spend in solitude with God to receive guidance, meditate upon Scripture, and appreciate creation. Be sure to gather after this solitary time to share what God may be saying to you and to others in your group.

...or think of your own!

Because Jesus is bigger than the things that stress me out, I'll "Walk It Out" by:

_____

_____

_____

_____

Walk It Out continued

After 10 minutes, get everyone's attention.

» **As we choose to serve Jesus and take his yoke upon us, Jesus takes our burdens and gives us *his* burdens in return. It's not just submission—it's a trade. It's us saying, "Jesus, I don't want this kind of life anymore; you died to take it away, so *take* it."**

As we allow Jesus to change our lives more and more into his life, the burden he places upon us is far lighter than the ones we laid at his feet. Let's pray:

‹prayer› **Jesus, you know our struggles better than we do—and you know the answers to those struggles better than we do, too. We ask you to reveal the areas of our lives we haven't given to you. Help us let go of them and commit them to you, and, as we do, help us to find our rest in you. Amen.**

Go Deeper

Dig deeper into ways to manage stress by checking out these great resources:

Boundaries: When to Say Yes, When to Say No to Take Control of Your Life by Henry Cloud and John Townsend (Zondervan)

Freedom From Tyranny of the Urgent by Charles E. Hummel (InterVarsity)

Margin: Restoring Emotional, Physical, Financial, and Time Reserves to Overloaded Lives by Richard Swenson (NavPress)

For the Love of Money

"*...or dishonest with money*" (TITUS 1:7B).

"*Don't store up treasures here on earth, where moths eat them and rust destroys them, and where thieves break in and steal. Store your treasures in heaven, where moths and rust cannot destroy, and thieves do not break in and steal. Wherever your treasure is, there the desires of your heart will also be*" (MATTHEW 6:19-21).

In this session, we'll journey..

from ————————————→ **to**

confronting how we really feel about our money and possessions...

discovering the attitudes God wants us to have toward what he's given us.

Before gathering, make sure you have...

○ a variety of snacks✳

○ a dollar bill for everyone✳

✳See **Leader Notes**, page 185, for details.

Come and See

(about 10 minutes)

Set out snacks before starting the session. Encourage everyone to get a snack and then find a partner with whom to discuss these questions: ⎯⎯⎯⎯⎯⎯⎯⎯⟶

Allow five minutes for discussion, and then regain everyone's attention.

》 We've started today's session by talking about foods we've enjoyed—and maybe still do. Maybe too much, even. It might be a comfort food you still turn to, something you once enjoyed but grew out of, some food you wish were still around, or even a food you ate so constantly that you finally got sick of it.

Let's take these ideas and apply them to what's often a much bigger craving—our finances and possessions.

◎ Why did you choose the particular snack you did?

◎ What's one snack or other food you've regularly craved, either as a kid or more recently? If you could have that food item every day, would you? Why or why not?

Seek and Find

(about 30 minutes)

Discuss: ⟶

Form groups of four.

》 **Take turns reading each of the passages listed, and note what each passage says about money and possessions. Especially note how God says we should view them. You'll be looking at God's Word from a variety of angles, so as you read, also think about how these passages relate to one another. When you've finished reading, discuss the questions that follow. Let's get back together in 20 minutes.** ⟶

- Psalm 24:1
- Psalm 37:16–19, 25–26
- Proverbs 30:7–9
- Ecclesiastes 5:10–20
- Matthew 6:19–34
- Philippians 4:6–14
- 1 Timothy 6:5–10, 17–19
- James 4:13–17

Allow 20 minutes for discussion, and then bring people back together to share highlights and insights with one another.

◎ Think about a significant purchase you made on an impulse or because you felt pressured to—and then wished you hadn't. What took place between the time you bought it and when you regretted buying it?

◎ Now think of a time you didn't have the money for what you wanted but were able to get by without it. What did God teach you during that time?

◎ One more question: How easy or difficult is it for you to talk openly about money or your possessions? Why do you think that is?

 Psalm 24:1; Psalm 37:16–19, 25–26; Proverbs 30:7–9; Ecclesiastes 5:10–20; Matthew 6:19–34; Philippians 4:6–14; 1 Timothy 6:5–10, 17–19; James 4:13–17

◎ Which phrases or ideas jumped out to you?

◎ Taken together, what do these passages tell you about the things God gives us?

◎ Practically speaking, in what ways do you find yourself relying on money or "stuff" instead of on God? Be specific. How is your relationship with God affected by it?

Go

(about 15 minutes)

>> **We've just looked at a variety of things God has to say about money and possessions, and at what our attitudes should be toward our stuff. Now let's look at one more list. Take two minutes to read the following list; then we'll talk.** ⟶

Stewardship is everything we do after we say, 'I believe.'

—*John Calvin*

After two minutes, discuss these questions: ⟶

10 Principles of Outward Simplicity

1. Buy things for their usefulness rather than their status.

2. Reject anything that's producing an addiction in you.

3. Develop a habit of giving things away *(especially if they fall into categories 1 and 2).*

4. Refuse to be propagandized by "the latest conveniences."

5. Learn to enjoy things without owning them.

6. Develop a deeper appreciation for creation.

7. View "buy now, pay later" schemes with healthy skepticism.

8. Obey Jesus' instructions about plain, honest speech.

9. Reject anything that contributes to the oppression of others.

10. Shun anything that distracts you from seeking first the kingdom of God.

Adapted from *Celebration of Discipline: The Path to Spiritual Growth* by Richard J. Foster.
Copyright © 1978 by Richard J. Foster. Reprinted by permission of HarperCollins Publishers.

◎ Which of these principles are speaking to you the loudest right now? What would you add to this list?

◎ How might practicing these things help you to better enjoy what God has given you?

◎ What would it look like for you to put these principles into practice? What (or who) could help you to start making that a reality?

Walk It Out

(about 5 minutes)

》 The following options are here to help you put what you've learned into practice. But if God has prompted you to do something else through this session, then by all means do that!

GROUP ▼

choose 1:

□ know it

Read and pray through this session's list of Scripture passages, as well as through the "10 Principles of Outward Simplicity." What does God want you to do? Identify at least one action point God is steering you toward. Ask God how he wants you to address it; then do what God is telling you to do.

□ live it

For the next seven days, write down everything you spend money on. At the end of the week, add up how much you spent on yourself, how much on necessities, and how much to bless God or other people. If God reveals a need to change your spending habits, resolve to make that change.

Also consider going on a "spending fast" this week. Buy absolutely nothing you don't truly need, and at the end of the week, see for yourself how much your life is affected by avoiding unnecessary purchases.

□ share it

Do some spring cleaning (whether it's spring or not!). Identify items you don't really need (or don't really need several "backups" of—such as shoes, clothes, TVs, or even computers). Then choose the best way to give them away. You could give them to a family that really *does* need them (a family that has lost its possessions in a fire or flood, for example), donate them to a charity, or have a garage sale to benefit others.

Form pairs, select the option you'd like to take on this week, and share your choice with your partner. Write what you plan to do in the space provided, and make plans to connect with your partner before the next session to check in and encourage each other. Take five minutes to do that now.

☐ ## go for it Spend your spending money on someone else. If you set aside a certain amount of spending money for yourself for the week (such as for buying a coffee every day or purchasing a new article of clothing), designate that money instead for someone who really needs it. That person will be blessed that you did.

☐ ## do it together

As a group, consider how you can pool your resources to have a bigger impact on others. Whether you decide to meet a crisis or an ongoing need, locally or abroad, take some time to gauge what's on your group members' hearts, and then figure out how you can help meet that need together.

...or think of your own!

Because God provides everything I need, and I want to use my resources instead of allowing them to use me, I'll "Walk It Out" by:

_____

_____

_____

_____

_____

Walk It Out continued

 Come back together.

》 If your wallets or purses are available, I'd like you to reach in and take a dollar or other bill out of it. If you've got extras, share them with those who don't have any. It's OK—you'll get your money back when we're finished.

Give everyone enough time to either locate a dollar bill or receive one from someone else. If necessary, give out the extras you have on hand, so everyone's holding a bill.

》 Close your eyes.

Think about the dollar bill you're holding. It's really just a piece of paper, isn't it? And yet this world—and we, too, quite often—attach so much value to it and to the things it can purchase that it overshadows everything else in our lives. Think about how our possessions affect the way others see us. Think about how we let our possessions affect the way we see ourselves. Now think about how we let possessions affect the way we see God.

Allow a minute of silence. Then ask everyone to quietly rejoin their partners from the beginning of this session.

》 **Let's ask God to help break us of our dependence on material things. Think again about how you've become dependent on stuff and how the dollar bill you hold represents that. As I begin to lead us in prayer, hand your bill to your partner. As you do so, think of it as exchanging your riches for God's. It's all God's, anyway.**

Let's pray.

Lord, forgive us for how we've let the things you've given us—or the things we want—come between us and you. We know that you only give us good things, and yet we've all been guilty of wanting to add to your goodness. Help us make the changes we need to make to receive every good thing you want us to have.

⊖prayer

Help us also to remember that change doesn't usually happen overnight and that we may still have to pay for some of the decisions we've made in the past. But also help us remember that as we're faithful to you, you are even more faithful to us. Remind us daily that you'll carry us past those mistakes and closer to you and all the *truly* good things you have in store for us. In Jesus' name, amen.

Go Deeper

To dig deeper into how our finances can glorify God instead of enslave us, check out these great resources:

Stewardship and the Kingdom of God by Ronald Walborn and Frank Chan (The Christian and Missionary Alliance; cmalliance.org/resources/church/stewardship/pdf/stewtheo.pdf)

Margin by Richard Swenson (NavPress)

How to Manage Your Money by Larry Burkett (Moody)

Financial Peace Revisited by Dave Ramsey (Viking)

Freedom of Simplicity: Finding Harmony in a Complex World by Richard Foster (HarperOne)

Following Jesus to Work

"...or dishonest with money" (TITUS 1:7B).

"Work willingly at whatever you do, as though you were working for the Lord rather than for people" (COLOSSIANS 3:23).

In this session, we'll journey...

from ————————————————→ **to**
determining how (or if) we follow Jesus into our workplaces...

learning new ways to allow God to speak into our jobs, no matter what they are.

Before gathering, make sure you have...

O playing cards or 3x5 index cards–at least 5 per person

O pens or pencils

O a table or other flat surface for every four to five people (Groups can also gather at different ends of the same table if there's room.)

O doughnuts or some other "prize" group members would enjoy winning✳

✳See **Leader Notes**, page 186, for details.

Come and See

(about 15 minutes)

Give everyone at least five cards, and then ask people to form groups of four or five. Make sure you have at least two teams; if you have a smaller group, it's OK to have smaller teams, too. Show everyone the prize.

》 Welcome! We're going to start things off with a game. The object is to build the highest tower using your cards. The team with the highest tower after three minutes wins this prize. Here are the rules:

There *are* no rules. Whoever wins, wins. It's every team for itself.

If anyone has questions or objections, continue to insist on the "non-rules." Once everyone understands the game, let them loose and see what happens!

After three minutes, call everyone back together, and award the prize to the winning team. Then discuss: ⟶

Give a prize to anyone who didn't already get one.

》 Today we're going to explore another venue where the competition is probably pretty heavy and not always fair—our workplaces. You may or may not have a good job, but there are always plenty of opportunities to let our jobs take precedence over our walks with Jesus. Even if your workplace is your home, you know this can be true.

So let's consider what it means to follow Jesus to work and what that might mean for each of us.

◎ What did your group co to try to win?
What motivated you the most to win?

◎ Were you annoyed by other team's
actions, or did you see them as being just
part of the game? Explain.

◎ Did you approve of everything your
team was doing? And if not, why did you
go along with it?

◎ How would more instructions have
affected the way you played the game?

Seek and Find

(about 30 minutes)

》 A couple of weeks ago, we explored a passage of Scripture relating to our tempers. Today let's revisit that Scripture in light of how we behave in our workplaces.

Ask for a volunteer to read James 3:13–16. Then discuss: ──────→

Ask everyone to rejoin their earlier groups.

》 The following Bible passages contain some differing perspectives about work. Divide them among your group members; if someone needs to take more than one verse, that's OK. Read your verse to yourself first, and write down in your own words what it says about work.

When everyone has finished, share with your group what you've written. Then together, answer the questions that follow. ──────────→

- Genesis 3:17–19
- Ecclesiastes 5:18–20
- Luke 12:15-21
- 1 Thessalonians 4:11–12
- James 4:13–16

James 3:13-16

◎ Let's think again about our game. In what ways does this passage from James echo what happened as we competed against one another?

◎ When have you seen some of the attitudes in this passage in your own workplace, either in yourself or in others?

◎ During our game, we also had to decide what rules—or lack of rules—we were willing to follow. What are some unwritten rules you face at your job? How do you work within—or around—those rules?

 Genesis 3:17-19; Ecclesiastes 5:18-20; Luke 12:15-21; 1 Thessalonians 4:11-12; James 4:13-16

◎ Which of these perspectives—all of which are biblical—best describes your attitude toward work? Why?

◎ How would you reconcile these different perspectives? As a group, try to come up with a single statement you can agree upon.

Seek and Find continued

Call the entire group back together to share highlights and insights from their discussions.

》 **Last week we considered our attitudes toward money and the attitudes God wants us to have. Since work is where we earn that money, let's explore that idea a little further.**

Read the Dallas Willard quote on your group page, and then let's discuss the following questions: ⟶

◎ How do our attitudes toward money affect how we feel about our jobs? What other factors affect our attitudes toward our jobs?

> *If we truly see [Jesus] as the premier thinker of the human race—and who else would be that?—then we are also in position to honor him as the most knowledgeable person in our field...and to ask his cooperation and assistance with everything we have to do.*
>
> —Dallas Willard,
> The Great Omission

◎ What would be different if you believed Jesus was smart enough to teach you what you need to know at work? What keeps you from believing that—or living as if you believe it?

◎ What's one question you face at work (or somewhere else) that you'd like Jesus to answer?

(about 10 minutes)

Ask for a volunteer to read Colossians 3:22–24. Then discuss: ⟶

> *Let the Christian remain in the world...to engage in frontal assault on it, and let him live the life of his secular calling in order to show himself as a stranger in this world all the more.*
>
> —Dietrich Bonhoeffer, The Cost of Discipleship

Colossians 3:22-24

◎ How would "working for the Lord rather than for people" (verse 23) solve issues you face at work? Be specific.

◎ Which problems, if any, *wouldn't* it solve? What do you think God would want you to do in those situations?

◎ What changes would you make so "working for the Lord rather than for people" is something you really *do*? What's one step you can take right now?

Walk It Out

(about 5 minutes)

>> **The following options are here to help you put what you've learned into practice. But if God has prompted you to do something else through this session, then by all means do that!**

choose 1:

☐ know it

Set aside an hour to review and meditate on this week's Scripture passages. What would it really mean to follow Jesus to work? If you get stuck, ask Jesus to help you—he really *does* know everything and wants to teach you what you need to know.

☐ live it

Plenty of companies have mission statements articulating their focus and purpose. Create your own workplace mission statement. How would following Jesus to work look in your context? How will you respond in certain situations? What lines will you draw? How up-front will you be about what you believe? Write down everything you come up with, pray over what you've written, and then boil everything down into a one- or two-sentence mission statement for your life at work. Then share it with a mentor or a good friend who'll keep you accountable.

☐ share it

Following Jesus to work isn't just about sharing your faith. It's also about being there for other Christians you work with—being a visible presence to one another to remind yourselves you're not alone. If you know of other Christians in your workplace, set up a time to meet regularly for prayer. If your company allows it, meet on-site; if not, look for a nearby coffee shop. Your meetings don't have to be long, but spend enough time for prayer requests to be shared and prayed over.

Form pairs, select the option you'd like to take on this week, and share your choice with your partner. Write what you plan to do in the space provided, and make plans to connect with your partner before the next session to check in and encourage each other. Take five minutes to do that now.

go for it

At work follow Jesus' example of love in action. Offer to help a co-worker who's buried under deadlines. Give someone a ride to work when his or her car is in the shop. Do the little things that no one else wants to do—clean the coffee pot, refill the copier with paper or toner, or empty the recycling box. And if someone's facing a difficult situation, ask if you can pray for, or better yet *with*, him or her about it. Even non-Christians will usually welcome a genuine offer of prayer, and your care and attention will speak volumes about God's love.

do it together

Is your company participating in a service project outside the workplace? Join in! Get to know co-workers in a totally different environment, and show Jesus' love while doing it. Check with your human resources department about programs your company supports; then pick one and get involved.

...or think of your own!

Because I not only want to bring Jesus to work but *follow* him there, I'll "Walk It Out" by:

_____

_____

_____

_____

Walk It Out continued

prayer➲ Come back together. Ask group members to once again reflect silently on their answers to the question "What's one question you face at work (or somewhere else) that you'd like Jesus to answer?"

Allow 30 seconds for reflection, and then thank Jesus that he really *does* know everything—including the answer to every challenge we face at work, whether it's moral, emotional, or intellectual. Ask Jesus to reveal just the right answer for each person in your group. Ask him to show all of you how best to model his love and wisdom in your workplaces.

Go Deeper

Dig deeper into how to follow Jesus at work by checking out these great resources:

Business for the Glory of God: The Bible's Teaching on the Moral Goodness of Business by Wayne Grudem (Crossway)

Mastering Monday: A Guide to Integrating Faith and Work by John D. Beckett (InterVarsity)

Balancing Your Family, Faith & Work by Pat Gelsinger (Life Journey)

Your Work Matters to God by Doug Sherman and William Hendricks (NavPress)

The Practice of the Presence of God by Brother Lawrence

The Heart of Hospitality

"*Rather, he must enjoy having guests in his home*" (TITUS :8).

"*Then these righteous ones will reply, 'Lord, when did we ever see you hungry and feed you? Or thirsty and give you something to drink? Or a stranger and show you hospitality? Or naked and give you clothing? When did we ever see you sick or in prison and visit you?' And the King will say, 'I tell you the truth, when you did it to one of the least of these my brothers and sisters, you were doing it to me!'* " (MATTHEW 25:37-40).

In this session, we'll journey...

from ⎯⎯⎯⎯⎯⎯⎯⎯⎯⎯⎯⎯⎯⎯→ **to**
exploring ways we can, or
already do, open our homes
and lives to others...
expanding our definition of
hospitality.

Before gathering, make sure you have...

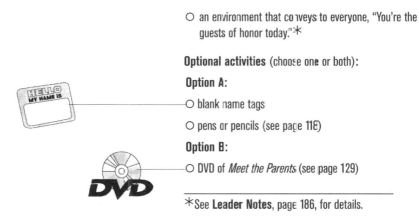

○ an environment that conveys to everyone, "You're the guests of honor today." ✳

Optional activities (choose one or both):

Option A:

○ blank name tags

○ pens or pencils (see page 118)

Option B:

○ DVD of *Meet the Parents* (see page 129)

✳See **Leader Notes**, page 186, for details.

Come and See

(about 15 minutes)

If you've chosen **Option A**, *read on.*
If you're doing **Option B**, *go to page 129.*

Give everyone a blank name tag, but ask people to leave them blank for the time being. Form groups of four or five.

» You're all going to have the opportunity to reintroduce yourselves today. You've each been given a blank name tag. Write down your name and one thing that others in your group probably don't know about you. It could be an accomplishment of some sort, a brush with fame, or anything else. Keep it simple.

Once you've finished writing, take turns reintroducing yourselves. Talk briefly about what you wrote on your name tag and why it's significant to you. Then discuss these questions: ⎯⎯⎯⎯⎯⎯⎯⎯⎯→

Allow 10 minutes, and then come together to share highlights and insights.

» Today we're going to talk about our homes. Our homes represent our lives, our privacy, and in a very tangible way, who we are. When we invite others into our homes, we're also inviting them into our lives. Today we'll consider how we can open those doors a little further.

Even if we don't have homes, there are other ways to allow people into our lives and our personal space. So let's explore how we can open our lives to those around us.

Come and See

◎ What do you like about wearing your label? What bugs you about it?

◎ If you were really meeting everyone here for the first time, would you have shared the same thing, something different, or nothing at all? Explain.

◎ Think about a time you were invited somewhere unfamiliar and were really uncomfortable. Why did you feel that way?

Seek and Find

(about 25 minutes)

» **First let's read some Scripture that will help us better understand God's definition of hospitality.**

Have a volunteer read 1 Peter 4:8–11.

» **On the surface, this passage seems to be jumping from one unrelated idea to the next. But let's take a closer look to see how these ideas might all go together.** Discuss: ————————————————→

Now let's look at a specific instance of hospitality that Jesus addressed.

Ask for another volunteer to read Luke 7:36–50. Then discuss: ————————————————————→

Ask everyone to stand.

» **We connect with others in lots of different ways, and sometimes we're not even aware of how we do it. Let's explore a few of those ways now. I'm going to call out a series of ways people can be grouped together. As I do, you'll join the people with whom you have those things in common. For instance, if I were to say "gender," you would join the men or women. You'll probably have to do a little more work than that with some of the groupings, and that's OK.**

1 Peter 4:8-11

 What connections can you identify between loving each other, sharing your home, and using gifts such as speaking and serving?

 What comes to mind when you hear the word *hospitality*? In what ways would you say you currently show hospitality?

 Luke 7:36-50

 In what ways did both Simon and the woman show hospitality? What was different about their approaches?

 Be honest: Which of these two would you be more likely to welcome into your home or life? Why?

Seek and Find continued

continued

> *They love one another. They never fail to help widows; they save orphans from those who would hurt them. If they have something they give freely to the man who has nothing; if they see a stranger, they take him home, and are happy, as though he were a real brother.*
>
> —Aristides, first-century Christian apologist

For this activity, you can either use the following list in its entirety or modify it to fit your group. Give everyone time to find their groups before calling out the next grouping. Do this four to six times before moving on to the questions.

》 So let's try this! Let's group together by...

- **those who are right-handed and those who are left-handed**
- **those who grew up in rural, suburban, or urban settings**
- **those who grew up in a church and those who didn't**
- **those who were an only child, those who had one or two siblings, and those with three or more siblings**
- **those who prefer country, rock 'n' roll, classical, jazz, or rap music**
- **those who prefer dogs, those who prefer cats, those who prefer birds, and those who don't like pets**

After the final grouping, have people remain with those groups and discuss: ⟶

》 It's easy to love people we have things in common with, but Jesus asks us to move out of our comfort zones. He asks us to show his love to everyone— even those we don't feel an immediate connection to. And for many of us, that's a lot of people. But Jesus tells us it's worth it.

◎ Were there any groups you thought you belonged to and didn't? If so, what made you think you were joining the "right" group?

◎ What are some characteristics that define your favorite groups? Why do you think those characteristics appeal to you so much?

◎ Without naming names, who do you think you'll never be able to connect with? You can think of a specific individual or a type of person. Why?

◎ How did our activity suggest that that might not actually be true?

Go

(about 15 minutes)

Have a volunteer read Matthew 25:31–40. Then discuss these questions:

>> **This week we're going to do the "Walk It Out" section a bit differently. Take two minutes to read the options to yourselves, and decide which one you're interested in doing. While we don't have to do something as a group, there's more opportunity than normal to work together as a group this coming week. So let's consider whether God might want us to do something together and what that might be.**

Allow two minutes for everyone to read the "Walk It Out" options; then allow another 10 minutes for discussion. Don't force anything here, but if there's an idea the entire group or some members of the group want to pursue, encourage them to hang out for a few extra minutes after the session to plan. If you're pressed for time, set up a separate meeting.

> *Let all guests who arrive be received as Christ, because He will say: 'I was a stranger and you took Me in.'*
> —The Holy Rule of St. Benedict

Matthew 25:31-40

◎ What does this passage tell you about the importance God places on hospitality? What forms does hospitality take in this passage?

◎ How does Jesus' perspective affect what it means for you to show hospitality to others? What might that look like?

◎ As we've worked through this session, who do you sense you need to make an extra effort to reach? How might you be able to do that? How can God—or this group—help you make that happen?

Walk It Out

(about 5 minutes)

》 **The following options are here to help you put what you've learned into practice. But if God has prompted you to do something else through this session, then by all means do that!**

choose 1:

☐ **live it** One of the simplest and best ways to care for others is to invite them into your home or, if it's more convenient, take them out for lunch or a cup of coffee. Use this time to discover who they are—their ideas, interests, and dreams. If you have opportunities to share what Jesus has done in your life, by all means do so. But don't force it.

☐ **know it** Reflect on Matthew 25:31-40. Ask God to show you who among "the least of these" you can show hospitality to. Ask him what you can do right away to start making that happen. Then do it!

☐ **share it** Would you like to invite someone to join this group? Go ahead and do it. Share how God has been speaking to you through these sessions and how it has affected your life. Or you might offer a Bible study in your home to friends who don't know Jesus or to friends who know Jesus but are "drifting" right now. You need only a few people for a study like this— maybe just you and two others.

Write what you plan to do in the space provided.

☐ **go for it *and* do it together** Think of an event your group can sponsor that reaches out to your neighborhood or beyond. Here are just a few ideas:

- Host a movie night.

- Have a conversational lunch that moves from house to house within a neighborhood.

- Reach out to a group you don't normally reach out to, such as the homeless, shut-ins, or the developmentally disabled.

Those you serve will begin to see you and your group in a different light. They'll begin to know what makes you tick and why you do these things. And they might become curious about who you do them for.

...or think of your own!

Because Jesus wants me to open my house and my life to others, I'll "Walk It Out" by:

_____

_____

_____

_____

_____

Walk It Out continued

prayer⊙
After your discussion time, pray for the people you want to reach. If ideas for reaching out as a group have surfaced, pray over each one. Ask God which one(s) he wants your group to pursue and how to do it. Thank God that he loves each of you enough to reach out to you. And ask God to give each of you the heart to do the same.

SEEING IT DIFFERENTLY
Come and See—Option B

LEADER Instead of the name-tag activity and questions, watch and discuss a scene from *Meet the Parents.* Cue the movie to 54:00 (DVD Chapter 11), where Kevin says, "Now for the floor you're walking on…" Stop at 57:32, at Greg and Pam's facial reactions to Kevin saying, "…considering I carved it all by hand from one piece of wood." (For those not familiar with the movie, it may also be helpful to point out that [a] Kevin is Pam's ex-fiancé; [b] Kevin is close friends with Pam's father, Jack; and [c] Jack doesn't like Greg, who's Pam's fiancé now.) Then discuss:

GROUP

◎ Why do you think Greg was reluctant to talk about himself? What, if anything, could Kevin have done to make him more comfortable?

◎ Think about a time you were invited somewhere unfamiliar and were really uncomfortable. Why did you feel that way?

Pick up at the leader statement beginning with **Today we're going to talk about our homes,** on page 118.

To dig deeper into how to practice hospitality in all its forms, check out these great resources:

Untamed Hospitality: Welcoming God and Other Strangers by Elizabeth Newman (Brazos Press)

The Gift of Hospitality: In Church, in the Home, in All of Life by Delia Touchton Halverson (Chalice Press)

Field Guide to Neighborhood Outreach (Group)

Making Room: Recovering Hospitality as a Christian Tradition by Christine D. Pohl (Eerdmans)

Radical Hospitality: Benedict's Way of Love by Daniel O. S. B. Homan and Lonni Collins Pratt (Paraclete Press)

Loving What's *Really* Good

"*...and he must love what is good. He must live wisely and be just*" (TITUS 1:8).

"*Yes, everything else is worthless when compared with the infinite value of knowing Christ Jesus my Lord. For his sake I have discarded everything else, counting it all as garbage, so that I could gain Christ and become one with him*" (PHILIPPIANS 3:8-9).

In this session, we'll journey...

from ⟶ **to**

exploring what God loves and why it's important...

determining what things—even good things—we need to surrender to God, so we can receive his better things.

Before gathering, make sure you have...

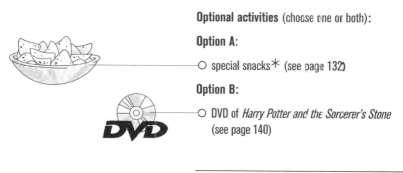

Optional activities (choose one or both):

Option A:

○ special snacks✳ (see page 132)

Option B:

○ DVD of *Harry Potter and the Sorcerer's Stone* (see page 140)

✳See **Leader Notes**, page 187, for details.

Come and See

(about 15 minutes)

If you've chosen **Option A**, *read on.*
If you're doing **Option B**, *go to page 140.*

As you share your snacks, discuss: ⟶

> **Over the last several weeks, we've talked about some of the things we value—family, work, and relationships. And we've explored how God can use us wherever he's put us. Today, we're going to move past even that.**

God has often blessed us by giving us the desires of our heart. The thing about following Jesus, though, is that he keeps us moving. In fact, we're never going to reach our destination here on earth. If we're following Jesus, we're always going to be moving forward, even if it doesn't always feel that way. And moving forward almost always means leaving things behind—even good things. At the very least, as Jesus changes us, our relationships with whatever or whoever comes along with us will also be changed.

As Jesus changes us, we begin to let go of whatever keeps us from following him. Sometimes that's sin. Sometimes it's our personal agendas or ambitions. Sometimes we let go of lifelong dreams because they've become our idol. Sometimes we even let go of something good so God can give us something better.

Today we'll discover some of the good things God wants for us *right now*.

Your life is shaped by the end you live for. You are made in the image of what you desire.

—Thomas Merton

We need to care for our hearts because they're ambivalent. Our hearts are corrupted, but still they're our source of life.

—Joshua Choonmin Kang, **Deep-Rooted in Christ**

◎ Think about the last major purchase you made or a goal that you worked toward and accomplished. How long did it take before that thing started losing its appeal? How long did it take to start striving for something else?

◎ How is that similar to the snack you're "enjoying" right now?

◎ How do you think your priorities might change over the next 10 years?

Seek and Find

(about 30 minutes)

Form three groups, and assign one of the following passages to each group: Mark 8:27–38; Luke 10:38–42; and Hebrews 11:8–19. If you have more than 15 people, keep group sizes to four or five, and assign the same passage to more than one group.

》 We're going to explore a few stories in the Bible in which God challenged someone to give up something good for something better. In your group, take 10 minutes to read the passage assigned and discuss these questions: ⟶

After 10 minutes, come back together and share highlights and insights. Then discuss: ⟶

Seek and Find

 Mark 8:27-38; Luke 10:38-42; Hebrews 11:8-19

◎ What good things did the person in the story give up? What better things did God offer, and why were they better?

◎ How did those good things stand in the way of what God really wanted for the person?

◎ Tell about a time God prepared you for something, but it meant letting go of something else. Why do you think God wanted you to let go of it? What were the results?

◎ Now tell about a time you gave something up to God, and he gave it back to you. What had changed, and why?

◎ Why do you think God often doesn't show us "the better thing" until we've given him the thing he's asked us to give him?

◎ How can something we enjoy, or something we find rewarding—even something we know God gave to us—become wrong for us, even sinful? Be specific, if possible.

Go

(about 15 minutes)

》 I'm going to ask a volunteer to read a Scripture passage, and I'd like the rest of you to close your eyes and really listen to and reflect on that passage. Afterward, we'll take a few minutes to quietly reflect on what this passage means.

Ask for a volunteer to read Philippians 3:7–14. Encourage him or her to read the passage slowly and deliberately.

After the reading, ask people to close their eyes, and allow 30 seconds of silence.

》 While your eyes are still closed, consider what this passage might mean for you specifically. Here are a few questions to think about.

Pause for 30 seconds between each question to give everyone time to reflect.

》 • What's the one thing—no matter how good or bad it is in itself—that you sense God is calling to you to surrender right now?

• What better thing do you sense, even now, that God may want to give you?

• Even if the answer to the last question was "I don't know," are you willing to trust God anyway?

» If something did come to mind, decide now in your heart that you'll commit to giving that thing to God. Decide that no matter how many times you might fail—how many times you take it back—that as you come to trust God more and more with that thing, he *will* help you to let it go. Ask God quietly right now to help you so that he can give you the things he really wants for you.

If you're comfortable doing so, while everyone's eyes are still closed, turn your palms downward as if you're releasing that thing. (Pause.) Now turn your palms upward to receive what God wants to give you—even if you have no idea what it is.

Allow another minute for everyone to respond, and then close this time with a brief prayer. Then move forward:

» Find a partner, and look at the Walk It Out options together. Once you've decided what you each want to do, pray for each other. God may have brought up something very personal during this session, and we want to keep that private as we close. But we also want to make sure you've got someone to help you bring that something to God—now and after we leave. Share as much as you're comfortable sharing with each other, and then pray together about what God has shown each of you. When you've finished, you're free to leave [or quietly hang out until everyone's finished, if you're in a small-group setting].

Walk It Out

(about 5 minutes)

》 The following options are here to help you put what you've learned into practice. But if God has prompted you to do something else through this session, then by all means do that!

choose 1:

☐ know it

Reread this week's Scripture passages. Consider how God's goodness was evident even when God's requests were unwelcome or hard. Ask God's forgiveness for those times you chose something other than God—even if at the time you thought you were choosing the right thing. Then ask God to help you know and follow his leading now.

☐ live it

Fasting is an excellent way to practice giving things up for God. It's also a good way to remove distractions that might be preventing you from hearing what God is trying to tell you. If you're not used to fasting, start with a meal, a half-day fast, or even a 24-hour fast. Drink plenty of water. Instead of eating, use mealtimes for prayer, discovering how God satisfies in ways food never can. Consider what other "good things" God might want you to be less attached to and how you might be able to set them aside for a time.

☐ share it

Who do you know who's trying to deepen his or her relationship with Jesus (or deciding whether to follow Jesus) and just seems *stuck*? Commit to helping that person for a season. Meet with him or her for coffee or lunch. Talk about his or her struggle, and then pray about it together. When it's relevant, share times God got you unstuck, and how God did it. Become someone this person can trust, and trust God to show you how best to minister to him or her.

Form pairs, select the option you'd like to take on this week, and share your choice with your partner. Write what you plan to do in the space provided, and make plans to connect with your partner before the next session to check in and encourage each other. Take five minutes to do that now.

go for it
God makes it clear that we don't truly love him if we're unloving toward others (1 John 4:20–21). This week, connect with a person you've wronged, and set things right. Move past the things that irritate you about someone. Fulfill a promise you made and didn't follow up on. Ask your partner to keep you accountable as you commit to doing one of these things.

do it together
Jesus calls us in no uncertain terms to reach out to those in need: the homeless, the stranger, the hungry, and the incarcerated (Matthew 25:31–46). Organize a group visit to people in the local jail; organize a social outing for children of the incarcerated; or volunteer in a soup kitchen, homeless shelter, or crisis pregnancy center. Think about how you can make this a regular practice rather than just a one-time event.

...or think of your own!

Because God always has better things for me, I'll "Walk It Out" by:

_____

_____

_____

_____

_____

SEEING IT DIFFERENTLY
Come and See–Option B

LEADER   Instead of the opening snack, watch a scene from *Harry Potter and the Sorcerer's Stone*. Begin at 1:32:15 (DVD Chapter 24), where Harry, an orphan studying wizardry at the Hogwarts School, is walking up to the mirror. Stop at 1:36:35, after Dumbledore says, "It does not do to dwell on dreams, Harry, and forget to live." (Note: Ron uses the phrase "bloody hell" in this scene. If you feel this will be a problem for your group, start at 1:34:22, where Ron says, "I'm Quidditch captain too..." Everyone should still get the point, even without the additional back story.)

Discuss these questions:

GROUP

◎ What do you think of Dumbledore's statement "It does not do to dwell on dreams, Harry, and forget to live"? How were Harry and Ron in danger of doing that?

◎ When has a dream caused you to "forget to live," even briefly? What snapped you out of it?

Pick up at the leader statement beginning with **Over the last several weeks, we've talked about some of the things we value,** on page 132.

Go Deeper

Here are some great resources to help you dig deeper into how to exchange the good things we have for the better things God wants to give us:

Living the Cross Centered Life: Keeping the Gospel the Main Thing by C.J. Mahaney (Multnomah)

Idols of the Heart: Learning to Long for God Alone by Elyse Fitzpatrick (P & R Publishing)

The Pursuit of Holiness by Jerry Bridges (NavPress)

Desiring God: Meditations of a Christian Hedonist by John Piper (Multnomah)

The Cost of Discipleship by Dietrich Bonhoeffer (Touchstone)

The D-Word (Discipline)

" *...He must live a devout and disciplined life"* (TITUS 1:8).

"So I run with purpose in every step. I am not just shadowboxing. I discipline my body like an athlete, training it to do what it should. Otherwise, I fear that after preaching to others I myself might be disqualified" (1 CORINTHIANS 9:26-27).

In this session, we'll journey...

from ————————————→ **to**
exploring the connections between—and benefits of—discipline and self-control...

discovering how we can have more disciplined lives.

Before gathering, make sure you have...

O a bowl of small candy, such as M&M's, with a sign in front of it saying, "Take only one piece."✳

O a newsprint tablet, blackboard, or white board✳
(If you're in a small-group setting, a notepad is OK.)

✳See **Leader Notes**, page 188, for details.

Come and See

(about 10 minutes)

ONLY TAKE
ONE
PIECE OF CANDY

Place the bowl of candy in the midst of your group, and invite everyone who hasn't already taken a piece to take one—but only one.

» In our last session, we committed to pursuing the better things God has for us. Today we're going to look at how discipline and self-control can help us do that. A lot of us hear words such as *discipline* and *self-control* and think, I just don't have that. If you're one of those people, you're wrong, and I'll prove it right now.

• How many of you are thinking, I'd really like more than one piece of candy? (Pause.)

• What's stopping you from taking another piece of candy, then? Is it just because you were told not to, or is there something more to it? Explain. (Pause for responses.)

Let's try another example. And it's OK to be honest; no one here will be offended or judge you.

• Before you came today, how many of you thought, even briefly, I could skip this session today? (Pause.)

• Why are you here today, then? (Pause for responses.)

See? It's not that we don't have any self-discipline. It's just that in many cases, we simply choose not to exercise it. We look at a goal, we think about what it'll take to reach it, and we decide it's not worth the effort—even though it often is.

Of course, not everything is a matter of willpower. Many people—and probably many of us—struggle with habits, self-destructive patterns of thinking, even addictions, that can seem overwhelming and unconquerable. But the Bible tells us that "overwhelming victory is ours through Christ" (Romans 8:37) and that Jesus has "overcome the world" (John 16:33). So if we believe in Jesus, we also need to believe what he tells us and act accordingly.

But life change usually doesn't happen overnight. It takes the Holy Spirit to guide and help us, and it takes—you've got it, *discipline*—the willingness to faithfully do what we know is best for us, even when we don't want to do it.

The good news is God is on our side. He wants us to get where he wants us to go. But this requires our cooperation. So let's explore what our part of the deal might look like.

> " *If you can convince yourself that you are helpless, you can then stop struggling and just 'let it happen.' That will seem a great relief—for a while.* "
>
> —Dallas Willard,
> The Divine
> Conspiracy

Seek and Find

(about 30 minutes)

Discuss this question: ⟶

Write down everyone's responses for all to see, acknowledging them as you do so. Once you have a good-sized sampling of responses, ask: ⟶

As people identify one or the other, mark natural disciplines with an X and spiritual ones with a star. Then discuss this question: ⟶

◎ What comes to mind when you hear the word *discipline?*

◎ Which of these would you call "natural" disciplines, and which would you consider "spiritual" ones?

◎ What would you say is the difference between these two categories? How are they similar?

> Many today are notoriously careless in their living...We have liberty, we have money, we live in comparative luxury. As a result, discipline practically has disappeared. What would a violin solo sound like if the strings on the musician's instrument were all hanging loose, not stretched tight, not 'disciplined'?
>
> —A.W. Tozer,
> Men Who Met God

Seek and Find continued

》 **Let's read 1 Timothy 3:1-5, 8-13. While this passage is addressed specifically to elders and deacons, there's nothing in it that doesn't apply to all of us.**

Ask a volunteer to read the passage; then discuss: ─────────→

Add the answers to the last question to the list the group created earlier.

Then continue the discussion: ─────────────────→

1 Timothy 3:1-5, 8-13

◎ What positive results of these disciplines does Paul mention?

◎ What disciplines are mentioned in this passage that we didn't list earlier?

◎ Do you normally think of all of these disciplines as spiritual? If not, why not?

◎ Let's look at our list again. What connections are you starting to see between the two types of disciplines? How do you see them work together in your own life?

It is inbred in us that we have to do exceptional things for God; but we have not. We have to be exceptional in the ordinary things to be holy in mean streets, among mean people, and this is not learned in five minutes.

—Oswald Chambers

Go

(about 15 minutes)

Ask for a volunteer to read 1 Corinthians 9:24-27, and then form groups of four or five to discuss: ⎯⎯⎯⎯⎯⎯⎯→

Come back together and share highlights and insights. Then pair up, and go on to "Walk It Out."

> *The job of a football coach is to make men do what they don't want to do in order to achieve what they've always wanted to be.*
>
> —Tom Landry, former NFL coach

1 Corinthians 9:24-27

◎ Tell about a time you really had to "put your nose to the grindstone" to accomplish something. How did it feel when you started? as you progressed? afterward? What kept you going?

◎ What goal have you been working toward recently? How close or far away does that goal feel right now, and how are those feelings affecting your efforts?

◎ How could the disciplines we've discussed keep you moving forward, no matter what you're feeling? Who can help keep you accountable as you start using those disciplines?

Walk It Out

(about 5 minutes)

>> **The following options are here to help you put what you've learned into practice. But if God has prompted you to do something else through this session, then by all means do that!**

choose 1:

☐ **know it**
Read the book of
Galatians this week.
If you can, read the
entire book every day.
Keep a brief journal
about your experi-
ence, reflecting on
these questions: How
easy was it to start this
devotion time? What
distracted me? What
did I learn from today's
reading? How can I
apply it to my daily life?
At the end of the week,
share with someone
how the daily discipline
of studying God's Word
has affected you.

☐ **live it** Identify one area of
your life in which you lack self-control,
and think of a discipline you could use to
counter it. Practice that discipline every
day. At the end of the week, reflect on what
God has taught you as you've sought to
become more Christ-like in that area of
your life. Thank God for what he's done so
far, and ask him to help you to continue
moving forward.

☐ **share it** With either a
Christian or non-Christian friend, agree
to become more disciplined in a certain
way. For example, you could start a diet
or exercise program or commit to reading
your Bible or praying for 30 minutes every
day. Then hold each other accountable.
But be sure to demonstrate grace because
you'll both probably stumble at least once
as you move forward.

Form pairs, select the option you'd like to take on this week, and share your choice with your partner. Write what you plan to do in the space provided, and make plans to connect with your partner before the next session to check in and encourage each other. Take five minutes to do that now.

☐ **go for it** For some of us, service is a discipline that doesn't come easily. Now might be the time to change that. What need have you noticed? Approach those who could use your help. Tell them you're willing to do whatever they ask, no strings attached. Then follow through, and show Christ's unconditional love to those you serve.

☐ **do it together**

Just coming to each of these sessions is a discipline. As a group, re-examine your commitment to one another, your expectations, and maybe even some bad habits you've fallen into. For example, it's easy to begin late each week or to enjoy each other's fellowship so much that you take your eyes off Bible study, prayer, and reaching out to others. Spend time talking about what's important to the group. Then encourage one another to practice self-control by living up to your agreement.

...or think of your own!

Because disciples need discipline, I'll "Walk It Out" by:

_____

_____

_____

_____

Walk It Out _{continued}

Come back together and form a circle. If possible, have people stand at least 3 feet apart, and try to make your circle 10 feet wide. If you have more than 10 people, form smaller circles. Ask people to close their eyes.

》 I'm going to read a series of statements. After each statement, take one small step forward if you agree with it. Keep your eyes closed as we do this.

Read the following statements, giving everyone time to respond after each:

- **I want to be better at the things I put my time and energy toward.**
- **I want to spend more time with God and more time in his Word.**
- **I want to be a better and more faithful friend, spouse, or parent.**
- **I want to overcome the habits, attitudes, or addictions I struggle with, and I know God wants to help me to do that.**
- **I want to seek God's will in all my decisions.**

》 Open your eyes.

Notice what's happened as you've focused on God and on bringing him into every part of your life. As we focus on God, God moves us closer together as well. And that's really what we often miss about discipline: When we get out of our own way, we're able to see one another's needs in fresh ways.

Close your eyes again, bow your heads, and consider what you've committed to today. I'll close in prayer.

Allow 15 seconds for everyone to reflect on their commitments, and close in prayer.

》 Lord, you've seen us express our willingness to seek you and to commit to being the kind of people you want us to be. We sometimes feel overwhelmed when we think about how far we are from being the people you ultimately want us to be. Forgive us, Lord, and don't leave us there. Help us begin to be faithful in small things. Help us to have the discipline to do what we need to do today and to allow you to carry us the rest of the way. Your Word says in 1 Corinthians 10:13 that you won't give us more than we can handle; help us take you at your word. In Jesus' name, amen.

⊖prayer

Go Deeper

Discover more about the importance of discipline by checking out these resources:

Growing Out: From Disciples to Disciplers, Season 1: Growing in Jesus by Carl Simmons (Group)

Celebrate Recovery: A Program for Implementing a Christ-Centered Recovery Ministry in Your Church by Rick Warren and John Baker (Zondervan)

Breaking Free: Discover the Victory of Total Surrender by Beth Moore (B&H Publishing Group)

Celebration of Discipline: The Path to Spiritual Growth by Richard Foster (HarperSanFrancisco)

The Spirit of the Disciplines: Understanding How God Changes Lives by Dallas Willard (HarperOne)

Standing in the Truth

> *He must have a strong belief in the trustworthy message he was taught; then he will be able to encourage others with wholesome teaching and show those who oppose it where they are wrong"* (TITUS 1:9).

"For our present troubles are small and won't last very long. Yet they produce for us a glory that vastly outweighs them and will last forever! So we don't look at the troubles we can see now; rather, we fix our gaze on things that cannot be seen. For the things we see now will soon be gone, but the things we cannot see will last forever" (2 CORINTHIANS 4:17-18).

In this session, we'll journey...

from ──────────────────→ **to**
seeing the importance—and   discovering where and how
cost—of persevering for   Jesus wants us to take a stand
Jesus...   right now.

Before gathering, make sure you have...

○ extra Bibles in case some people didn't bring theirs

Optional activities (choose one or both):

Option A:

○ Do Go as is (see page 162)

Option B:

○ DVD of *A Man for All Seasons* (see page 166)

See **Leader Notes**, page 189, for details.

Come and See

(about 20 minutes)

》 We've been together awhile and have dealt with a lot of ideas and issues this season. As we near the finish line, let's kick it up a bit for the final stretch. Everyone grab a Bible, find a partner, and form two lines. Partners will stand in separate lines, facing each other.

Give everyone time to pair up, stand up, and line up. Make sure everyone has a partner; if someone's alone, join him or her. Have partners stand at least a yard apart, but make sure they're directly across from each other. Give a Bible to anyone who needs one.

》 Everyone take two steps back from your partner. (Pause.)

Point to one line and continue:

》 Everyone in this line, turn to Romans 5, verses 2 through 5. (Pause.)

Point to the other line.

》 Everyone in this line, turn to James 1, verses 2 through 5. (Pause.) **Has everyone got the right passage? Good.**

Hold your open Bibles against your chests, turned toward your partners so they can read your passage to you out loud. Don't move toward each other, and don't extend your arms. Those holding James, read your partners' passage in Romans. Go!

Give pairs at least 30 seconds to attempt reading.

》 OK, Romans people, read the passage in James. Go!

Allow another 30 seconds.

》 **Now you can move as close to your partner as you want. Take a minute to read each other's passage, and then discuss these questions:**

Give pairs 10 minutes to discuss. Then, as everyone remains standing, call the group together to share highlights and insights.

》 **Today's session is about persevering in Jesus. If you haven't faced a time when it's been tough to stand firm for Jesus, you will. But as the passages we've just read and the stories we've shared remind us, God uses those times of testing, trial, and temptation to make us stronger—to give us more character—to deepen our hope—to make us more like Jesus.**

 Romans 5:2-5; James 1:2-5

◎ How did it feel to have to try to read your passages from a distance?

◎ Talk about a time God seemed far away. What helped you—or would have helped you—be faithful during that time? How did you get through that time, and looking back, how did you grow?

Seek and Find

(about 20 minutes)

>> **Turn to 2 Timothy 3:1. We're going to read a longer passage than usual today, going all the way to the end of Chapter 4. As we read, remember that this was written by Paul near the end of his life. He was trying to pass on as much as he could to his son in the faith, Timothy.**

Divide the reading of 2 Timothy 3:1–4:18 among your group members however you see fit, or ask one person to read the entire passage. Afterward discuss: —————————————→

I still believe that standing up for the truth of God is the greatest thing in the world. This is the end of life. The end of life is not to be happy. The end of life is not to achieve pleasure and avoid pain. The end of life is to do the will of God, come what may.

—*Martin Luther King Jr.*

>> **OK, let's all take a seat and talk about this some more.** —————————————→

2 Timothy 3:1–4:18

◎ What examples of faithfulness—or unfaithfulness—do you see in this passage?

◎ How was Paul affected by others' faithfulness or their lack thereof? How was Paul faithful, regardless of what other people were doing?

◎ At what point in this session did you begin to wonder, When are we going to sit down? Why do you think you started noticing it at that particular point?

◎ Likewise, in our walks with Jesus, when is it easier to take a stand for him? When isn't it so easy?

◎ Ultimately, how much do you let your feelings dictate how willing you are to take a stand for Jesus—and how you do it? Do you obediently suffer through it, talk yourself out of what you think God's telling you to do, or ignore what you're feeling and take a stand?

Go

(about 15 minutes)

If you've chosen **Option A**, *read on.*
If you're doing **Option B**, *go to page 166.*

Ask for a volunteer to read 2 Corinthians 4:7-12, 16-18.
Then discuss: ———————————————————————→

**》 Form pairs, and go on to Walk It Out. When you've
decided which option to tackle, go ahead and pray
for each other in your pairs for the things God has
brought up today. When you've finished, you're free
to quietly leave** [or quietly hang out until everyone's
finished, if you're in a small-group setting].

2 Corinthians 4:7-12, 16-18

◎ In what ways does the idea that we're already dying bother you? Why?

◎ Where is it costing you—or where do you sense it will cost you—to
follow Jesus? Who can help you carry that load?

Walk It Out

(about 5 minutes)

GROUP ▼

choose 1:

☐ **know it**

Paul's two letters to Timothy are filled with fatherly advice on how to persevere in Jesus. Read them this week. Better yet, read one of them each day, thus reading each three times. Allow God to challenge and inspire you. Then ask God what he wants you to do in response to your reading.

☐ **live it** One practical and time-honored way to identify with Jesus' suffering is to fast. Jesus himself fasted in the wilderness (Matthew 4:2), as did the church at Antioch before sending out Barnabas and Paul on their first missionary journey (Acts 13:2). Fast for a meal, a day, or longer. Donate the money you save by not eating to a hunger-relief organization.

☐ **share it** Maybe you know someone going through a trial or temptation that you've gone through yourself. Spend time listening to his or her feelings and experiences—how is it like what you went through, and how is it different? How did God meet you in that situation? What can you share that might help this person? Let him or her suggest a way you can help, and follow through with the suggestion.

Form pairs, select the option you'd like to take on this week, and share your choice with your partner. Write what you plan to do in the space provided, and make plans to connect with your partner before the next session to check in and encourage each other. Take five minutes to do that now.

☐ **go for it** Invite a not-yet-Christian friend to study Jesus' life with you. Read one of the gospels together, and ask him or her to keep a journal to record observations and questions as they arise. Use your conversations as an opportunity to point out Jesus' claims and the teachings that make Christianity unique.

☐ **do it together** Persecution of Christians is a terrible reality in many parts of the world. Commit to financially supporting and praying for an organization that supports the rights of Christians worldwide, such as Voice of the Martyrs, Open Doors, or Christians in Crisis. Or participate in The International Day of Prayer for the Persecuted Church (IDOP). You could also identify a specific international group of Christians who face persecution for their faith; then do what you can to support them through regular prayer and other practical ideas.

...or think of your own.

Because Jesus wants me to persevere—and to prevail—I'll "Walk It Out" by:

_____

_____

_____

_____

SEEING IT DIFFERENTLY
**Go**–Option B

LEADER   Instead of reading 2 Corinthians 4:7–12, 16–18 and answering the related questions, watch a scene from *A Man for All Seasons*. (It might help to explain that this scene takes place shortly before Sir Thomas More was beheaded for refusing to take an oath consenting to King Henry VIII's supremacy over the church in England.) Cue the movie to 1:36:22 (DVD Chapter 24), as Meg and William look away and Sir Thomas asks, "Well, what is it?" Stop at 1:38:48, after Sir Thomas says, "Finally, it's a matter of love." Then discuss these questions:

GROUP

◎ In what ways do both Meg's and Sir Thomas' arguments make sense here? What would you have done?

◎ In what ways has taking a stand for Jesus already meant dying to who you once were? Be specific.

◎ Where is it costing you—or where do you sense it will cost you—to follow Jesus right now? Who can help you carry that load?

LEADER   **Form pairs, and go on to Walk It Out. When you've decided which option to tackle, go ahead and pray for each other in your pairs for the things God has brought up today. When you've finished, you're free to quietly leave** [or quietly hang out until everyone's finished, if you're in a small-group setting].

Go Deeper

To deepen your understanding of what it takes to persevere in Jesus, check out these great resources:

Perseverance: A Long Obedience in the Same Direction (Christian Basics Bible Studies Series) by Eugene H. Peterson (InterVarsity)

Second Guessing God: Hanging on When You Can't See His Plan by Brian Jones (Standard)

When the Darkness Will Not Lift: Doing What We Can While We Wait for God—and Joy by John Piper (Crossway)

Foxe: Voices of the Martyrs by John Foxe (Bridge-Logos)

Biographies of notable or historical Christians, such as *Grace Abounding to the Chief of Sinners* by John Bunyan (Vintage, et al.); *The Hiding Place* by Corrie ten Boom (Barbour, et al.); *God's Smuggler* by Brother Andrew (Baker, et al.)

Merge With Care

"I'm not asking you to take them out of the world, but to keep them safe from the evil one. They do not belong to this world any more than I do" (JOHN 17:15-16).

In this session, we'll journey...

from
reflecting on where we've allowed God to intersect more with our daily lives...

→ **to**
identifying where God wants to take us from here.

Before gathering, make sure you have...

○ snacks✱

○ a plan✱

✱See **Leader Notes**, page 139, for details.

Come and See

(about 20 minutes)

Set out snacks for everyone to enjoy.

》 **We've made it to the end of this season. Give yourselves a pat on the back. Then help yourselves to a
snack, and make yourselves comfortable. Let's talk
about the journey God has taken us on together over
the last few months.**

*Your life is not
something from
which you can
stand aside and
consider what it
would have been
like had you
had a different
one...You are not
separate from
your life, and in
that life you must
find the good-
ness of God.*

—Dallas Willard,
    The Divine
    Conspiracy

Ask for a volunteer to read Colossians 4:5-6. Then discuss these
questions: ——————————————————————→

》 **As we've seen again and again during this season,
Jesus wants our faith to be woven more deeply into
every part of our lives. In this way we can grow deeper
in our faith. We can encourage other Christians by
sharing how God has been faithful as we've obeyed
him. And those who see our faith lived out might desire
to have a relationship with Jesus as well.**

**Let's take some time today to reflect and to celebrate
what God is already doing in our lives—and the even
better things he has in store for us.**

Colossians 4:5-6

◎ Over the last few months, in what ways have you seen your faith and everyday life become more "mixed"? How has that changed you? How has it challenged you?

◎ How have others in your life—both Christian and non-Christian— been affected by those changes?

Seek and Find

(about 20 minutes)

》 If anyone doubts that Jesus wants our faith to inter-sect with every part of our lives, let's put those doubts to rest right now. We're going to explore a prayer that Jesus himself prayed—and prayed specifically for us.

Ask for a volunteer to read John 17:9–26. Then form groups of four or five to discuss: ──────────────────────→

> *The way to be truly of use on this earth is to be genuinely heavenly minded—and to live as one of the places where, and the means by which, heaven and earth overlap.*
>
> —N.T. Wright

Gather after 10 minutes, and share highlights and insights.

John 17:9–26

◎ What does Jesus pray for in this passage? How have you seen this prayer play out in your own life? Give examples.

◎ Throughout this season, we've explored different opportunities for our faith to enter our daily lives. As we've done so, what examples have you seen in the lives of others—either here or elsewhere—that have prompted you to think, I wish *I* could live out my faith that way?

◎ What do you think God might want to do with that desire?

Go

(about 20 minutes)

>> **Let's bring this study full-circle by ending where we began.**

Ask for two volunteers to read Titus 1:5–9 and Matthew 5:13–16. Afterward, discuss these questions: ⟶

>> **This week we're going to "Walk It Out" a little differently. You've just thought of someone God has given you a heart for, so really, you already have your assignment. Now find a partner, and spend the next 10 minutes in prayer. Pray for each other and for those God has put on your hearts.**

If you want to share more—or you really don't know where God wants to take you next—share that, too. God wants our honesty, but he also wants us to move forward, so make the most of your time by spending most of it in prayer for each other.

Titus 1:5-9; Matthew 5:13-16

◎ What are some ways you've discovered you can let your faith shine that you weren't aware of or didn't realize you've already been doing?

◎ Who do you see as your mission field right now (whether that's one person or a specific group)? Put another way: Who has God put on your heart?

◎ What are you doing about it—or what can you do? Who can help you take the next steps?

Walk It Out

(about 10 minutes)

prayer⊙

Allow 10 minutes for pairs to share and pray, and then gather everyone together.

》 We're going to close by making Jesus' prayer in John 17 our prayer. Close your eyes, and think once more about the things Jesus asked God for. Realize he asked them for *you*…and that God has answered that prayer. As we pray, ask Jesus to help you believe that and to walk it out in the days—and years—to come. (Pause.)

Lord, we ask that you *don't* take us out of this world, but we *do* ask that you protect us from the evil one as we go out into the world. You call us yours, and because of that, we *don't* belong to this world anymore. Thank you again for that truth. Make us holy by your truth, and teach it to us more and more so we *can* be holy. Just as you sent Jesus into the world, you send us. Help us to appreciate the awesome privilege—and responsibility—that truly is.

And just as Jesus gave himself as a sacrifice for us, help us to sacrifice what we want for the sake of what others need—you. Help us, as your church, to be one in you so that the world will see and believe you came for them, too, and that they will come to believe that you love them as much as you love us. Help us to remember how much you love each person you've created, and form us more and more into the people you want us to be. In Jesus' name, amen.

> *But we are still on a journey, and we are truly travelers. We are not wanderers, but we are wayfarers. We have discovered that he is the way, but we are still on the road. Our faith is a pilgrim faith essentially at odds with place and settlement.*
>
> —Os Guinness,
>   The Call

Because my faith and my daily life need to cross paths more regularly, I'll "Walk It Out" by:

_____

_____

_____

_____

_____

_____

_____

_____

Go Deeper

To dig deeper into how your faith can intersect more with your daily life, check out these great resources:

The Externally Focused Church by Rick Rusaw and Eric Swanson (Group)

Organic Church: Growing Faith Where Life Happens by Neil Cole (Jossey-Bass)

This Beautiful Mess: Practicing the Presence of the Kingdom of God by Rick McKinley (Multnomah)

The Radical Reformission: Reaching Out Without Selling Out by Mark Driscoll (Zondervan)

Instruments in the Redeemer's Hands: People in Need of Change Helping People in Need of Change by Paul David Tripp (P & R Publishing)

General Tips

- **Read ahead.** Although these sessions are designed to require minimum preparation, read each one ahead of time. Highlight the questions you feel are especially important for your group to spend time on.

- **Preview DVD clips.** The copyright doctrine of fair use permits certain uses of very brief excerpts from copyrighted materials for not-for-profit teaching purposes without permission. If you have specific questions about your intended use of copyrighted materials, consult your church's legal counsel. Your church can obtain a blanket licensing agreement from Christian Video Licensing International for an annual fee. Visit cvli.com, or call 888-771-2854 for information.

- **Enlist others.** Don't be afraid to ask for volunteers. Who knows? They may want to commit to a role such as teaching a session or bringing snacks once they've tried it. However, give people the option to say, "No, thanks" as well.

- **Be prompt.** Always start on time. If you do this from the beginning, you'll avoid the tendency of group members to arrive later and later as the season goes on.

- **Gather supplies.** Make sure to have the supplies for each session on hand. (All supplies are listed on the opening page of each session.) Feel free to ask other people to help furnish supplies. This will give them even more ownership of the session.

- **Discuss child care.** If you're leading a small group, discuss how to handle child care—not only because it can be a sensitive subject, but also because discussing options will give your group an opportunity to work together *as* a group.

- **Pray anytime.** Be ready and willing to pray at times other than the closing time. Start each session with prayer—let everyone know they're getting "down to business." Be open to other times when prayer is appropriate, such as when someone answers a question and ends up expressing pain or grief over a situation he or she's currently struggling with. Don't save it for the end—stop and pray right there and then.

- **Let others talk.** Try not to have the first or last word on every question (or even most of them). Give everyone an opportunity to participate. At the same time, don't put anyone on the spot—remind people that they can pass on any questions they're not comfortable answering.

- **Stay on track.** There are suggested time limits for each section. Encourage good discussion, but don't be afraid to "rope 'em back in."

- **Hold people accountable.** Don't let your group off the hook with the assignments in the Walk It Out section—this is when group members apply in a personal way what they've learned. Encourage group members to follow through on their assignments.

- **Encourage group challenges.** Also note that "Do It Together"—the last weekly challenge in Walk It Out—is meant to be done as a group. Make ̲u̲r̲e̲ that ̲g̲r̲o̲u̲p̲ members who take on these challenges are both encouraged and organized.

- **Pray.** Finally, research has shown that the single most important thing a leader can do for a group is to spend time in prayer for group members. So why not take a minute and pray for your group right now?

Session 1

- If you haven't already, read the General Tips beginning on page 179.

- If this is the first time you're meeting as a group, take a few minutes before your session to agree on a few simple ground rules. Here are three important ones:

  1. Don't say anything that will embarrass anyone or violate someone's trust.

  2. Likewise, anything shared in the group *stays* in the group, unless the person sharing it says otherwise.

  3. No one has to answer a question he or she is uncomfortable answering.

- Being able to grow as a Christian is often dependent on being confident in one's own relationship with Jesus. If some group members are still unsure whether they have a personal relationship with Jesus, direct them to passages such as Romans 10:9-10 and Ephesians 2:8-9. Sometimes it's as easy as showing people what *God* says, rather than what they believe about themselves.

  But in other cases, the issue goes deeper than that. If either you or they still have doubts, set aside time when you can talk one-on-one, or promptly refer them to your pastor or another Christian leader you trust.

- For this week's snack, provide an unsalted version of a salty snack (such as pretzels, popcorn, chips, or unsalted saltines). Make sure there's enough so everyone can get a handful. Chances are that's *all* they'll want, but you can make more available if you like. There's a good chance that people will make the connection to Matthew 5:13 once they taste the unsalted snack. If our field-test group is any indication, it's likely that people will be making faces and sticking their tongues out once they sample their very bland snacks. Enjoy their reactions.

- At the conclusion of this first session, make a special point to remind group members of the importance of following through on the weekly challenge each has committed to in the Walk It Out section.

Session 2

- If new people join the group this week, use part of the Come and See time to ask them to introduce themselves, and have members of the group pass around their books to record contact information (page 18). Summarize the points covered in Session 1.

- Marriage may be a difficult subject for some in your group. There may be singles in your group who either don't know what to do with the subject of marriage or wish they *could* do something with it. On the other hand, there may be divorcees in your group who are still hurting and may be bitter about the dissolution of their marriages. Some people may be struggling with their marriages right now. In any case, strong feelings might surface during the discussions, so be prepared to listen and show the compassion of Jesus. If necessary, stop and pray for people on the spot. Completing a session takes a back seat to bringing healing to people's lives.

- Try to create a datelike setting for this session. You could light some candles, play romantic music, maybe even get dressed up, greet people at the door, and escort them to their seats. Be creative.

- If there is an uneven number of people for the Seek and Find activity, either join in or bow out, depending on your current role as leader. Either way, make sure everyone—married or not—has a partner.

  By the way, this was a powerful activity during field testing. Spouses who now had a captive audience raised serious matters they hadn't had the chance to discuss in depth previously; others were moved to realize that their spouses really *had* shared some of their concerns but hadn't been heard.

- During the coin activity, you'll permanently give up one coin to each person in the group, so make sure you're comfortable with whatever coins you offer.

- During the closing prayer, consider asking for volunteers to pray for requests that were shared. You could also minimize the time you spend sharing prayer requests by just diving into praying. If certain requests need to be explained, discuss those requests afterward so people know how to pray for one another during the week.

Session 3

- As with last week, the literal subject matter of this session isn't for everyone. There are likely people in your group who don't have children, possibly those who haven't been able to have children, or even those who have lost children. It's also possible that some in your group have children who are either rebelling or simply headed the wrong way (or at least in a way the parents don't approve of). Some of these issues, in fact, came up during our own field testing, as well as less-than-positive memories of group members' own parents.

  As painful feelings arise, be prepared to listen and show the compassion of Jesus to those who are struggling. Don't blow past what people are feeling; *do* help them to process those feelings so you can all move on together. Your compassion might just be the best lesson you could teach today.

- Make sure the items you choose for this week's activities are expendable, as some of them could be ruined in the course of the session. It's OK if different groups have different sets of supplies.

- Are you praying for your group members regularly? It's the most important thing a leader can do for a group. If you haven't already, take some time now to pray for your group.

Session 4

- During the field test, the opening activity held extra surprises for group members. Just when they were starting to think, Oh, we're going to get into groups and do the activity, it was revealed that forming a group and selecting a leader *was* the activity. The element of surprise helped people challenge the assumptions they automatically make about who is and who isn't a leader.

- Now that you're a month into this season, you may find it helpful to make some notes right after your session to help you evaluate how things are going. Ask yourself, Did everyone participate? and, Is there anyone I need to make a special effort to follow up with before the next session?

Session 5

- Remember the importance of starting and ending on time. If necessary, remind your group of this, too.

- Prepare the salt water before people arrive. Try to use noniodized salt, to help prevent possible allergic reactions, or check about possible allergic reactions in advance. In our field test, people made lots of funny faces as they tasted the salt water. So be sure to have fresh water or other drinks available, too!

- For the second activity in Seek and Find, you may want to set up stations prior to your session.

- This was a powerful session during field testing. One participant said, "I really wish I hadn't come"—not because he didn't ultimately benefit from and enjoy it, but because it brought him face to face with some forgiveness issues he'd been ducking up until then.

- If you need to spend more than just one week on a given session—and if you're not tied to a calendar and *can* spend some extra time—then do it! Taking the time to understand what God wants to tell your class, group, or accountability partner(s) is *way* more important than "covering the material."

Session 6

- A gentle warning to leaders: During the field test, I, as the leader, was pelted with stress balls. (Apparently this helps groups de-stress as well.) So be prepared!

- The books can be either hard cover or soft cover and should be fairly heavy. Just don't make them too heavy too soon for the activity you'll be doing. Also make sure to choose books you don't mind damaging because they're likely to be dropped in this experience. As the leader, be prepared to wind up holding all the books.

- Try to have some relaxing music playing in the background. You don't want anyone getting *too* stressed during this session, after all.

- This would be a good time to remind group members of the importance of following through on the weekly challenge each has committed to in Walk It Out.

Session 7

- Congratulations! You're halfway through this season. It's time for a checkup: How are the sessions going? What's worked well so far? What might you consider changing as you approach the remaining sessions?

- About those snacks: Don't break your budget, but make sure there are different types to choose from (such as sweet, salty, and healthy).

- For your closing activity: Although you'll encourage people to draw from their own wallets and purses (and share), have your own reserves ready just in case. (The specific denomination isn't all that important, actually; in fact, larger denominations might make your closing prayer time *more* powerful.)

Session 8

- For the opening activity, make sure there's enough of whatever "prize" you've chosen so everyone can have one after the initial prize has been awarded. Chocolate is almost always a good choice.

  Also, be prepared for teams to "get vicious." Ours did. Cards were thrown at opposing groups; towers were blown over; tables were shaken. However ugly it gets (as long as it doesn't get physically violent, of course), welcome it. It will make the point of the session that much stronger.

Session 9

- Create a setting that makes everyone feel at home and special. Personally welcome everyone, play music that appeals to everyone, or serve a favorite snack. If you normally occupy a favorite chair or location, sit in a less prominent place, and let someone take your spot.

- For your regrouping activity in Seek and Find: If you modify the groupings to fit your group, highlight both differences and similarities between your group members. Use a progression similar to the one we provided—that is, start with more clear-cut questions and move on to group-ings that will surprise group members and cause them to say, "Really? I didn't know *that* about you!" For instance, in our field test, one rock 'n' roll person was surprised to discover that the subgroup of three people he joined was actually composed of jazz fans.

- Are you praying regularly for your group? Pray for them now, if you haven't already.

Session 10

- OK, here's the secret: Your opening snacks shouldn't be very special at all. In fact, they should be stale. You could use pretzels, mini-sandwiches with hardened bread, or cold pizza. Make sure everyone gets a sample before you start your session. If possible, pass the snack around as you begin the session, so people are eating while you're discussing.

  Also have some fresh, tasty snacks—the same kind, if possible. Just don't make them available until after everyone's sampled the stale snacks.

- As you work through this session, some people may be tempted to get into a discussion about "the perfect will of God" versus "the permissive will of God." *Don't go there.* All theological issues aside, that's not the point of this session. What's really at stake here is obedience to God and what that might cost. It's likely that the Spirit will bring up some important issues in people's lives. Be supportive, and keep pointing to Jesus.

- Here's another approach to using the movie clip: You could go ahead and enjoy the opening snack, and instead show this scene at the beginning of Go before reading Philippians 3:7-14. This could set up a powerful moment as group members realize they're relying on things rather than on God's promises. So set your session up with this DVD clip, or drive the point home with it. Your group, your call.

- One more thing: This is a tough session to work through, and for that matter, was the toughest one in this entire series to write. (I knew *exactly* what good thing I needed to give up for God's better thing as I wrote it.) That's OK. Let the deep discussions begin, and let the tears flow. God will start great things in your lives through them. And I can attest to *that,* too.

- Now is a good time to do another group checkup—especially if you're planning on doing another study together after this. Ask yourself, Is everyone participating? and, Is there anyone I need to make a special effort to follow up with?

Session 11

- During your opening activity, you'll ask people why they're not taking extra pieces of candy. Be prepared for knee-jerk reactions such as "Because you *told* us not to," but allow time for people to explore their motives further. They'll think of other reasons. With this and the follow-up question about skipping today's session, the idea is to get people to realize they already exercise discipline in their lives whether they're aware of it or not.

  During field testing—and despite the sign—several people cheated, grabbing handfuls of M&M's candies—sometimes more than once. They thought they were rebelling against the leader (me), but they actually helped make the point of the lesson even stronger and exposed some of the real reasons we choose not to be disciplined.

- During Seek and Find, encourage people to come up with a variety of disciplines if they don't automatically do so—spiritual disciplines such as worship and prayer, physical disciplines such as diet and exercise, intellectual disciplines such as study and memorization. Work is a discipline, too, and so is anything people do to keep themselves doing the best job they can. Someone might even suggest "getting out of bed" as a discipline (and in fact, someone did during field testing). Have a good laugh; then write it down—the wise guy who suggested it isn't entirely wrong, you know.

For the follow-up question, if there's debate over which category a given discipline falls in, mark it with both an X and a star. Disagreement can be healthy—and it will make your point stronger later on.

Session 12

To order copies of *Season 3: Growing in Your Gifts,* visit your local Christian bookstore or group.com.

- Since your next session will be the last of this season, begin discussing with the group what to do after this study. Will you go on to *Season 3: Growing in Your Gifts*? Or will you study in greater depth a topic that arose this season? Will you break up and head to different classes? Make your plans now.

- Make sure everyone remains standing from the opening activity until you instruct them to sit down during Seek and Find. If someone has a serious problem standing, let him or her off the hook; otherwise, anyone capable of standing should do so. If anyone asks, "When can we sit down?" simply reply, "Soon."

Session 13

- Since this is your group's last session of the season, make sure you have a plan for next week and beyond.

- For this closing session, offer foods that feature two or more ingredients that go well together: trail mix, fruit salad, ice cream sundaes, peanut butter and jelly sandwiches, or omelets, for example. Or have the group create its own trail mix. Select ingredients; then at the beginning of the session, have the group work together to combine the ingredients. Enjoy the trail mix during your discussion time.

  As you share, the "aha" of how different things go together will become clear. It certainly did in our field test. We came away with a deeper sense of how God had "mixed" us and brought us closer during our season together. And that's what *Growing Out* is all about.

- One question near the end of the session, "Who do you see as your mission field right now?" and its clarifier, "Who has God put on your heart?" produced a *lot* of responses in our field test. One gentleman looked me in the eye and said, "You've just opened up a door for me." He went on to describe a guy at work whose lifestyle is pretty much killing him and whom he felt the need to reach out to. That prompted others to describe their yearnings to reach out to family members, local volunteer organizations, and friends. One person in our group who recently returned from the mission field shared that she was now seeking direction about her mission at home.

  We closed this season with a deeper desire to invest ourselves in the people around us. And that's exactly what we had set out to do.

- To celebrate your time together, do something special after the session, or plan a separate time together. No matter what you do—congratulations! We hope God has blessed your time together these past few months, and that you'll continue to let God lead all of you forward together.

Outstanding praise for Drew Ferguson
and *The Screwed-Up Life of Charlie the Second*

"*The Screwed-Up Life of Charlie the Second* is a funny, honest, and engaging book told with attitude and style. Drew Ferguson is a talented writer with great comic timing, and an eye for the absurd."

Bart Yates, author of *The Brothers Bishop*
and *The Distance Between Us*

"Drew Ferguson's debut novel is equally funny and smart, and will strike eerily familiar chords in anyone who remembers the edgy, frustrating, sex-obsessed days and nights of high school. You'll love his narrator, Charlie, and you'll also love this book."

Scott Heim, author of *Mysterious Skin* and *We Disappear*

"Look out Napoleon Dynamite, here comes Charlie the Second! In this page-turning laugh riot, Drew Ferguson captures the voice of Today's Teen conquering the daily drudge that is Life in the Midwest. Colorfully candid, unapologetically explicit, yet touchingly tender, *The Screwed-Up Life of Charlie the Second* serves as a reminder to those who've escaped from Small Town USA as to the reasons why!"

Frank Anthony Polito, author of *Band Fags!*

"A terrific debut novel. Drew Ferguson is one of the most authentic new voices in contemporary fiction."

Steve Kluger, author of *Almost Like Being in Love*

Please turn the page for more advance praise!

The Screwed-Up Life
of
Charlie the Second

drew ferguson

KENSINGTON BOOKS
http://www.kensingtonbooks.com

ISBN-13: 978-0-7582-2708-9
ISBN-10: 0-7582-2708-6

First Printing: September 2008
10   9   8   7   6   5   4   3   2

Printed in the United States of America

For Mom and Dad—
and no,
neither of you
is anyone
in this book.

ACKNOWLEDGMENTS

My sincere thanks to John Scognamiglio and Peter Senftleben of Kensington, their insights and comments made this a much better book; to my agent Jennifer DeChiara, who "got" Charlie and believed in him from the start; to Charlie's spiritual godfathers: Randall Alders, who gave Charlie his heart, and Eric Smith, who gave Charlie his . . . let's just say, appetite; to Erick Gerrard and Bruce Broughton, for reading drafts of the book and offering encouragement and critique; to Joanne Asala, for her early proofreading; to the folks in Columbia College's fiction-writing department—particularly Andrew Allegretti and Ann Hemenway; to Chris McCaughan for letting me name-check The Lawrence Arms; to my bartenders; and most of all to my friends and family for basically managing to put up with me. My apologies to the city of Crystal Lake and South High School for bending you to my will.

Saturday, August 25

Okay, so maybe getting my scrawny ass pushed into the back of a Crystal Lake cop car wasn't the smartest thing I've done, but Dana's party last night—it sucked. She should thank me. The only thing anyone'll remember about the party is me getting busted.

My folks, on the other hand, won't let it go. They say I'm this big embarrassment to them. What else is new? After spending seventeen years listening to them say that I don't "apply myself," I'm giving up. Not in the good-bye-cruel-world sort of way. I'm not in this huge rush to swipe a Ginsu knife from the kitchen and make Swiss cheese of my intestines. It's just that when you're in a damned-if-you-do, damned-if-you-don't situation, it's best if you don't. It's easier.

Only, my parents don't see it that way. According to them, I need to grow up and try to make something of myself, which means writing this stupid personal essay for my college applications. So I said I'd start my personal essay.

My name is Charles James Stewart, II. Charles the Second. My friends call me Charlie. First (AKA Charles James Stewart, AKA Dad, AKA McHenry County's next state's attorney) calls me Chip at press conferences, but around the house, I'm usually Smart-ass. Everyone else calls me Ass Bandit or Fudge Packer. I'm seventeen years old, scarecrow gangly at all of 6'4", and a buck-fifty dripping wet. My nose and ears are way too big, my voice cracks all the time, and I've never passed my driver's test. (Six failures, but who's counting?) As you can probably tell, I'm one of the cool kids. While some guys in my class already have hair on their chests, I just started getting pubes. And to make me a bigger freak, all three of them are growing in straight. I also don't have their "cool" half-a-pint-of-gel-and-two-hours-in-front-of-the-mirror-to-look-like-I-just-rolled-out-of-bed hair, puka shell necklaces, designer hoodies, or K-Swiss shoes, either. I do have their dirty jocks, though, 'cuz they shove 'em in my face all the time.

I'll be a senior at South. I'd've graduated already, but in grade school I was held back 'cuz I was, as First half-jokes, "socially retarded."

My extracurricular activities include soccer, being a total music and comics freak, and jacking off like a retarded monkey. C'mon, I'm seventeen, and it's not like I've gotten any action, short of the one time Bob Collins beat off in front of me after a soccer game (and then freaked and totally stopped talking to me).

After high school, I want to . . .

Who cares?

So naturally, Dana Flannigan's not the only person who thinks I'm a jerk. Everyone does. That's why Dana didn't even want me at her end-of-summer-we're-gonna-be-seniors party. It didn't matter to me. The only reason I even went to the thing was because Dana is dating Bink, my best friend since second grade (second grade round two, that is). Bink made me go.

I guess the fact that Bink's always making me do things is how the two of us ended up friends in the first place. He jokes that we wound up being friends 'cuz "all the really cool superheroes have sidekicks." He says it 'cuz he knows it'll get a rise out of me. I tell people we ended up friends 'cuz we wanted each other's meat. It pisses him off, but it's true—sort of anyway.

During the first week of second grade, I made sure I always sat by him in the school cafeteria during lunch. Even back then, I thought he was cute—cute like I wanted him near me, not cute like I wanted him *in* me. Anyhow, this one day toward the end of the week, Bink opened his lunch bag, pulled out a plastic-wrapped corned beef sandwich on white bread, and stuck a finger in his mouth, pretending like he was going to puke.

"I hate corned beef," he said, pouting. "What do you have?"

I opened my plastic lunch box and looked inside. "A ham sandwich."

"I'm not supposed to eat those."

"Why?" I asked, wondering if he was like this one girl in class the year before who ate something that touched a peanut at some point, and almost died.

"Because I'm Jewish," Bink said. He looked like a little kid who'd just been told to hug a great-aunt who always wears costume jewelry sharp enough to puncture a lung, tells you how big you're getting, and then drags her chin whiskers across your face as she gives you one of those slobbering kisses that border on intergenerational incest.

"What's Jewish?" I asked.

"It's like being grounded for life for not believing in Jesus.

3

You can't eat ham. You have to wear stupid hats. Every Friday night they force you to go to a place where everyone talks funny. Once a year, you have to wait at the table until some guy named Elijah shows up for dinner. He never does 'cause he's dead, but they don't tell you that at first. The worst part is you don't get Christmas. I don't want to be Jewish."

"Me neither," I said, wondering, at the time, if it was something you could catch from a girl or from sitting on a public toilet seat.

I felt bad that Bink didn't get to have Christmas, so I gave him my sandwich. He practically shoved the whole thing in his mouth, telling me between chews that I was his best friend in the whole wide world. Looking back on it now, it wasn't the smartest thing to do, but what did I know? I was, like, eight. And, I didn't know that Mrs. B would fly off the handle when she found out.

I like to imagine the second-grade version of Bink, walking home from school all pissed-like and letting Mrs. B have it. He marches into the house, metal screen door slamming behind him, throws his book bag on the floor, puts his fists on his hips, stares at Mrs. B, who's sitting on the couch watching some TV judge tell a hillbilly he's gotta pay for the cell phone he stole from his truck-stop girlfriend. Mrs. B looks at him and asks, "What's a matter, honey?"

Then Bink gets all high and mighty, and lays into her about how Moses, Methuselah, Maccabaeus, Meir, and Menachem had it wrong.

Bink says to his mom, "You lied to me. There's nothing wrong with ham. In fact, it tastes really good—especially on rye bread with Swiss cheese."

I can see Mrs. B going into this state of total apoplexy—bulging eyes, trembling lips, jaw practically to the carpet—but none of that seems to bother Bink. He just wants to know what else she lied about—bacon, shrimp, cheeseburgers, shellfish, bacon cheeseburgers, and probably even his foreskin. Okay, so not his foreskin. I'm the only freak who'd bring it up.

I don't know how it really happened, but Mrs. B found out about Bink eating ham, and she actually did blow a gasket. She called the school and, I imagine, demanded that the principal tell her what Nazi sympathizer was feeding her son pork products, why the school was letting some kid single-handedly ruin the Jewish diorama (or whatever she called it), and if West Elementary would teach kids to remember the Holocaust by selling Anne Frank-furters at lunch.

The principal ended up calling my mom, and we had to go into his office for a meeting with Bink and Mrs. B. I got grilled on why I gave Bink the sandwich even after he told me he was Jewish and wasn't supposed to have it.

" 'Cuz he doesn't get Christmas."

As a defense, it didn't fly. It just led to some boring let's-find-exciting-new-ways-to-celebrate-our-differences discussion that made both Mom and Mrs. B happy, especially when the principal made the two of us promise to be friends and swear that we would only eat the lunches that were packed for us. The part about us being friends held. The second part didn't. Bink still takes my ham sandwiches whenever he gets the chance.

When Bink pulled into my driveway last night about two hours late, I wasn't in any hurry to leave. I had actually hoped he'd forgotten me.

Fat chance. Bink nailed the horn of his rusted-out, bumper-attached-with-baling-wire Volvo and I peeled my skinny butt off of the couch, slammed through the screen door, and slumped shotgun next to him.

"How was your summer?" Bink asked. He reeked of his dad's

knockoff cologne—*"If you like Polo, you'll love Lacrosse."* Most people don't expect Neil Binkmeyer to be much of a talker. Hell, at first glance Bink looks like a jockstrap with a pulse. He's one of those guys who's like a puppy that hasn't grown into its body yet.

We hadn't talked much lately. He'd been too busy with football practice, carpooling his kid sisters, and, of course, Dana. It's weird, 'cuz there was a time when we were really close. My mom and Mrs. B were always saying if you wanted to find one of us, look for the other one. Sure, we'd argue about whether the Star Trek *Enterprise* could take out the *Death Star.* (Ummm, no . . . Prime Directive, anyone?) But at least we were talking. But this last year, it's been different. Mom says it's my fault. She says I'm jealous that Bink's spending more time with Dana than he is with me. So, she's right. What if I am jealous? Bink gets to go off and spend all his time with his girlfriend and my dating life's about as active as a comatose eighty year old on a respirator. Might as well pull the plug.

"My summer was pretty lame," I said. "I spent most of it beating off and playing *Grand Theft Auto*." I pretended like I was lying, but I really wasn't. I adjusted my seat so my knees wouldn't knock out my Adam's apple. Bink slipped the car into reverse and backed out.

"Actually, things suck," I continued. "There's this new rich kid on the soccer team. His dad got him on the team without a tryout. No one knows if he's any good. Then there's First. He spent the summer telling me how I was wasting my life, how I should get a job, try to make something of myself . . . you know, his whole, pull-yourself-up-by-your-bootstraps, no-son-of-mine-is-going-to-sit-around-all-summer-eating-Ho-Hos-drinking-grape-Nehi-and-watching-rerunsof-bad-sixties-TV-shows routine. What are bootstraps any-how?"

"Your dad's an ass." Bink rolled his eyes. We both grinned. His tongue was stained little-girl pink from the gum he always chews. I turned the radio down—the tuner was permanently stuck on WAIT, Crystal Lake's Home of Easy Listening—and watched Bink as he drove to Dana's house in Turnberry, the rich side of town.

He looked different—more college junior than high school senior. He'd bulked up a lot and he had a farmer's tan that almost hid the freckles on his arms and face. A few strands of glowing copper chest hair poked from the Velvet Underground T-shirt he wore under a loud-ass Hawaiian shirt. Christ, I should've known Dana's party was gonna be some kind of Don-Ho-Goes-Freaky-Tiki-Last-Days-of-Pompeii theme. I didn't care. I was with Bink. It was hard to think of him as the same guy I'd grown up with . . . kiddie birthday parties, fishing for minnows in the creek near his house, and catching lightning bugs until it was dark enough for games of kick-the-can. You aren't supposed to want to do it with someone who's practically your brother, right?

Part Two of the College Essay I Won't Be Writing 'Cuz It's Way Too Embarrassing:

I've been a walking hard-on for four years now. I can't help it. Sex is the only thing I think about even though I'm this total virgin dork and don't know jack about it. The guys at school talk about getting head and stuff. But I don't get how it's done. What do you do with your teeth?

I'm worried that I'm a total perv. The alarm clock'll

go off in the morning and my dick'll be poking through the Y-front of my Jockeys, frantic-like. I'll pull out last year's yearbook, flip to the two-page wrestling spread, and hump a load into the pillow between my legs. I even suck the spooge out of the pillowcase so Mom doesn't get any ideas. It's not like I'm the only guy who's ever tasted his own spunk, right?

It's even worse at school. I constantly wanna rub one off there. It doesn't have to be the locker-room-jocks-in-the-shower stuff. Odds are the guy sitting next to me in second period can get me burrowing out of my button flys. Or a guy with a fresh haircut—all those just-shaved hairs at the base of his neck. I'll see something like that and boom, I've gotta major case of wood poisoning.

Which sucks 'cuz there aren't many places at South you can actually make knuckle babies. The bathrooms are too busy, and besides, the stall doors don't lock. So that leaves the library stacks and daydreaming about the hockey team's "soggy biscuit" initiation, where all the guys jack off onto a slice of Wonder Bread and the last guy to shoot eats it.

Sorry, Toni Morrison; I promise I'll eventually read The Bluest Eye *instead of tearing it apart page by page for come rags.*

Honestly, I probably jerk off way more than other guys my age. It's so bad I don't even moan anymore. I could do it at a funeral and no one'd know.

"How was your summer?" I asked Bink.

"Crazy. Mom had me drag my sisters to swimming lessons, ballet classes, and to a bunch of other crap. My dad hounded

8

me to retake the SATs for a better score. Football practice has been hell. The only cool thing was Dana went on the pill. Damn, Charlie, if she'd made me wait any longer, I swear I would've died."

"So?" I said, reaching into my pocket and pretending like my jeans'd been riding up. I adjusted my dick.

"It's weird. Doing it, I mean." Bink's voice cracked. He mopped a few beads of sweat from above his lip onto his forearm. "She says she likes it, but I don't know. I think I'm too fast. She hasn't said anything to me, but I think she told her friends. I'll walk past them and they'll huddle together and giggle, you know?"

He was being stupid so I laughed.

"Screw you, homo. What do you know about pussy?"

"Just that you're acting like one."

At first, Bink wasn't totally cool with me being into guys. Even now, when we both go to the john to piss, he'll use a stall. If I space out for too long, he'll sometimes think I'm checking him out and he'll jab me in the arm and tell me to knock it off. Bink's parents were cool from the start, though. They were the ones who insisted I stay with them when First kicked me out last summer after he found my jack-off stash under my mattress. That's not exactly fair. I was the one who left. I couldn't take it. And it wasn't 'cuz First went into some kind of you're-dead-to-me, no-son-of-mine rages that ended where, warmed only by my own bitter tears, I stood on our front porch, shaking my fist at First and vowing that I would never go straight or hungry again. No, I left 'cuz First went silent—the cold, vacuum of space kind—and that's what freaked the hell out of me.

See, when it comes to me, it's not like First's ever been able to keep his mouth shut. He's never said it—he hasn't had to—but he's never been exactly thrilled with the way I've turned out. In a way, I actually understand it a little. It's the name thing—Charles James Stewart the Second, not Charles James Stewart, Junior. It's like he sees me as the new version of himself—First 2.0—and each and every one of my failures and setbacks are a reflection on him. Seriously, how screwed up is it to give your son your own goddamn name? It's like pinning your dreams to a ghost.

I think that's why things went radio silence between us after he found my visual aids, or as I like to think of them, my collection of photos of future ex-boyfriends: an Abercrombie & Fitch catalog, one of the Binkmeyer girls' teenybopper mags filled with pictures of shirtless guys with names like Jeremy and Zach, and a photo spread from one of First's old copies of *Hustler* featuring two blond guys at a barbecue with some chick they didn't seem interested in.

Last year, when this all happened, my grades in trigonometry had been pretty crappy, and when after-school tutoring didn't help matters, First decided I had to be on drugs. It was the only thing that made sense.

So one Friday night after I got a D on a trig pop quiz (I'd messed up, again, on sines and cosines), First went on a hunt for the source of my reefer madness.

When I got home from practice, the parental units weren't around. I walked to the fridge to grab a can of Coke or something, and out of the corner of my eye, I saw my whack-off material splayed out across a countertop. Out in the open like that, the magazines felt dirty. Obscene. The crime scene photos of a murder victim shoved at the suspect in custody. My heart stopped. For a second, I actually hoped—believed—that destroying the evidence would erase the crime. And then

I heard First and Mom upstairs. I sneaked up the stairs and stood just outside their bedroom.

"I don't understand it," First said. He sounded tired, like his voice had given up on expressing emotion.

"There's nothing to understand," Mom said. "It is what it is."

"And what, I'm supposed to just accept it?" First's voice jumped into sharpness. "Am I supposed to pretend that this isn't going to make his life harder?"

"You don't have to pretend anything. You just have to be there for him. I'm not saying it's going to be easy. I've always wanted a daughter-in-law . . . grandchildren. This . . . it breaks my heart."

"You'll talk to him?"

"We both should."

"I can't. Not yet."

I felt like I was going to throw up, so I sat on the second stair from the top of the landing. Part of me wanted to run into the room and say I was the same person I'd always been, that nothing had to change, that we could all go back to acting like they didn't know the truth. But another part of me was pissed. Me being into guys, it wasn't about them. It was mine—a private part of me—and their stupid asses had to go rooting around for it. It was their own fucking fault if they discovered shit they couldn't handle.

I was so pissed and scared and hurt, that I was crying into my hands and didn't know it.

"Charlie?" Mom said. She and First had left their bedroom, and she was leaning down to me, her arm shepherding my shoulder. "Don't worry. We'll figure this out. We'll figure everything out in time."

I looked to First for confirmation. His eyes were empty

as sinkholes. That hurt. It really fucking hurt. Even today, I don't know if there's anything worse than a guy looking at his father and seeing nothing behind his eyes—no glimmer, no spark, just muted disappointment.

The three of us went downstairs to the kitchen, where First started cleaning the mess of masturbatory aids from the counter. The *Hustler*, he dumped in the trash, the rest he left in a stack to the corner. I know now that she was trying to be patient and understanding and all, but Mom was giving me the third degree.

She wanted to know if this was a phase—*no*—if I was confused or experimenting—*no*—had someone, a friend, a relative, a teacher touched me—*hell no, don't be sick*—if I was having sex—*it's none of your business*—which apparently it was as long as I am living under her house—*I'm not having sex with anyone but myself, is that what you want to hear? Just leave it alone, okay?*—did I have a special friend—*like a retread?*—no, was I seeing anyone special to me—*no* (with a huge disgusted sigh)—was Bink gay—*no Mom, he's not gay, he's just Jewish*—did I want to see anyone for help—*I'm gay, not crazy, but if you ask me any more questions I'll be both*.

The whole time she was drilling me—and yeah, I was kind of shitty to her—I kept looking at First. I was waiting for him to jump in and say something. I actually wanted him to yell at me. I really did. I wanted him to say what a disappointment I was and how this was yet another one of my illustrious screwups. He didn't, and that's what killed me. No lecture, no study guide, no after-school tutoring, no new game plan, no extra practice, no him breathing down my neck and refusing to let up for even a goddamn second—nothing was going to help. By saying nothing, it felt as if he was telling me that he was done with me. That's why I had to leave. I couldn't be around him when he made me feel dead at sixteen.

I spent the next few days, until Mom said that First had come around a little, with the Binkmeyers. Things were freaky, partly because Bink's parents are so much older than everyone else's and partly 'cuz it was three days of Binkmeyer family powwows about my dick and how I hoped to use it. Mrs. B is big on "dialogues," which are her solution for anything that can't be fixed by a "strongly worded" letter-to-the-editor, protest march, or boycott. She's this flower child gone to seed who's always lecturing Bink and me about how she'd been to Woodstock and marched for civil rights in Selma or Alabama or some place, I forget. Anyhow, Mrs. B droned on and on about all the homos in history who lived wonderful, normal lives. (*Oscar Wilde—no, they were awful to him. Prison, then dying broke in France. Well, Charlie, he's not a good example. But what a tomb! If you're ever in Paris, you really should see it.*) And Mr. B, being a high school biology teacher—excuse me, "man of science"—kept saying that in the animal kingdom there are muff-diving sheep and circlejerking chimpanzees.

Bink's parents tried acting cool, but every night Mrs. B'd sneak into the basement where I was sleeping and shine a flashlight on me. She wanted to make sure I hadn't gone all Sylvia Plath and stuffed my head in their gas clothes dryer. C'mon, give me some credit. I took world lit with Ms. Puckelwartz and shop with Mr. Sturng. I know it was an oven and I know I'd have to at least disconnect the gas line. *Yep, Mrs. B, still alive . . . go back to bed.*

One night, when I was jonesing to escape, I climbed out a basement storm window so I didn't have to hear any more history lessons (*Alan Turing—a brilliant mathematician who broke the Nazi's code . . . No, Charlie. Forget about him.*

They put him on hormones and he killed himself. Sad, really.)
or about animal orgies. (*Male walruses sometimes bond and
have sexual intercourse with each other. It's also been ob-
served in bison, antelope, sage grouse, and . . .*)

I walked out into the backyard. Bink was sitting Indian-
style in the grass and staring up at a sky that was charcoal
purple and littered with stars like debris from a riot. He
brushed a hand along his hairy legs, shooing mosquitoes or
gnats, and patted a spot of ground beside him. I sat—a good
two feet from him—my legs stretched out, leaning back on
my palms.

Bink said something, maybe "sorry," but I wasn't sure.

"Me, too."

"What?"

"Nothing," I said.

Bink fumbled in his pocket for the hard pack of Marlboro
Reds and Zippo he'd lifted from his dad. I caught a whiff of
kerosene and watched Bink study the end of his square before taking a long, slow drag.

"I had to get out of there." His head bobbed back toward
the house. "They're making me nuts."

"They already think I am," I said. "Your mom's convinced
I'm going to off myself. Last night, I caught her taking the
Clorox out of the laundry room. She claimed she spilled red
wine on something. Tonight, she came downstairs and took
the laces out of my shoes so I won't hang myself. She didn't
even bother making up an excuse."

"You wouldn't, would you?"

"Nah. If I did, First'd probably just dig me out of my grave
to lecture me on how a noose should have thirteen knots
and mine only had eight or something."

"You're such a dork, Charlie." We laughed. Bink leaned a
hand against my shoulder, stood, took one last puff, and then

14

flicked the butt into a neighbor's yard. "I should go to bed. If my parents check on me, they might think I ran away 'cuz I got wigged that you're a homo."

Bink offered me his hand and pulled me to my feet. Things were as normal as they could get between us.

That is, they were until last night.

When we got to Dana's—way late—she answered the door, fighting back a horse-sized poodle. "Down, Jacques," she said. The dog galloped off.

Dana was hammered, and she looked ridiculous. Her hair was a mess and topped off with what looked like a basket of wax fruit. Around her waist was this Hawaiian print skirt that looked like a tablecloth for a family of cannibals. Her bikini top had two very large and very dead starfish sewn over the nipples.

"You're late," Dana said, giving Bink a quick peck on the cheek and totally glaring at me.

I stuck my tongue out at her. Real mature, I know, but I wasn't the one dressed like a four year old who'd decided to marry the Hawaiian Punch mascot.

"Thank God my parents won't be home until Sunday," Dana said, listing to her side. She burped loudly and smacked her lips. Her breath smelled like bratwurst and beer.

"The house is *sooo* trashed. We've gone through two kegs . . . and . . . and . . ." She snorted and pressed her palm against her upturned piggy nose. "And for some reason, everyone thought I had a pool. I don't, Neil. I just don't." She traced a fingertip across Bink's chest and smiled. If Dana didn't pass out, Bink was totally going to get laid. "Everyone's out back."

Dana laced her fingers with Bink's and led him, dog-on-a-leash, through the hallway—or *"foy-yay"* as Kim Green

15

called it an hour later, when Kyle Weir's index finger wormed under her red swimsuit and past her pubes. *(Kyle, oh God, Kyle, not here in the foy-yay!)* I followed. When we were out back, Dana half-moaned, half-squealed the straight-girl mating call *(God, I'm* sooo *drunk!)* and disappeared with Bink.

Couples like Bink and Dana are so dumb that I want to beat them. Hard. They act like they're the only ones in the history of the world that have ever been in love. They think everybody else wants to see them making out with each other. Like seeing them so happy together is the only reason the rest of us don't close the garage door, climb into the car, turn on the ignition, and end our pathetic little lives.

Anyhow, the backyard looked like the site of a plane crash— trampled blue Solo cup empties, burned-out tiki torches, shoes and sandals snared in a collapsed volleyball net, paper plates piled with half-eaten food, used rubbers, cigarette butts, and a pair of speakers pumping Pearl Jam. The yard was infested with an assortment of frat-boy larvae so plastered they didn't bother hiding the woodies throbbing in their swim trunks; girls who wore too much makeup with fresh razor burn dotting their bikini lines like chicken skin; guys wearing coconut bras and grass skirts; fat, bottle-blonde chicks from South's pommie squad who were too ashamed to wear anything that'd expose their dimpled thighs and huge hips; flabby junior varsity linebackers dry-humping soon-to-be sophomores; business-in-the-front–party-in-the-back posers head-banging and strumming air-guitar; and last year's prom princess blowing chunks in the bushes.

I planted my ass in a wooden deck chair, nursed a Coke, and tried to ignore the dickweeds sprouting up around me. It wasn't easy. About ten minutes into the nightmare, Dana came back outside and started bitching about all the "white boy" music—a bunch of metal bands fronted by guys who had bigger hair and better legs than she did. Ever since last year when Kyle Weir and his friends dressed up like members of the Latin Kings—complete with bandannas and baseball bats—during the Winter Carnival's Mexican Fiesta Day (¡Viva Mexico!), Dana's decided it's her job in life to end racism. She forced Elian Arnez to embrace his "heritage" by wearing a dashiki (he's actually from the Dominican Republic), organized an informal field trip to what's left of the Cabrini Green projects so we all could see "how black people live," and I swear, she wanted to hold a fund-raiser for the Asian kids at South so they could afford to buy silverware and stop eating with sticks.

I cringed, rubbing my eyes and shaking my head.

Dana's always pretending she's morally offended that her parents are filthy rich. *My father may be an investment banker, but I'm a revolutionary. A socialist. The people of Latin America, I share their struggle.* Before you could ask how she was suffering when she had a full scholarship to Vassar or Sarah Lawrence or one of those lesbian-until-graduation colleges, she'd start in about how some guy named Jose Cuervo or something was the true hero of Cuba.

Behind me, the sliding glass door skidded open. I wasn't alone on the patio anymore. Bink was in the doorway with Dana's Clydesdale of a mutt.

"Well, in or out, already?" With the side of his foot, Bink shoved the poodle outside and it bounded away, barking at the moon. Some bare-chested guy I didn't know tried to squeeze past Bink. He was holding a shirt stained with strawberry Kool-Aid, probably spiked with Everclear. Bink caught his arm and spun him around in one motion. The T-shirt dropped with a splat.

"Hey, sorry about that. Dana didn't mean to spill. She gets clumsy when she's drunk," Bink said. "She's cool, though. I'm Neil, by the way. Rob?"

"Yeah, Rob Hunt," he nodded. "I moved next door a few days ago."

Rob saw me watching him and grinned, all dimples. I think we were checking each other out, but I couldn't be sure. He was shorter than me (who isn't?) and cute in an easy, lazy kind of way. He had dark black hair that was mussed, a few strands falling toward his eyes. His ears stuck out just a bit (not like my Dumbo monsters). The rest of him looked good, too—a mostly smooth torso with a Y-shaped shadow of hair; a tight, slightly pumped chest with penny-sized nipples the color of raspberries; and a thin treasure trail snaking from his belly button to his low-hanging Bermuda shorts. My cheeks burned.

"Where'd you move from?" I asked. I tried being casual, but my voice chipped like cheap paint.

"Manhattan." His bluish eyes kept looking at me, which made me think I was getting a zit (I was—just popped it a minute ago). "Well, actually my parents lived in Manhattan. I went to the Phelps School in Pennsylvania."

"Your parents sent you to boarding school?" Bink asked. "Man, that sucks."

Rob shrugged and picked up his shirt. "It made sense at the time."

"Boarding school?" Bink said, like he couldn't believe it. "Like shirts and ties and blazers?"

"Well, formal, yes."

"No girls?"

"No . . . no girls."

"Damn, that had to suck."

18

"Well," Rob stopped looking at me and twisted his shirt, raining Kool-Aid on the patio bricks, "we had dances with our sister schools—Purnell and Grier."

"Still . . ."

"I should probably rinse this," Rob said to no one in particular and ducked back into the house.

Once Rob was out of earshot, Bink closed the sliding door and pulled me aside. "You know what Dana heard?"

"What?"

"She heard Rob got sent away 'cuz he got some chick pregnant. Supposedly, Rob's dad was pissed Rob was out banging some chick when his mom's really sick. He wasn't gonna pay for an abortion."

"That's retarded," I said, sounding pissy.

"It's true."

"Sure it's true. Just like when Dana said Joan Hawkings was a big lesbo and they caught her rubbing her crotch against a gymnastic beam."

Bink scrunched his face and belched pure-grain alcohol.

"I'm gonna be sick."

Bink went green, chest and throat retching, and vomited on a pile of clothes. I gagged on the smell. I should've checked to see if he was all right, but I needed to piss—bad.

Inside, I got lost looking for the bathroom. Smug family portraits of the whole damn Flannigan family covered every wall. There were Flannigans wearing the same Christmas sweaters, Flannigans at Disney World, sepia-toned Flannigans dressed up in Wild West outfits. I stumbled into a room filled with Precious Moments figurines and hand-stitched quilts. Another door led to the kitchen. There were Flannigans at somebody's wedding, Flannigans under the Eiffel Tower, Flannigans at Mount Rushmore acting out that famous Hitchcock movie. Another room, this one filled with shelves of books and coffee tables littered with issues of *The National Review, The Economist, Forbes, Fortune,* and the *Wall Street Journal* before coming to the *foy-yay. (Oh, Kyle, that feels sooo good . . .)* Finally, a bathroom. *(Can ya wait a goddamn minute, asshole?)* I went upstairs: a girl's room, all peaches and cream, filled with stuffed animals and horseback-riding trophies. The Flannigans in a lab discovering a cure for cancer. Door number two: twenty toes sticking out from a sheet (ten with nails flaking red polish, the other ten, thick and hairy hammertoes). Another door: towels, linen, cotton balls, Kotex. Door four: a guest bedroom, a cheesy paint-by-numbers of a kneeling Jesus praying at a rock; the Flannigans feeding fishes and loaves to the poor; the Flannigans walking on water.

Door five: finally an empty bathroom—hand towels crumpled on the floor, a quarter sheet of toilet paper left on the roll, yellow bubbles of piss in the toilet. This wasn't the time to be picky. My knees were shaking so badly I almost couldn't pull it out in time. The cold-jerk, piss-shiver through my shoulders, two taps, flush, and to the faucet. A dish of soaps shaped like sea horses and conch shells.

After the toilet stopped racing, I heard a piano I somehow hadn't seen.

I went downstairs into what I'm guessing Kim would've called the "salon." The half-dozen or so people still at Dana's had migrated there: Joan Hawkings, Bink, Dana, Shannon Debold, Bob Collins, Jon Bales, Grace Peterson. Bink was on a couch, his mouth clean of vomit, with Dana on the floor, nestled between his legs. She was stroking the back of his calves while he rubbed her shoulders and laughed at Shannon, a hammered cheerleader whose skirt was hiked so far past her knees everyone could see the daddy-longlegs hairs creeping from her panties. Bob laughed, too late and too hard, snapping one of the rubber bands on his braces against the roof of his mouth. He reeled backward and collided with the grand piano, bringing its lid down with a slam.

"Idiot," Grace said, leaning into Shannon.

The guy at the piano—Rob, still shirtless—glanced at Bob and went back to playing that classical music from the Peanuts Christmas special.

"Hey, Schroeder, quit playing that crap or eat out Peppermint Patty," Bales said. Dana swatted his leg and whined that he was being gross.

Rob looked up just in time to duck the flip-flop Shannon'd drunkenly tossed at his head. It hit the Venetian blinds behind Bink.

"Watch it, woman," Rob smiled. "Play nice."

"Then you play something nice," Shannon said. "Not the crap you've been playing."

"Okay, but only because you asked so politely," he said. It seemed like he was flirting with her, but I couldn't tell. It pissed me off anyway, 'cuz, let's face it, I wanted him to flirt with me.

Rob's shoulders rolled, his fingers dancing the length of the keyboard. I plopped on the couch and threw a leg over Dana's shoulder. She was too drunk to notice.

"I know this! It's the 'Minute' Waltz," Bink said, surprising even himself. "They did this at my sisters' ballet recital. It's by Chop-in."

"*Show-pan*, you pig," Kim Green corrected him, coming into the "salon" from upstairs. Kyle followed her, tugging at his shorts like he was showing off what was left of his boner. "It's pronounced *Show-pan*."

"Pigshh. All my friendshh are pigshh," Dana said, her face in the carpet.

"It's fag music," Kyle said, high-fiving Bink and knocking my leg off Dana. He curled into a couch with Kim.

Rob flipped Kyle the bird and then played a bass-heavy version of "Fascinatin' Rhythm," making it sound as if he was playing two pianos at once. He wasn't concentrating on the music. His whole body moved, hands trilling white here, spanking black there, and he had this huge, dimple-making smile on his face. When he'd finished, the girls applauded and the guys look ticked, like Rob'd deliberately tried to show them up in front of "their" women.

"Thanks," Rob said. Blushing, he closed the piano, flipped on the stereo, and sat next to Dana.

"You know what we should do?" Jon asked. He made one of those tough-guy, silent chin thrusts at Kyle, letting him know he needed to look up Shannon's skirt. "We should totally play Truth or Dare."

"Hell, yeah," Kyle said. "Dana, you start."

Bink jabbed his knee into Dana's back. She snapped up and blinked like she couldn't figure out where she was.

"Bob," Dana said, "truth or dare?"

"Dare."

"Fine. I dare you to get me some water and an aspirin."

Bob's face sank. He raced out of the room, returning with a bottle of Tylenol and a Dixie cup so fast I wondered if there was another bathroom I hadn't discovered.

"My turn," Bob said, licking his lips and eyeballing Shannon. She whispered to Grace. "Shannon, truth or dare?"

"Truth."

Bob looked at his crotch, then back at Shannon. "Spit or swallow?"

"Swallow. Same as you." Kyle and Jon howled. Shannon put a hand on Rob's thigh. *Slut.* I was jealous. "Joan, truth or dare?"

"I'm not playing."

"Chickenshit. C'mon, truth or dare?"

"Okay, truth."

"Ever have sex . . . with a guy?"

"Yeah." Everyone's jaw dropped. Rob shifted his leg and Shannon's hand slipped away. *Good. Keep her whore hands off you.*

"No way. Who?" Grace asked.

"What is this? An interrogation?" Joan sighed. She wasn't gonna get off that easy, not with this group. "Oh, all right. Tom Vodak. He was . . ." She wiggled her pinky finger. The girls laughed. When Bob swallowed hard, I smiled. I was glad I wasn't the only guy with a reason to get self-conscious. "Charlie, truth or dare?"

"Dare."

Dares are safer than truths. Sure, I ran the risk of being dared to make out with the dog or lick a toilet bowl, but that beat Joan making me admit that when I got home, I'd jack off thinking about Bink and Rob.

"I dare you to . . ." She scanned the room. "Kiss Neil."

"Hell, no," Bink said, curling into a fetal position and shielding his face with his arms. "I'll quit."

"Baby," Joan said like she couldn't be bothered. She searched the room. Jon and Kyle glared at her. "Fine. Kiss Rob."

I froze. My face burned. My throat was so dry it felt like I'd swallowed sand. Play it cool, I told myself. Just give him a peck on the cheek. But as I crossed the room, Bob—the jagoff—tripped me. I fell, landing on top of Rob. Our bodies were hip-to-hip, our faces practically colliding. The guys moaned,

"Gross," trying to outdo each other's straightness with their disgust. Eyes closed, I leaned in, expecting to get Rob's cheek, but I got his lips. My jaw went slack. I'm not sure, but I swear I felt his tongue trying to get in my mouth. My dick switch-bladed up and I jerked away. A strand of spittle linked us mouth to mouth, then broke. He dried his lips on the back of his hand. I wanted to know if he was wiping away the taste of me.

The game went on. I got Bales to admit he spanked it while sniffing a pair of his sister's dirty panties. Grace kissed Dana. Joan mimicked Tom Vodak's come face. Bales finally got to french Shannon. Kyle admitted to nicknaming his prick "The Shotgun" because it "fired from both barrels." If my eyes could groan, they would have. Dana dared everybody to get her more water, then made Bob get her slippers, then a quilt, then a grilled cheese sandwich. Rob frenched the girls. Bob confessed to being the guy on the hockey team who ate the Wonder Bread.

"Shannon, truth or dare?" Grace asked with a wink. They were in on something.

"Dare."

"I dare you to feel Rob's dick—under his shorts."

Shannon slipped her hand up Rob's leg. He tried to squirm away, but Kim and Joan pinned him by the shoulders.

"I'm not wearing underwear." His face tensed. Shannon smiled.

"What's it feel like?" Grace asked.

"It's warm . . . kinda heavy. His balls aren't hairy."

"Does he have an erection?" Kim asked. *Foy-yay. Show-pan. Erection.* If she wanted people thinking she was classy, she didn't need to throw around a bunch of big words. She could start by not letting Kyle and Bob make her into a whore sandwich.

24

"Sorta, I guess . . . I don't know." Rob looked panicked and embarrassed.

"Let's see," Grace said.

Rob kicked, but Shannon and Grace tugged Rob's shorts an inch or two past his hips, flashing a patch of black pubes. They looked soft, not wiry. I wanted to touch 'em.

Rob leapt from the girls, red faced and sweating. He somehow lost a shoe as he hiked up his shorts.

"Look, Shannon," Bob said, pointing at Rob's crotch. Of course, Mr. Closet Case would notice. "He's got a hard-on."

"Do not," Rob said. He was tenting his shorts.

Rob forced himself between Bink and me. Rob's arm touched mine. His skin felt hot. I got hard and part of me hoped Rob would notice.

"Dude, it's totally cool," Kyle said. He grabbed his crotch. "Man, The Shotgun would totally dig three chicks going after him."

Shannon sighed, bored with the boy-bonding, macho-posturing. I couldn't blame her. It was like all the guys were suddenly Rob's best friends just 'cuz his dick stiffed for chicks. So what? My dick doesn't need a reason to get hard and I don't see anybody throwing a party for it.

Shannon turned to me. "Charlie, truth or dare?"

"Dare," I said, hating them and hating myself more for being there.

With the exception of Bink, it's not like I was friends with any of them. Hell, even though we'd been in the same classes for like ten years, we barely knew jack about each other. They knew I liked guys, which, depending on which one of them was talking, put me on a spectrum somewhere between one of those cute little dogs that socialites accessorized with, the Ken doll best friend that went to school dances with the fat girls, almost normal (except for all the other things

25

about me that made me a freak—like not wearing the right clothes), a social pariah, a sitcom character's snarky best friend, and a kitten rapist. And I knew, or at least hoped, that after high school, they'd all end up fat, bald, mortgaged to the eyeteeth, and nursing a litter of ankle-biters and a six-pack-a-day drinking habit.

Kyle saddled up to her, whispered something in her ear, then looked at me.

Prick.

Shannon nodded.

Bitch.

"Charlie, I dare you to go skinny-dipping in the O'Reillys' pool next door."

It was a setup, but what was I going to do? Chicken out? If I did, I'd just have to listen to Kyle and Jon's crap about being afraid of everyone seeing my pin dick. And, compared to the guys I've seen in gym class, it is. Like that's something I want to advertise.

I kicked off my shoes and socks, peeled off my shirt, not caring who saw my bony ribs, and barreled out of the room, dropping my jeans. Sober now, Dana chased me, pleading and saying something about an alarm. I didn't listen. I jerked the sliding glass door open and tore off my underwear when I was sure no one could see anything more than my butt. I crossed the Flannigans' backyard and hopped the O'Reillys' fence.

"Damn it, Charlie. Stop," Dana said. She grabbed the fence and tried hoisting herself over, but she couldn't get any traction with her slippers. "Stop it, Charlie! You're gonna get us busted." *Not my problem.* "Neil, stop him."

Kyle and Bink bounded over the fence, charging me at full speed, but I was already mid-dive.

Underwater, I missed all hell breaking loose. The pool's motion detector triggered an alarm. Window after window in the O'Reillys' house blazed with light. Bink and Kyle scrambled back over the fence. Everyone scattered, running back to Dana's or to their cars. I swam, feeling relaxed for the first time all night. Some old guy—Mr. O'Reilly?—peeked through the blinds, cordless phone in hand.

After about twenty laps, there were two cops at the pool's edge, their hands hovering over gun holsters.

"Hey, kid," the fat one said, hitching up his pants. "Out of the pool. Now."

What were the little pigs gonna do if I said no? Wade in after me? Fish me out with a skimmer? Shoot me?

"All right, I'm coming." I slapped my hand on the pool's surface, a spray of water just missing the legs of their polyester uniforms. The piggies jumped.

I climbed out, got knocked to the ground, and tasted concrete. One of them jerked my hands behind my back, cuffed me, and bitched, "Jesus, he's naked." The fatter of the two hauled me past the front of the O'Reillys' house and crammed me into the backseat of the squad car.

"Stupid stunt, kid," said This Little Piggy Had Roast Beef, slipping into the driver's seat. He radioed the station. "What's your name?" I knew that once they called the parental units, First'd go bat-shit crazy.

"Sir," I said, "let me apologize and then we can call it a night."

"Not likely, kid," said Roast Beef. "The homeowner wants to file trespassing charges. Look, make it easy, kid. Give me your name and we'll drop the public indecency stuff." That wasn't gonna happen. If First found out what I did, he'd make sure I got charged with everything they could just to teach me a lesson. I'd be dead before my name ever made the police blotter section of the *Northwest Herald*.

The Little Piggy That Said Wee Wee Wee climbed into the car. He had my jeans and shoes. "I think there was underage drinking going on."

"You think?" asked Roast Beef. He wiped his mouth, then grabbed the steering wheel like he needed the grip to stop himself from beating the stupidity out of his partner.

"Now, kid. Tell us your name. You'll get your clothes and everyone can go home."

I did and they radioed it back to the station. They weren't happy when the dispatcher told them my dad was the assistant state's attorney and wanted to straighten things out himself. They were gonna have to wait and they were pissed. They wouldn't let me get dressed. If I was gonna ruin their night, they'd ruin mine.

Forty-five minutes later, First arrived at the O'Reillys'. He managed to convince the guy not to press charges, promising that what he had in store for me was worse than anything the juvie courts could dish out. Wee Wee Wee let me out of the squad car.

After they uncuffed me, I winced, started dressing in the clothes the cops'd been able to find. I didn't have underwear so I hopped on one foot and yanked at the waistband, cupping my crotch to hide dick and nuts.

"Maybe you should have worried about everyone seeing you naked before you pulled this little stunt," First said. "Get in the car." I scrambled to his Oldsmobile, the asphalt biting my bare feet.

Back home, I stalked off to my bedroom and slammed the door. First threatened, so help him God, that if I ever slammed the door again, he'd break it down and he wasn't going to be responsible for what happened next.

*   *   *

It's late. First is downstairs hollering that he wants my personal essay finished in a half hour. It's the only time he's said anything to me since this morning when he laid into me how this college essay wasn't his way of punishing me. It was his way of making me see how much of a mess I've been making of my life. According to him, it's supposed to a real eye-opener.

I gotta come up with something better for this essay quick. If he sees what I've got now, I'm dead.

Sunday, August 26

My family fights like most people fart in church—silently and with this crippling fear that someone might notice.

The Ps are so concerned with what the neighbors might think that they never have a good, knockdown, drag-out, why-can't-we-have-nice-things, this-is-the-thanks-I-get, minia-ture-Franklin-Mint-reproduction-of-a-Ming-dynasty-vase-hurled-at-First's-head battle royal. At the first sign of conflict, First and Mom don't tear open the silverware drawer, grab the nearest Lillian Vernon holiday-topper cheese knives and try to shiv each other on our TruGreen front lawn. No, they throw down like good little WASPs, which means discreetly closing the blinds, turning on all the faucets, the vacuum cleaner, the TVs, the stereo (Mom's gotta go digging for *Document* and that lame-ass REM patter song; First, he prefers Twisted Sister—*yeah, dude, you're hard core, way to rock out with your cock out*). Then, when the Ps are 100 percent convinced that they've created their own impenetrable Phil-Spector-Wall-of-Sound, that's when they go at it—giving each other looks that could defrost turkeys, whispering threats about how if the toilet seat doesn't get put down, the tooth-paste tube doesn't get squeezed from the bottom, the check-book doesn't get balanced, the stationary bicycle doesn't start getting used for something other than a $400 tie rack, well then, things definitely are not going to be pretty.

Lately, it seems like the two of them are fighting all the time. I'm not supposed to hear them, but I do. They're con-stantly bitching about money, about how neither of them is ever happy, how First's running for state's attorney was sup-posed to make him happy and hasn't, how Mom's sick of being just a wife and mother, how neither of them imagined nearing 40 with nothing but a mortgage to show for it.

I've never heard them say it—even when they're really pissed at each other—but sometimes, I think they blame me for all their problems. They weren't much older than me when Mom got pregnant. It was college. First was a senior and, ap-parently, charming; Mom was a sophomore and, apparently, either drunk or crazy. The condom was defective. The wed-ding was shotgun.

That personal essay for college . . . it's supposed to include something about my family, right? For what it's worth:

My parents haven't always hated each other or re-sented me. They actually—get this—were normal once. Well, as normal as the Ps can be. Mom did more than the other kids' moms, because she was so much younger—taking me to swimming lessons, T-ball games, helping me set up a lemonade stand in the summer, teaching me division using a batch of homemade cookies that she'd lined out on the kitchen table to cool. (She called division "goes-intos" to make things easier—Chip, three goes-into nine how many times?)

Hell, First and I once got along, even after he started being such a totally overbearing control freak that it was like my umbilical cord had been attached to him. I wasn't allowed to ride a tricycle if I wasn't wearing Kevlar knee and elbow pads and a near-military-grade helmet. When I started kindergarten, the guy ran background checks on all my classmates, their parents, their parents' neighbors, my teacher—hell, even the bus driver. If I had a runny nose, Mom'd practically have to snatch me out of First's arms to stop him from taking me to the emergency room for a chest X ray. I'm not kidding. This year, I had to make my doctor tell him not to follow me into the exam room for my annual physical. There was no way in hell I was gonna listen to him give Dr. Gumatay the third degree on why I was still underperforming in the dangly bits department. Basically, First's MO has been let's-give-Chip-a-peptic-ulcer-by-preschool-an-AA-membership-by-eight-and-psychiatric-bills-larger-than-the-GDP-of-the-Republic-of-Slovenia-by-his-sophomore-year.

Still, First was the one who got me started with soccer. And he was the one who explained how I had to repeat second grade, telling me at the Tastee-Freez over a chocolate-dipped soft-serve that Miss Gunther said I was so special that she wanted me to stay with her and act like the best big boy I could to show the other kids how they needed to be.

I gotta say, though, when it's just between me and Mom or me and First, the fights are different. With Mom, it's not that we're fighting as much as fencing—feints and parries, and hits with no real sting. Most of the time, we don't even make it to a full-on fight. Like this summer, Mom was pissed that I was wasting my life and she kept harping on me to go outside and blow the stink off my body. So, me being a total smart-ass, I grabbed her hair dryer and an extension cord, pulled the shirt off my skinny chest, plopped my ass down on the front stoop, and air-blasted my underarms. Mom, from the other side of the screen door, laughed and told me to get dressed, and the two of us went out for lunch.

That's not how it is with First. Ever since I started high school, it's like the two of us have been locked in this eternal, man versus nature struggle. He's the gardener and I'm the bonsai tree he spends every day keeping small, shaping as he sees fit, bending to his will. When I'm feeling cocky, I like to think of myself as the Colorado River and he's the Grand Canyon; he may be old and some people might find him impressive, but I know that little by little, I'm eating away at him.

Needless to say, after the crap I pulled Friday night, I wasn't expecting the Ps to go easy on me. If I was lucky—and that was one whackin' big *if*—the two of them would ground me for life plus five. But it's not like that would've been a big deal. It's not like I've got this great social life where hot guys line up to let me grope 'em. I really didn't care what they did to me as long as I got to stay on the soccer team. I'd go nuts if I had to come home right after school every day. That's why I set my alarm for earlier than normal. I wasn't about to give Mom and First more reasons to rag on me. *Must be nice to sleep in, Mister. I would have liked to, but your mother spent the night trying to convince me that a fifty-fourth trimester abortion wasn't an option.*

Still groggy, I took a quick shower, somehow managed

not to play with myself and got ready for church—clean white shirt, tie, slacks, dress shoes—and went downstairs. I started making breakfast Mom came into the kitchen in her bathrobe, wet hair in a towel, like she'd pulled another all-nighter trying to get First to understand that the stupid crap I pulled was just that—stupid teenaged stunts—and it wasn't—at least not entirely—an orchestrated attempt on my part to make his life miserable.

Behind me, Mom ran the faucet, added water to the coffee-maker, and flipped on the radio—Star 105.5, Billy Joel She hummed along and since she hadn't started in on lecturing me yet, I kept my mouth shut and pretended to concentrate on scrambling the eggs. When the coffee was finished, she poured a cup and sat on a kitchen stool kitty-corner from me. I dumped the eggs into a bowl, covered them with a towel to keep them warm, and went to the fridge for some bacon. Mom stopped me.

"You look nice," she said, fixing the knot in my tie and smoothing my hair. *A compliment?* I was screwed. There are times when a compliment is the cigarette before being walked out in front of the firing squad.

"I'm dead, aren't I?" I asked as I fried the bacon. She didn't answer. "I knew it."

"What'd you expect, Charlie? That we'd appreciate a phone call dragging us out of bed in the middle of the night?"

"I know—"

"I don't think you do " she said, setting her mug on the counter. "You don't know what it's like getting a phone call and not knowing where your son is. You could've been dead for all we knew."

"Like Dad would care "

"Enough. I don't want to hear it."

33

"Sorry."

"If you're sorry, why'd you do it? You knew it was stupid, right?"

I knew this was a trap, so I didn't answer. I forked the bacon from the skillet to a paper-towel-covered plate.

"Your father is expecting an explanation."

"I don't know why I did it, okay? I don't. It's just that—"

First, already dressed for church, stepped into the kitchen. He'd probably been listening for a while. He grabbed a mug of coffee and crossed behind me to stand by Mom.

"It's what?" Mom asked.

"It's not easy being me." Even I had to admit that sounded whiny.

"So this is what you do?" First asked, eyeballing me over the brim of his mug.

I looked at him and saw everything I hate about myself— my gangly build, big goofy ears, the giant schnoz my grand-parents say makes me like some old-time Hollywood actor, my pointy chin. When we smile, First and I have the same dorky, Cheshire-cat-who-ate-the-canary, playing-card joker grin. Sometimes, I'll stare at guys like Bink or Kyle and think they're not much better looking than I am, and that somebody, some-where, might actually think I'm hot. Well, okay, maybe not hot, but at least kinda cute. Well, at least not dog-scaring ugly. Then I remember what a screwed-up geek I am.

"Look, Chip," First said, "things have to change. Understand?"

"Yes."

That was it. We ate in silence.

I didn't get off so easily at church. I never did—not since Steve Marshall and I got caught cheating on our Ten Com-mandments test in confirmation class.

I'm not sure if this is about religion or academic integrity, but:

34

Cheating was a cinch. All you had to do was write all the "thou shalt nots" on the side of your shoe, cross your leg, and copy the answers. Steve Marshall—a weasely little jackass—tried telling me I'd go to Hell for cheating in church. But I said Lutherans don't go to Hell for cheating, we get eternal damnation for having self-esteem. We could lie, cheat, and steal as long as we believed in Jesus, never felt a sense of pride or self-worth, and avoided Pastor T's "fish-breathed, bead-counting Mary-lovers."

Today, church was really bad. We opened our hymnals to "Eternal Ruler of the Ceaseless Round," a classic Lutheran tune composed for a bunch of fat, tone-deaf Germans who can plow through four mind-numbing verses without once sounding joyful or inspired. Look, I'm a pretty good tenor, I've been in choir for three years, but even I was chipping notes right and left. The only person who wasn't was some baritone a few pews in front of us. Rob Hunt. Mister I-Went-to-Phelps-and-Girls-Like-Touching-My-Enormous-Cock. *Show-off.*

Announcements came next. Our hopes and prayers were with our boys in uniform in Iraq and Afghanistan, with Mrs. So-and-So recovering nicely from surgery for a deviated septum, and with the list of old farts who kicked the bucket. Pastor Taylor then asked that we join him in giving a warm welcome to the congregation's newest family. Mr. Hunt and Rob made their way forward and thanked Pastor Taylor, who asked Mr. Hunt to say a few words.

Dork the Elder introduced himself. He was Paul Hunt. They'd moved to Crystal Lake from Manhattan, which'd been an adjustment since he'd never been west of the Mississippi. It was a lame joke, but the congregation laughed. He'd got-

35

ten married in this very church to his lovely wife, Kathy. *She's the wind beneath my wings.* She grew up in the area. A few years ago, she'd been diagnosed with eh-Alice, which meant she probably wouldn't be around much. (I asked Mom what eh-Alice was. *"Not 'eh-Alice.' ALS. Lou Gehrig's disease. Ask your father."*) Mr. Hunt worked in advertising, but he'd be working from home most days. Blah, blah, blah. I stopped listening until he introduced Dork the Younger.

"Hi, I'm Rob," he said, giving an awkward elbow-tucked-into-the-hip wave. He looked at me and smiled. I blushed. Behind me, Shannon Debold giggled. *Great.* He'd smiled at her. Could I be more pathetic? "I'll be a senior this year at South."

After the service, Dork the Elder stood in the middle of Luther Hall, the church's multipurpose room, thanking the umpteen-millionth woman for asking about his wife and politely declining her offer to "bring something over to the house, maybe a nice hot dish." They were convinced Mr. Hunt was "a good Lutheran," even though he was from New York. *You know it's positively crawling with I-talians, A-rabs, and Catholics.*

We went up to meet Dork the Elder. First clasped both his hands around one of Mr. Hunt's and pumped it vigorously while pigeonholing him in the corner next to the Boy Scout trophy case. He didn't let go, not even when Mr. Hunt politely tried to pull away.

"It's great meeting you, Paul. I'm Charles Stewart. This is my wife, Laura. My son, Chip."

"Charlie," I corrected for all it mattered.

Mom and I shook Mr. Hunt's hand as he glanced past us, like he was wondering how he'd ended up stuck here. I was used to it. Nobody ever wants to be around First. Most people shower with a Brillo pad after meeting him. Okay, so I exaggerate. But there is something about First that makes people seem a little uncomfortable. Maybe it's the whole politician thing—that hey-little-buddy-we're-all-in-this-together-and-I-feel-your-pain vibe that he gives off almost every time he opens his mouth.

"Sounds like our boys'll be at the same school," First said. "Maybe they'll have a few classes together."

"I doubt it," Mr. Hunt said, checking his watch.

"Well, Chip's smarter than he looks. Aren't you?"

I shrugged. He wanted me to brag, but I didn't like it. First's jaw clenched as he did one of those mental relaxation exercises Mom tells him to do when I'm getting on his nerves.

"Oh, I'm sure Charlie's very smart. But school's not exactly Rob's strong suit."

"Too busy with the girls, eh?" First winked, nudging Mr. Hunt with frat-monkey familiarity. Mom gave First a leave-the-man-alone-already look, but he ignored it.

"Something like that." *Yeah, something like spreading their legs and pumping them full of his boy juice.*

Mr. Hunt leaned past First, looking for somebody to rescue him. It didn't happen, 'cuz, and I'm guessing here, nobody wanted to hear his spiel for campaign contributions. "So, you're in advertising. Write any jingles I know?" First asked.

"I don't write the music." Mr. Hunt grabbed my elbow and smiled at the Ps. "If you don't mind, I'll have Charlie show me to the men's room."

"I can show you," First said, not realizing that this was Mr. Hunt's plan for an escape.

"Please, I don't want to steal you from your wife."

"Steal me from her? You can have her." Mom elbowed him. "What?"

We ducked away, Mr. Hunt nodding at well-wishers.

"Nice save," I said, leading him to the bathroom across from the church office.

"He seems like a nice enough guy. A little aggressive. You're lucky to have him."

"Maybe."

"Give him time. You'll be surprised how smart he gets when you're twenty-five." *Yeah, maybe then monkeys'll fly out of my ass.* Do adults ever realize how dumb they sound? I mean, really. *First, smart?* Please.

"The bathroom's to the left." I pointed down a small hallway.

"Actually, I need to make a call," he said, pulling a cell phone from his pocket.

"It's quiet in the office."

Mr. Hunt thanked me. Through the window, I saw him say something to Pastor Taylor's secretary. She gave his arms a gentle squeeze and excused herself. I couldn't be sure, but I think she dabbed tears from her eyes. Everyone was treating the Hunts like they were so fragile and precious. Like if you breathed on 'em, they'd shatter. It was ridiculous.

Even if Mr. Hunt didn't, I needed to take a leak. I walked to the farthest urinal of the three and unzipped. Steve Marshall walked in and stood at the urinal next to me, *sooo* violating the Men's Room Code. Everyone knows that when there're three johns and two guys, the one-urinal-buffer rule's in effect. Both of you take the ones at the end, leave the middle open, and stare straight ahead. But Marshall didn't. He went right for the middle one and made this big production of pulling his dick out, like he was daring me to look.

Marshall's not a homo, just a perv. His whole family is a bunch of nymphos. His little sister accused a junior high gym teacher of fondling her mosquito-bite tits, even though she totally flirted with him, sitting in his lap and stuff. I never believed it, 'cuz when I was in junior high, Mr. Forde seemed like he was more into Steve. Forde always watched us showering, pointing out the guys with small dicks. He even popped a boner when he used Bill Minor to demonstrate some wrestling move. Anyhow, the school bought her story and Mr. Forde got canned.

"Is it true, Charlie?" Steve asked after he'd flushed. "Did you ruin Dana's party?"

"What?" I stared at him.

Steve's one of those guys who, even though he's a senior, still looks like he's ten. A real midget—the kind of guy who gets asked if he needs a booster seat at restaurants.

"You know, getting arrested for skinny-dipping." He nodded his head, all excited like.

"I didn't get arrested."

"Yeah, that's what I thought. You're too big a pussy."

"Screw you. The cops were there. They cuffed me."

"Really? That's awesome." He folded his arms across his sweater-vest. "You know, I was gonna go to Dana's—"

"But you weren't invited?"

"Jerk," he said, pouting.

Back in Luther Hall, First and Mom now had Rob Hunt cornered.

"Speak of the devil; Rob, this is our son, Chip," First said, roping an arm across my shoulders.

"Charlie," I said. Mom patted down one of the cowlicks in my hair. I could've died. I wanted to ask if we could go already, but First would've bitten my head off.

"Hey," Rob said, his dimples flashing.

He'd taken off his suit coat, loosened his tie, and unbuttoned the top three buttons of his shirt. Staring at the V under his Adam's apple, I wondered what he'd look like naked. Rob must've asked me something, 'cuz everyone was waiting for my answer.

"Huh?"

"Your mom said you're in choir and on the soccer team, too."

"Yeah. You play?"

"Forward. My dad sent my game tapes to the coach. I guess I'll be playing varsity. Is the team any good?"

I wanted to tell him not as good as Phelps School's team, which probably got its field re-sodded after every practice and had World Cup players as coaches.

"We almost went to state last year. We've got a strong chance this year. Conference's definitely a lock."

"Who's goalie?"

"Charlie is," Mom said, glowing. "He's been voted to the All-Conference team three years straight."

I glared at her.

"What? You're shy all of a sudden?" Rob grinned.

"Hey, sport," Mr. Hunt called to Rob, not wanting to get within ten feet of First. "Let's get a move on."

"Well, see you tomorrow," Rob said, then nodded at the Ps. "It was nice meeting you both."

We left, too, grabbing lunch at this Cantonese place we always go to. Over egg rolls and Mongolian beef, Mom and First lectured me about seeing my guidance counselor, about taking my SATs or, hell, even the ACTs, and trying to find some college that'd take someone like me.

When we got home, I went to my room—my Fortress of Solitude—and put a CD in the stereo. Yeah, I'm a total dork for treating my room like a superhero hideout. And it is as bad as it sounds. It looks like it did when I was an eight year old obsessed with outer space. Mom and I had stenciled larger-

than-life scenes from her dad's old comic books on the walls—
Flash Gordon locked in a sword fight with Ming the Merciless, Buck Rogers blasting his ray gun, Clark Kent peeling
open his shirt to reveal the top of the "S" on his costume,
stuff like that. The only thing that's changed is the smell. It's
total locker room: the funky musk of sweaty jockstraps and
undershirts, generic body spray, and spooged-on socks.

I spent the afternoon getting ready for school tomorrow,
cramming new folders, notebooks, and a handful of pens
and pencils into my backpack. I called Bink for a lift in the
morning, but he'd promised Dana a ride. He wasn't gonna
have both of us in his car, especially when Dana had vowed
she "was *sooo* going to kill" me.

I hung up and tried on some of the school clothes Mom
bought for me last weekend. There was no way I'd ever be
cool. The jeans she made me get suck. *I'm not getting you
those. They look worn out*. The shirts she'd picked were the
cheap, no-name, store-label kind. *Not at those prices, Charlie. Here, take these*. No matter what I wore, I still looked like
a freak. I was too bony, my face was too pink, and my ears
were way too big. In the bathroom mirror, I pinned them
back with Scotch tape to see if that helped any. It did. But
it's not like I could go to school with my ears taped.

I looked kinda hot. Well, hot enough that I figured if they
could clone me, I'd make out with myself. Well, if the clone
and me were the last two "people" on Earth. And yeah, I actually got hard, sat on the toilet, and pulled my pud, fanta-
sizing about a hockey team circle jerk, then Bink and Rob
wrestling around naked, and then Bink sticking his dick in
Rob Hunt's mouth. I washclothed the goo off my stomach,
put on my clothes, and went downstairs.

"What's with the tape and the ears?" Mom asked.

I'm pathetic. Really, truly, sadly pathetic.

41

Monday, August 27

School sucks—there's a shocker.

> FIRST PERIOD: CREATIVE WRITING
> SECOND PERIOD: STUDY HALL
> THIRD PERIOD: CHOIR
> FOURTH PERIOD: GYM (Actually, it's a study hall until soccer's over.)
> FIFTH PERIOD: LUNCH
> SIXTH PERIOD: LATIN IV ('Cuz First thinks I'll be a lawyer—if I don't end up in prison before spring semester.)
> SEVENTH AND EIGHTH PERIOD: ADVANCED PLACEMENT BIOLOGY
> NINTH PERIOD: PRE-CALCULUS

It's only a matter of time before I catch crap for being the only senior taking the bus, which I'll be doing until I apologize to Dana or pass that damn driver's test. I'd rather walk than tell her I'm sorry. But nobody noticed today. Everyone was too busy *ooohhhing* and *aaahhhing* about Rob Hunt driving to school in a black BMW. At South, crap like that's important. The kids here practically demand your parents' tax return to see if you're worth talking to. Apparently, nobody told Rob there wasn't a dress code, 'cuz he climbed out of the beemer wearing dark slacks, a white shirt (with cuff links even), and a tie. For a second, Mr. Fuller, one of the school deans, actually thought he was a student teacher.

Anyhow, South's the same as it ever was. All of the preps, jocks, and cheerleaders still sit in the Pit, a gigantic sunken atrium smack in the middle of the school. Last year, when my ancient civilizations/world history/Latin teacher, Mrs. Lardner, described the Hindu caste system, she drew a whackin' big diagram of the Pit on the chalkboard. With Mrs. Lardner everything's either "whackin' big" or "cute little"—whackin' big cathedrals, whackin' big pyramids, cute little monks, cute little Earth goddesses. On her diagram, she marked the Brahmans (rich kids, varsity jocks, cheerleaders), the Vaishyas (JV jocks, kids whose parents owned retail stores, girls that put out and didn't get pregnant), Shudras (stoners who sold cheap, band and choir geeks, the Vocation Ed and Home Ec types, the girls who put out and got pregnant), and the rest. We, the Untouchables, weren't allowed near the Pit. We got the cafeteria.

I ended up at a table with a few geeks from the academic team and the *Guns & Ammo*-reading ROTC psychos who were itching to go into Pakistan and kick Osama's ass.

Soccer practice was cool. Rob's good—crazy good. He'll take diving headshots, but he'll pass if someone's got a better opening. During one drill, Josh McCullough was getting covered too closely and he passed the ball, way too hard, across the field to Rob. The ball slammed Rob's ribcage. Rob didn't miss a beat and drew the ball into a juggle rolling it thigh-to-thigh, then thigh-to-chest-to-thigh, before dancing it past a fullback for the goal. It was the only shot I missed.

Rob's not as big a jerk as I thought. We talked after he offered to drive me home—well, at least not about him frenching me on Friday, but that's probably 'cuz I imagined the whole thing. I asked what classes he had and he blushed. Basically, he's in remedial everything. He said the only things he didn't have trouble with were soccer, singing, and playing the piano.

43

I couldn't help checking him out, especially since he didn't shower or change with everyone else in the locker room, just took off his cleats and shin guards. He's got really pale skin, like marble, and the veins on his hands and arms sort of pop out. I wanted to trace them with a finger. His hair was still damp, and there were dark circles of sweat in the armpits of his jersey. He smelled good. Slightly musky.

I should start on my homework. We're supposed to write a credo for creative writing tomorrow. Credo, Mrs. Bailey told the class, is Latin for "I believe." *Duh, excuse me, Latin IV here.* I've also got pre-calc and a chapter to read for AP Bio. It'll all have to wait. The little man's knocking the Jockeys, and it looks like I'm going to have to take matters into my own hands.

Tuesday, August 28

The bus was late, which was okay, 'cuz it meant skipping this morning's Rot-See Nazi discussion on whether the Chinese Air Force could destroy the U.S. Navy. Some clever prick's already figured out the combo for the MasterLock on my locker. Whoever it is, he opened it and re-locked it so the dial faces the wrong way. *Real cute.* I spent, like, ten minutes twisting and cranking the lock around so I could work the combo upside down. By the time I got it unlocked, I only had two minutes to get to class. I chucked everything into my locker except for my creative writing folder and notebook. Excuse me, *journal*; writers keep journals, as Mrs. Bailey had to say nearly eight million times yesterday. I slammed my locker shut and practically skidded through Mrs. Bailey's door as the bell rang, collapsing into the same seat I was in yesterday.

Mrs. Bailey gawked at me from behind her big owl-eye glasses as I caught my breath.

"Charles, what's wrong?" she mewed like a half-drowned cat.

If it weren't for Mrs. Bailey, I wouldn't have written "mewed like a half-drowned cat." I would've stuck with "asked." But Mrs. Bailey totally has a hard-on for similes and metaphors. During class today, she wouldn't shut up about "the need for efficiency of language in our writing" and how Gustave Flaubert was so poor he couldn't afford a thesaurus and he spent eight hours one day trying to get *le mot juste*, "the right word." We were lucky, she said, that we could—no, *should*—use our thesauruses when writing. We'd save ourselves from Flaubert's fate, which, according to Bailey, was getting arrested in Paris for stealing a loaf of bread. "Just like *Les Mis*," gushed some girl in class. "Exactly; Flaubert was the model for Jean Valjean," Mrs. Bailey said. She's full of it. I'm pretty sure she's an alky, too.

"Charles, I mewed you a question. What's wrong?"

Hell if I knew. My fly wasn't open—I checked—but the class was still staring at me.

"Nothing's wrong."

"Really?"

She stepped closer to me. The smell of patchouli oil and cat piss steamed off her sweater and old-lady polyester fat pants. She was pulling one of those Wonder-Woman-lasso-of-truth mind jobs on me.

"Would anyone care to tell Charles what's wrong?"

Twenty hands rocketed into the air, propelled by twenty

sets of ass cheeks squirming in their chairs. Everyone *oooh-oooh-ooooohhh*-ed to be called on.

"Class, you don't need my permission to find your voice," Mrs. Bailey said, all Lane Bryant Buddha-like. "You must find your own voice."

Shannon actually scribbled that in her notebook.

"Charles is in the same seat he was in yesterday," Kim Green said, smirking. I wanted to ask her how many guys she'd had in her seat yesterday.

"Exactly," Mrs. Bailey said. "We can't be truly inspired unless we let ourselves be surprised. Now, Charles, sit at my desk and I'll sit here. Even the teacher can learn from the student. Now shoo, Charles."

I got up and went to her desk.

"Class, take out your credos and we'll begin sharing ourselves."

Kim's gonna ace this class. She's definitely nailed the sharing herself thing.

We went around the room, reading our credos aloud. *I believe in the power of love. I believe I can make the world a better place. I believe that I'm beautiful just the way I am. I believe that children* are *our future. I believe in the music of my soul. I believe in life's simple wonders—a stranger's smile, the fleeting solidness of a comet's tail, the dangers of such closeness.*

I believed I was gonna be sick. My credo—at least the one I read in class—was just as crappy and just as Hallmark-plagiarized. It was something about me believing I was the captain of my fate. But while everybody read their stuff out loud, I added more to mine to keep from going nuts. When Mrs. Bailey said she was going to collect them—*to experience, not to grade*—I started crossing out what I'd written in class.

That was a mistake. It just got her attention. She snatched my notebook and got this:

~~I believe this assignment is totally retarded.~~
~~I believe that Mrs. Bailey really needs to get electrolysis for her mustache.~~
~~I believe my parents want to ruin my life.~~
~~I believe I'm the only faggot at South—well, except for Bob Collins and Andy Moore, but who'd want to do Andy?~~
~~I believe, some days at least, I'm not the geek everyone thinks I am.~~
~~I believe Dana Flannigan hates me because she's jealous and she really knows—deep down—Bink likes me more than he likes her and that pisses her off.~~
~~I believe I'll never be normal; I'll always be a freak.~~

"Some beliefs aren't worth having," Mrs. Bailey said, spitting her words in my ear. Her breath made my skin feel like it was melting.

Soccer practice was okay. We've got an away-game against Woodstock on Friday. Not to sound cocky, but I think we'll beat 'em. Their forwards start off strong, but don't have any stamina and their fullbacks pretty much blow.

Rob's still not taking showers after practice. After I had mine, I asked if I could bum a ride, but he was meeting Shannon once she finished cheerleading practice. She'd volunteered to tutor him in history. *Right*. We ended up hanging out until Shannon showed up, and Rob dropped everything to follow her like a puppy. He even opened the passenger side door for her.

I bet they're still in his car somewhere right now, doing it. Him pinning her ass to the leather seats, all sweaty, with his shorts and jockstrap tangled at his ankles. Their shirts thrown to the backseat. His butt clenching as he mechanically pumps her.

Okay, so I *totally* have a crush on him. But, hell, I'd've helped him with history. Magna Carta? 1215. The six wives of Henry VIII? Divorced, beheaded, died, divorced, beheaded, survived. Charles II? Beheaded. An omen?

Friday, August 31

Since Dana was out sick today, Bink risked it and gave me a ride. He's got really bright hazel eyes and a crooked mouth I'd kill to kiss straight. He was wearing a *Never Mind the Bollocks Here's the Sex Pistols* T-shirt, canvas skateboard pants, and Vans sneakers with no socks. He's got little sandy hairs at the top of his ankles.

What is it with me and guys' feet? Christ, I see a bare foot and my dick twitches like it's a goldfish that's jumped the bowl. I swear to God—and yeah, I know it's way pervy—but I'd dry hump the bottom of Bink's foot. Hell, I'd screw his armpit. Anything to get close. I need to stop. I blushed and the tops of my ears burned. Bink smiled. I pressed my head against the window and tried thinking of something other than what it'd be like to run my hands along Bink's chest or, you know, really kiss him, tongue and everything. It was so bad that I had to cover my crotch when we got out of the station wagon.

I'm not delusional or anything. I know Bink's not gay. If he was, I'd probably be too dorky for him to go out with.

Instead of me, he'd mess around with some hot punk rocker from Central High that he'd meet at a show at the VFW.

There's this unwritten rule at South that says if you want a guy to stick it up your butt, you have to transfer to Central. Bill Minor did, right after all those emergency room doctors supposedly pumped buckets of jizz from his stomach.

Yeah, I'd jump Bink's bones, but I'm not in love with him or anything. Not really. It's just that I miss him, I guess. During our freshman and sophomore years—heck, even before that—it was us against everyone. It didn't matter that Bink was better looking than other guys or smarter or better at most sports; since Bink's family is Jewish *and* poor, in Crystal Lake, that's about as unforgivable as molesting kids or voting democratic.

One time in junior high, Kyle Weir started acting like a total fucking dick, saying how the Jews shouldn't bitch about the Holocaust 'cuz Hitler gave 'em new clothes, free train rides, room and board, dental work, and indoor plumbing. I kept looking at Bink, but he just stood there and took it, like he wasn't supposed to do anything. So I did. I took a swing at Weir, and Weir proceeded to use me like toilet paper— wiping my skinny ass all over Lundahl Junior High's football field. If Bink hadn't pulled Kyle off me and knocked two of Weir's teeth through his bottom lip, I'd've ended up as fertilizer for the thirty-yard line.

But now that Bink's dating Dana, all that crap's stopped. It's like Bink got a lifeboat in Dana, and I got left behind to swab the decks of a sinking ship.

Enough whining. Bink and I have study hall together, so it's not like I'm never going to see him.

The first football game of the year was tonight, so of course, South had to have a lame-ass pep rally this afternoon. It's sad, but there are actually people in this school who think that if we hadn't cancelled ninth period to show our support for the team, Cary Grove would've beaten us by seventy points instead of just forty-nine. The whole damn school, all fifteen hundred of us, filed into the main gym and parked ourselves in the bleachers while the marching band played a really crappy rendition of "Do Wah Diddy" 'cuz the band director, Mr. Locke, had seen *Stripes* and wanted to be like Bill Murray. I'd rather die than be a 37-year-old suburban high school teacher who thinks he's cool.

Somehow, Rob ended up behind me in the bleachers, his feet planted on both sides of me. If I'd leaned back, my head would've been in his crotch. The PA system kicked on and Yello's crappy "Oh Yeah" thumped through the gym. The pommie squad waddled front and center and shook their cellulite and big hair around. They acted like everyone was supposed to think they were *way* hot, but they actually looked like a herd of poorly choreographed cows slowly dying of heat stroke. I cupped my hands to my mouth and booed.

I wasn't the only one. Other kids booed, too. Before any of the pommies burst into tears and the entire school had to go to some dumb, don't-make-fun-of-fat-chicks sensitivity workshop, some guys from the football team ran out and joined the pommies. They were dressed like cheerleaders—bad makeup, Kleenex-stuffed bras, miniskirts showing hairy legs, and mops for wigs. The guys waved their poms around for a while, then they basically gave up and started feeling up each other's fake tits. When the music stopped, the pommies raced underneath the basketball hoops as fast as their chubby little legs could carry 'em.

I felt something warm and slick in my ear. I turned around. Rob was sucking his index finger.

"Wet willy," he said, taking his finger out of his mouth and smiling.

"You're such a retread," I said, body checking his left leg. He mussed my hair.

Principal Michael grabbed a microphone and made some dumb crack about "all the cute girls" at South this year. He talked about it being the best school year ever and how he knew the team'd win the big game tonight. *Yeah, maybe if they let the pommies play instead. At least they were built for defense.* He handed the microphone to Marshall, who was the football team manager/towel boy/dirty-jockstrap-picker-upper, and in a squeaky voice Steve introduced each member of the team—all of them now in their green-and-gold dress jerseys.

The band tore into the school fight song with way too much enthusiasm. The cheerleaders did some routine. Our school mascot had a boxing match with someone dressed as the Cary Grove mascot—a Trojan—and an inflated condom wound up on the gym floor. Principal Michael took the microphone again, asking, sport by sport, for each of the fall teams to stand and be recognized. When he got to boys soccer, I tried standing, but Rob pushed me down by the shoulders.

"Schmuck," I said after he let me up. He left his hand on my shoulder. It felt nice. Like it belonged there.

The pep rally ended, and I grabbed my soccer gear and headed for the bus.

We creamed Woodstock seven-zip. After the game, I helped Coach Mueller drag the team's stuff back to the locker room. Most of the guys had showered and changed, but I passed Rob sitting on the bench. Only his cleats were off.

I slowly stripped out of my Umbros, still sore from a diving save I'd made, and hit the showers. The hot water felt good.

"Shower up, Hunt," Coach Mueller bellowed at Rob. "Nobody wants to smell you all the way back to South."

At first, I didn't see Rob in the showers. I was too busy washing off the Vaseline I used on my eyebrows to keep the sweat from my eyes. But when I rinsed shampoo and soapsuds from my face, I saw him checking me out over his shoulder, almost staring. When I caught him, Rob turned away. While he shampooed, I bent down to scrub the grass stains and dried mud from my knees. I peeked. He was bigger than me, thicker, too. I gulped. He started getting hard.

"It just happens sometimes," he said. He sounded embarrassed.

"Me too."

Maybe it was crazy, but I let myself get stiff. I needed to know if he'd look. He did and my dick felt hot as a curling iron. I squeezed more liquid soap into my hands and lathered my chest and legs. Rob turned to rinse his back. He had a smooth, totally white bubble butt. As we toweled off, I noticed a bead of pre-come leaking from the head of Rob's dick. I almost reached over to touch it. From the locker room's entrance, Coach Mueller shouted that he was leaving with or without us. We dressed fast, ran to the bus, and found an empty seat in the back.

We sat with our calves pressed together. His skin was warm and it felt good against mine. He's got little black hairs down his legs that are like corn silk. I don't even have peach fuzz. Rob rested a hand on the vinyl seat. I touched his fingers, barely, and he didn't move away. I noticed he was still tenting his shorts. I wanted it to mean something, like he was into me, but I knew better. Hard-ons don't have meaning. Guys'll do anything when they're horny. I mean, there's a reason for all those jokes about farmers and sheep, right?

When we got back to school, I asked Rob if he wanted to hang out. He said he had to go home and help with his mom, but we could hang out this weekend. He offered me a ride home, but I was nervous I'd make a move on him and he wouldn't be cool with it. Rob fished a pen and some paper from his book bag and wrote down his number. I stuffed it into the back pocket of my shorts.

"Call me," he said, ducking into his car. He flashed his headlights at me before pulling away.

I walked from the parking lot to the football field. The second half had just started and South's cheerleaders had pretty much given up. We were down by 36, and Bink's only completed passes of the game had been interceptions. I dodged the halogens, ducked under the bleachers, and stuck a hand through my fly. After four pumps, I was tucked back in and grinding boy syrup into the dirt with the bottom of my Chuck Taylors. Since then, I've tenderized my meat twice while thinking about Rob. If I don't do it again, I'll never get to sleep.

Monday, September 3

This weekend with Rob—awesome. I think the Ps only let me spend the weekend with him 'cuz it meant not having to deal with me for two days.

Did I say how awesome this weekend was? Rob and I *sooo*

did the nasty—like total contortionist-on-a-trapeze, porn-star-mattress-surfing, screeching monkey love.

Yeah, right. Like that happened. With his dad and mom around all the time, there wasn't much we could do without getting caught. But we did enough.

When Rob picked me up on Saturday, he was way nervous and talking so fast I could barely understand him. *Charlie, my mom's got Lou Gehrig's disease. She's in a wheelchair, okay? It's not contagious, and don't freak, she'll see it. It's kind of like she's paralyzed. And God, if she says something—her speech isn't great. She's almost locked in.*

It kind of bugged me that Rob was worried about how I'd act around his mom. Did he think I got my jollies pulling the wings off butterflies or dragging my foot across lightning bugs so I could make a glowing line with their ass juice? What did he think I'd do to her? Throw rocks?

Rob must've seen I was ticked, 'cuz he apologized for acting stupid and dropped his fist on my thigh.

"You mind me just driving for a bit?" he asked. I shook my head. He pressed a button and all the car's power windows went down. Rob punched a few buttons on the MP3 wired to the stereo.

"We're gonna kick it old school," Rob joked.

The car zipped past newly emptied cornfields. My shoulders rolled with the doooo-rooo doooo-rooo bass groove. Rob bobbed his head and let his left hand air surf outside the window as he lip-synched. We had to look ridiculous—two goofy boys acting all straight gangsta mack.

Being with him felt good. I wanted us to kiss.

"I'm glad you're coming over," he said.

"Me too."

"I guess I'm, you know, nervous about people coming over and getting scared by my mom."

"Well, Shannon was over, right?"

Rob nodded, then clammed up. Leave it to me to say the stupid thing. *Did I mention my mouth perfectly fits a size sixteen shoe?*

"She's totally hot for you."

"I'm not into her like that," Rob said. He turned left on Huntley Road and headed to Turnberry.

"Everyone thinks she's cute."

"Well, everyone else can date her."

"Everyone else has."

Rob's house was big, but nowhere near as confusing as Dana's next door. We went upstairs and I dumped my bag in his room—unmade queen-sized bed, a desk, bureau with a TV and DVD player on top, posters of soccer players, a bookcase filled with CDs and a couple of trophies. The floor was covered with sheet music, tennis shoes, soccer cleats, and dirty clothes. Rob scurried around, picking stuff up and shoving it into a walk-in closet. I started helping, grabbing a stray sock that was damp and sticky. I didn't say anything, just kicked it under his bed. As he led the way downstairs, I put my palm to my nose and wondered whom Rob'd been thinking about when he'd taken care of things.

"We're out back, guys," Mr. Hunt called as we stepped into the kitchen.

They were on the deck. Rob opened the screen door and Mr. Hunt stood, setting a hairbrush on the patio table. Rob's mom was facing away from us, an oxygen tank strapped to the back of her wheelchair. Mr. Hunt had been combing her black hair. I freaked a little. More of a silent gasp than anything. Rob didn't hear me and Mrs. Hunt didn't see it, so it wasn't too bad. Still, would it have killed Rob to say, "Oh, and gee, before I forget, Mom's wearing an oxygen mask"?

We said our hellos. Mr. Hunt looked tired, dark bags under his eyes. Rob seemed worried.

"What's wrong?"

"She's okay now. We had some trouble at lunch. I called the nursing service. Julie came over to help," Mr. Hunt said, massaging a kink from his neck. "She'll be here tomorrow afternoon. I've got to run into the city to look at a new campaign."

"It's Sunday. Who works on Sunday?" Rob asked.

"It's a big project, Rob. Charlie, you haven't met Rob's mom yet."

Mr. Hunt turned the wheelchair. Even with an oxygen mask, she looked like Rob. They had the same white skin and cheekbones, even the same blue eyes.

"Charlie, this is Kathy. Kathy, Charlie."

"Hi, Mrs. Hunt," I said, offering a clumsy wave. Her eyes widened and—this sounds stupid—it seemed like she smiled.

"Charlie's the guy I've been telling you about," Rob said.

"Don't listen to him," I said, socking Rob on the arm. "I'm way better at soccer. Yeah, he scored four goals last night, but I was the one who kept Woodstock to nothing."

Talking to Rob's mom was easy, which kind of surprised me. Rob smiled and his retainer glinted in the sunlight.

"Of course, Rob didn't tell you that, 'cuz that'd mean admitting I'm better."

"In your dreams, Stewart," Rob said. He faked a jab to my gut. I flinched, tucking my arms to my chest. "We both know I'm better. I'll prove it."

He bounded to the corner of the deck, hefted a soccer ball into the air with his insole, trapped it with his stomach, juggled it, and then grabbed it mid-flight with his hands.

"Okay, punk. Someone needs to teach you some respect."

Mrs. Hunt looked at me like we were sharing a joke. I smiled and raced Rob to the backyard.

Rob grabbed two Frisbees and marked off a makeshift goal. I grabbed one of the Frisbees and tossed it in about four feet.

"What?" Rob asked, like he hadn't deliberately made the goal too wide.

"Putz. Like I don't know what twenty-four feet looks like?"

"I had to try." He launched a kick at me and I batted it away.

We played for hours, pretty much holding each other to even. At one point, I'd punted the ball a good thirty yards out. Rob dribbled it in a full-on charge. I dropped into my stance—knees bent slightly, arched on the balls of my feet, arms loose and ready. Instead of shooting, Rob stepped over the ball and dove forward, tackling me.

"Penalty, penalty! Flag on the play," I said. We rolled around, laughing, hands fumbling everywhere, until it was something more than roughhousing. I wriggled from under him, the grass staining my T-shirt, and grabbed Rob by his wrists, hoisting them above his head. I swung a knee across his waist, pinning him beneath me, trapping his hands. I tickled him and he squirmed, hips arching, ribcage brushing against the insides of my legs. It felt amazing. I wanted to lean down and plant one on his lips. He might've let me, too, but Mr. Hunt popped outside and shouted that we needed to come inside because it was getting late.

I beat Rob to the deck and raced him up the steps, blocking him with my hip whenever he tried passing. He swatted my ass and we ducked inside.

When Mr. Hunt saw us, he shook his head. "The two of you are filthy. Get cleaned up and then go get something to eat." He reached into his wallet and slipped Rob a hundred-dollar bill. Rob took it like it was no big deal. First'd give up a lung before he'd fork over that kinda dough to me.

"Pretend it's a date," Mr. Hunt grinned.

I couldn't tell if Mr. Hunt was kidding or if he actually was serious. Rob smiled back, but I couldn't tell anything from his expression. It was just a smile—the stupid, meaningless kind you'd expect to see in a yearbook photo.

We went upstairs and I grabbed my backpack for a change of clothes. Rob kicked open a door near the end of his bed and flicked the light switch. The bathroom. He snagged a couple of towels and tossed them to me.

"Your dad's okay with you . . . like. . . ."

I didn't finish what I was saying. I wanted Rob to fill in the rest to give me a better handle on the situation. *Dad's okay with me like what? Taking a hundred bucks? Yeah, he gives me cash all the time.* Or *My dad's okay with me like what? Like liking guys? Christ, he was totally kidding about that homo stuff. He'd flip if I liked guys, Charlie. That gay stuff is sick.*

"Okay with me going on a date? Why wouldn't he be?" Rob asked. He grabbed a shirt from the floor and sniffed it to see if it smelled clean. He alley-ooped it into an open hamper. It must've been too bad for a white trash dry-cleaning—ten minutes in a dryer with two sheets of fabric softener.

"You're cool with it, right?" Rob bit his lower lip.

"It's cool," I said. My heart climbed into my throat and throbbed so hard it probably looked like it was humping my Adam's apple.

Rob's teeth let go of his bottom lip and he exhaled. I think he'd been just as nervous as I was.

Sure, I'm into guys and all, but going on a one-milkshake-two-straws-Archie-and-Veronica-only-with-Jughead-instead date with a boy wasn't something I'd thought about. I just never figured I'd meet a guy who'd wanna go on one.

"I'll show you the guest bathroom," Rob said.

Okay, I'll admit I wanted to shower with him, get all sudsy, and, *oops, butterfingers,* drop the soap. But that stuff only happens in *Penthouse Forum* letters, and then only in prisons or military barracks.

After we'd showered and dressed, we thundered downstairs, hopped into Rob's car, and headed to the Village Squire. Rob'd driven past it once and thought it looked cool. I'd always thought it was hokey. Outside, it looks like an English cottage—all stone, wood, and ivy. Inside, it's pretty much like any other restaurant except for coats of arms on the walls and the two suits of armor flanking a soundstage for musicians.

Our waitress asked what we wanted to drink and I tried scoring us a couple of Mai Tais. I don't know what they taste like, I just like that they come in these Easter Island statue glasses. I got a nice-try-kid scowl, menus, and Cokes instead. (Diet for Rob, regular tasted too sugary, he said. "Yeah, but not metallic and artificial tasting," I said.) Rob's lips moved as he read the menu, and when he saw I'd noticed, he acted all shy, and asked me not to tell anyone. He was dyslexic and had learning disabilities, which was part of the reason his Ps'd sent him to Phelps.

The rest of dinner's a blur. Saganaki—*opa!*—with a squeeze of lemon juice, a pizza, another round of Cokes. The singer on break and Bowie over the speakers. Not "Heroes," but still, a total sign! Rob, total southpaw, eating left-handed. Grease mopped from chins. Playing footsie under the table. Rob, surprised I hadn't figured out he was gay sooner. *Sheesh, pup, the locker room? Yeah, but that coulda been anything. Well,*

what about Dana's? Truth or dare? Me trying to french you?
I thought you were making fun of me. More Coke. *We'll*
float out of here if we have any more. Me hard and hardly
breathing. The Thin White Duke returning. An eyelash on Rob's
cheek. Me brushing it to my fingertip, not caring who saw. Him
wishing on it and blowing it away. Squeezing hands under
the table, fingers intertwined. The bill paid, tip left, his hand
in the small of my back as we left. Then to Julianne's across
the street for frozen custard, eating our cones in the car.
And at a stoplight, a kiss almost, almost my first, my nose
Eskimo-ing his as he leaned in. The light changed and Rob
sighed, slipping the car into gear.

Back in Rob's room, we both acted awkward and skittish.
It was the bed. The thing was there, smack in the middle of
the room, but we both acted like if we went near it, things'd
get snack-time-in-the-Garden-of-Eden messy.

I was terrified that as soon as we started making out, he'd
figure out I was a virgin, and he'd laugh 'cuz it was so pathetic. Overreact much, Charlie? Nah.

Finally, Rob asked if I wanted to watch a movie. I didn't,
but I figured a movie'd keep him from seeing how much of
a dork I was. Rob popped in a DVD—*Labyrinth*—'cuz he noticed at the Village Squire that I liked Bowie, and 'cuz he liked
it when he was a kid—and kicked off his shoes. I toe-to-heeled
out of mine and nudged them under the bed, afraid they
might stink. Rob turned off the light and we climbed on the
bed, staying as far apart as we could—me at the foot, lying
on my stomach, Rob at the head, knees tucked to his chest.

We must've both dozed off, 'cuz when Mr. Hunt rapped
on the door, saying we needed to hit the hay, we jumped.
The movie was over. Rob found the remote and clicked off
the DVD player, leaving the room lit by the TV's blue haze.

He hopped off the bed, pulled his shirt over his head, dropped it to the floor, and shimmied down to his boxers. Rob sailed into the bathroom and grabbed his toothbrush. I dug through my bag for mine and stripped down to my Jockeys, worried I might get hard.

I joined Rob in the bathroom. He smiled at me in the mirror. His retainer was in a yellow case on the counter. He gargled, spit, and then slipped behind me so I could have the sink. I fumbled to squeeze a glob of Crest onto my brush as Rob wrapped his arms around my waist and stood on his toes. He pressed against me and his nipples grazed the skin of my back. It tickled.

"Quit it."

"No, I want to," Rob said.

His fingertips slid past the elastic band of my underwear. My dick jerked up and Rob snapped the waistband against Mr. Five-Incher's head. I winced and tucked him back into my Jockeys, and then went back to brushing my teeth. Mr. Five-Incher wasn't having any of it. A wet spot formed on the cotton fabric and Rob traced it with his index finger. My face went red. I stopped breathing and it felt like the bones in my legs had dissolved. Rob pressed his lips along my shoulder blade, kissing my skin, then he darted back to the bedroom and dove into bed. I followed, leaping after him as my toothbrush clattered into the sink.

How was I? More self-evaluation:

Compared to driving, I think I'm not all that bad with the making-out-with-guys thing. But that's not saying a lot.

I was really nervous the whole time. I kept thinking Mr. Hunt'd walk in on us going at it, our dicks

rubbing together like we were a couple of Boy Scouts
starting campfires in our underwear. Half the time
we tried kissing our teeth would clink together or I'd
jab him in the eye with my nose or bump his fore-
head with my chin. Or we'd roll over and our knees
would knock. I'd grab him and he'd flinch 'cuz I was
holding him too hard. I kept saying "I'm sorry," "oops,"
"so sorry," until Rob stuck his tongue down my throat
to make me shut up.

So there. I'm no James Brown sex machine or Rick
James superfreak. Rob's a lot more experienced. I can
tell. I've got the marks to prove it—whisker burn along
my jaw and hickeys down my ribcage. When was he
down *there? Oh, and he bites. Hard. Not that that's a*
bad thing. I'm just surprised I have ears left. My nip-
ples are still pretty sore, too. They're all swollen and
it almost hurts to wear a shirt. Actually, it feels kind
of cool, like he's given me love tattoos. That should be
the name of a lounge singer's band. And now, ladies
and gentlemen, it's my great pleasure to present to you
the incomparable song stylings of Charlie Stewart and
his Love Tattoos. He's here 'til Thursday. Try the veal.

Still, I'm good at spooning. Even though Rob's dick
poked my butt, I didn't reach around to play with it.
I didn't even play with mine.

I woke up way before Rob with a major case of morning
wood. I thought about humping his hand until he woke up,
but I really needed to take a leak in the worst way. I untan-
gled myself from Rob, tiptoed to the bathroom, and tried to
pee without making a mess of everything.

Girls have it easy. Sure, they have periods and babies and
menopause and all. Big deal. Try pissing through a hard-on.

Waiting for it to go away doesn't work. It's a proven fact that a teenaged boy can't lose wood if he's gotta piss. He can pound one off and then try peeing when it's back at half-staff, but sometimes he can't bust a nut if he's gotta go. He can try the cold shower routine, where he prays the freezing water will make him lose it before he sprays his chest. There's the screw-it-piss-through-it option. No guy'll admit doing it, but sometimes it's the only way to get the job done. You stand over the bathroom sink (or any sink for that matter) on your tippytoes, point Mr. Happy at the drain, and let it rip. Sure, it sounds gross, but it's just another one of those things guys don't talk about—like farmer blows in the shower or seeing if they can suck themselves off. I can't; I nearly sprained my neck trying.

I did a variation of the screw-it-piss-through-it method, 'cuz if a guy shoots in his shorts and lets it dry, things down there get stuck. He's gotta go slow with the undressing. If he's glued to his underwear, he can't do the Band-Aid thing—the fast tug so the scab doesn't come off—because that'd hurt way too much. So I uncemented my underwear with a few drops of water from the faucet and then managed to shimmy into the toilet sandwich position—my butt cheeks on the seat like the top slice of bread, the seat where the meat would be, and Mr. Five-Incher hooked under it like he was the bottom slice. I pushed him down at his base so he wouldn't spray the bathroom floor and soak my shorts.

When I finished, Rob was still asleep and drooling a little on his pillowcase, so I grabbed a pair of baggy basketball shorts and an oversized T-shirt, put them on, and went downstairs. I heard Mr. Hunt arguing with Nurse Julie.

The gist of the fight was that Mrs. Hunt would need a ventilator soon, maybe a feeding tube. According to Julie, she wouldn't last long without either. She said it'd be cruel if he didn't do something now. Mr. Hunt said he'd decide what was best for his family.

"Bullshit," Nurse Julie said. "I'm talking about a living, breathing person. She needs this treatment now or she'll get worse."

"Okay, we put her on your machines. Then what? She's never getting better. It must be nice knowing how other people should live their lives. I only know what she wants—and it sure as *fuck* isn't this."

Julie burst into tears. Mr. Hunt told her—in a voice so calm it was scary—to get her crap and get out of his house. I crept from the kitchen, making sure my bare feet didn't make any sounds on the hardwood floor. When I felt carpeting, I turned and saw Mrs. Hunt's profile. She was in her chair, facing an open window. She'd heard them. I felt sick. When she saw me, her eyes smiled. She struggled to say something, but no words came. I sat across from her on an ottoman and touched her hand. It wasn't withered or anything, just curled into a fist.

"It's pretty bad now, isn't it?"

Her eyebrows arched. Was that a yes?

"And Rob doesn't know?"

Her eyes closed, then opened slowly. No.

I didn't know what to say. *Gee, sorry you're dying. That's kind of a bummer, isn't it? Can I getcha something? No? You sure? Coffee, maybe? Okay. Why am I standing here with my thumb up my ass, looking sorry for you? 'Cuz I don't know what else to do. The whole dying thing isn't exactly a conversation-starter. Wanna see the hickeys your son gave me last night?* That'd go over real well.

What I couldn't figure out was why Mr. Hunt hadn't told Rob his mom was in such bad shape. Maybe he was worried

Rob couldn't handle it. That he'd totally lose it and turn into this chain-smoking, vomit-and-piss-stained, raging drunk guzzling rubbing alcohol straight from the bottle; crashing at flophouses; selling blood, plasma, sperm, spinal fluid, and the fillings from his teeth to scrounge up a handful of change for a bottle of Mad Dog 20/20 banana-flavored wine. Or maybe he was freaked Rob would off himself and he'd find him swinging from the rafters in the attic, bicycle chain around his neck, toppled chair at his feet. I decided it was probably best just to keep my mouth shut for once. *Hard to believe, right?*

Half an hour later, Rob came downstairs wearing only his Calvin Klein underwear and rubbing sleep from his eyes. He conned his dad into letting us skip church, but only if we made sure Rob's mom had her medicine and her Robert Ludlum book-on-tape, and that we checked on her once in a while.

Rob asked why Julie couldn't do it, and Mr. Hunt said he'd let Julie go. She couldn't provide the support he needed anymore. I guess it wasn't a total lie, but still. Rob shouldn't worry, though. Mr. Hunt was looking into other options.

We spent the day playing video games, talking about which guys on the team needed to play better, telling stupid jokes, and bragging about all the crap we'd do once we were out of school. Rob said that if they'd let him in, he'd go to some famous New York music school. What was weird was Rob talking about the stuff he'd do with his parents—like going back to New York to visit family over Thanksgiving and finding a way to get Mrs. Hunt to one of our games.

After dinner, Rob drove me home. He didn't want me to leave—I think he wanted more bed time, too—but Rob needed to practice for an audition he has on Tuesday with some piano teacher in Chicago. I guess the guy plays for the symphony or something big like that and only takes the best students. Afterward, Rob and his dad are going to visit Rob's uncle in Lakeview.

Rob was really cute when he pulled into my driveway. Every time I tried to get out of the car, he'd grab my shirt, pull me in, and we'd kiss. Then he'd complain I did it wrong and said I had to keep doing it until I got it right.

We were in the middle of a long kiss—Rob's hand cupping the back of my neck—when he stopped and jerked away. He grabbed the steering wheel, white-knuckling it, and sighed really hard. Rob looked at me, opened his mouth, stopped, and then blurted out something so fast it sounded like he was speaking Korean.

"What?" I asked.

"—go out with me. Be boyfriends?"

I *ummm-ummm-ummm*-ed and couldn't stop myself. My throat started making these weird choking and gurgling sounds. I must've seemed like a complete moron. All I managed was a tiny, "Okay."

"Awesome, pup," Rob said.

I smiled. I could get used to him calling me pup.

He pulled my face into his. We kissed, only this time it was different. It was slow, like there was this charge between us. An electrical current arcing from his lips to mine. I didn't want it to stop, but Rob pulled away. He needed to get going or his dad would kill him. I promised to call on Monday, gave him one last peck on the cheek, and got out of his BMW. He flashed the car headlights at me. I waved good-bye and he pulled away.

Inside, the Ps had left a note—they'd gone out and would be home later. Fine by me. If they'd seen how giddy and bouncy I was, they probably would've gotten all D.A.R.E.-this-is-your-son-on-drugs suspicious, sat my ass down, shined a flashlight into my eyes, and checked my arms for track marks. With the house to myself, I raced upstairs and stripped. My boner snagged on my Jockeys as I tugged 'em off. I hopped on the bed face down, humped the mattress, and frenched the pillow, pretending Rob was under me.

I have a boyfriend. Not that I can really tell anyone without getting a prison-style beat down, but still, I have a boyfriend.

Today sucked though. First made me help him replace a bunch of his "Elect Stewart" campaign signs. Seems someone has been changing the L in "Elect" to a J, which had First ready to chew 16-penny nails and made me kinda wish I'd thought of it.

Since First had me out most of the night, I just now got a chance to call Rob. Mr. Hunt answered, saying Rob was in bed already. I insisted he tell Rob I called. I didn't want Rob thinking I'd freaked out about being his boyfriend. I must've sounded panicked, because Mr. Hunt only stopped laughing to say, "Relax, I'll tell Rob you called. Now go to bed, Charlie."

It's 11:30 p.m. and I still have homework.

I have a boyfriend. How cool is that?

Tuesday, September 4

I finally did it. I bit the bullet and told Dana I was sorry for ruining her party. Actually, she browbeat me into doing it. Doesn't matter either way. It's done.

Before first period, I looked for Rob, forgetting he had

67

his piano audition today. I stupidly walked into the Pit where Kyle Weir—just 'cuz he's an asswipe—tripped me. My books skidded out of my hands and a bunch of seniors grabbed 'em and passed them around the Pit. As I got on to all fours, Josh McCullough stepped on top of one of my hands to keep me from getting up, calling me a fag. My face burned and my eyes watered. I shoved McCullough off me, got up, and rushed to creative writing, not even trying to get my books. That would've made me look like a bigger dork.

The room was empty. Mrs. Bailey was probably in the teacher's lounge spiking her coffee. Not that I blame her. I'd drink, too, if I had to spend my mornings listening to vitamin D-deprived-pseudo-Goth girls reading poetry about how the color of their souls was black. I found a desk I hadn't sat in yet. With my luck, today Bailey would announce that the mark of a true genius was finding one's place on a well-crafted seating chart.

"I don't know why I'm doing this, but here."

It was Dana. She dropped my stuff on the desk.

"Gee, Dana. Thanks," I said with zero appreciation.

That was a stupid move. If I had faked some sincerity, she would've left. Instead, she jerked a desk around, plopped in it, and tugged at the bottom of her T-shirt. Her nipples were pointy and hard and one of 'em poked out so far the eye of the Latin American revolutionary on the shirt looked like it was about to explode. It was gross.

I don't know what Bink sees in her. To hear him talk, he likes everything about her—the plaid schoolgirl skirts, knee-high white cowboy boots, cheap plastic butterfly barrettes, the smell of her shampoo, even that she was "quirky." *Quirky?* For God's sake, quirky isn't something you date; it's something you make fun of until it totally loses it, runs to its bedroom, throws itself face down on its Barbie comforter, and sobs into its diary about how everyone's so *mean*.

"You know what I don't understand, Charles?" she asked. Her voice let me know she wasn't interested in my answer. "Why do you have to hate everyone as much as you hate yourself?"

She opened her handbag, grabbed a tube of out-out-damn-spot lipstick, and slathered a coat of war paint across her pucker. Dana eyed herself in her compact and smacked her lips, making this disgusting popping sound.

"Look, Dana," I said, still with no enthusiasm. "I'm sorry. I'm sorry I was such an ass at your party. I'm just sorry."

"You *are* sorry."

She stepped from her desk and planted a kiss in the middle of my forehead. My fingers touched the lipstick.

"Don't bother, it's practically waterproof." She smiled at me. "Truce."

Soccer practice was shorter than usual—running laps and free weights mostly. Afterward, I wanted to call Rob to see how his audition went—hell, just to talk to him—but First was in the parking lot, leaning against the Oldsmobile's fender. I pretended not to see him, but he ran after me, grabbed my shoulder, and spun me around.

"Where do you think you're going?" he asked. "You're going to learn to drive if it kills me."

"Kills us both is more like it," I said, yanking the keys from his hand. As I got behind the wheel, First made this big production about how, even in a vacant parking lot, my driving was the same as playing Russian roulette with a revolver with only one empty chamber. I wanted to gun the engine and drive us into a lamppost. With my luck, I'd end up a paraplegic and First'd insist on teaching me how to drive my motorized wheelchair.

Having your dad teach you to drive's no rite of passage. It sucks. It really, really sucks. We spent two hours in that damn car, drove thirty miles, and never left the lot.

Chip, check your mirrors.

Why? Is my mascara running?

Let's try to parallel park again. Don't use that tone of voice with me. What are you going to do when they make you parallel park during your road test?

Find a valet?

It wasn't fun for either of us. First had to be praying he'd hear from the God of the Old Testament—the one he empathized with; the divine micromanager who got off on asking fathers to kill their sons. Screw any Johnny-come-lately angel types telling him to stop 'cuz it'd only been a test of faith. First'd not only demand a grade, he'd be a total apple-polisher, saying how he was the only one that actually finished the test, how his knife was sharper than Abraham's, how Abraham had only bound Isaac, but First'd trussed me up and even made a lovely sage dressing with walnuts and prosciutto.

After driving with First, I knew I should call Rob, which wasn't exactly as easy as it sounded, mostly 'cuz I was worried about total chickenshit things. Like, what if my voice wasn't deep enough, and Rob, thinking I was some four-year-old girl who'd mistaken a real phone for her Fisher-Price version, hangs up? What if I talked too much and then revealed every single embarrassing moment of my life—like how when I was two First made Mom take me to the pediatrician 'cuz he thought my potty training was taking too long to kick in and I wasn't getting "housebroken" fast enough—and Rob realized just how big of a freak I am, decided he could never speak to me again, and begged his dad to send him back to boarding school? What if I didn't say anything? What if he didn't? What if the two of us just sat with the phones glued to our ears, trying not to breathe too heavily into the mouthpiece?

Overanalyze much, Charlie? Maybe, but what was I supposed to do? It's not like the people that I know who are together are stellar examples of the art of conversation. Bink and Dana? What they do can't really be called talking, it's more like Bink blocking out Dana's incessant car-alarm complaints about how nobody cares about the suffering in Uganda or Utah; how her summer trip to Europe taught her that Americans are fat, sinful, and lazy 'cuz they can't make *real* coffee, they insist on indoor plumbing that includes both *hot* and cold running water and they think cheese is an appetizer (*it's a dessert, Bink*); and how the Irish saved civilization and the French saved culture (from whom exactly? England, Germany, Russia, the United States, or just about any other country whose population includes a small asthmatic child with a slingshot or really sharp, dirty fingernails?).

And the other couples I know aren't exactly role models. Mom and First? All they seem to do anymore is fight about car payments, who didn't refill the gas tank, missed anniversaries, Mom's nylors being draped over the shower curtain, and First's boxers and black dress socks never making it to the hamper. Mr. and Mrs. B? I suppose they talk and all, but it's all about boring stuff like social justice and school carpools for Bink's sisters.

So after an hour or so of beating myself up over what I'd say to Rob and how I'd sound, I *carpe diem*-ed and picked up the phone.

"Hi, is Rob there?"

"Hey, pup. What's going on?"

"It's me, Charlie."

"I know. I'm not the kind of guy who calls telemarketers pup."

"Oh, okay. That makes sense, I guess," I said, practically choking on my own stupidity. I blushed and was *sooo* glad Rob couldn't see me. "Ummm . . . yeah . . . I was just calling to say hi."

"You already said hi. Are you going to hang up now?" Rob laughed, sounding completely relaxed. Me on the other hand, I sounded like somebody had put my lungs in a vise and was quickly squeezing the air from them. If I did end up suffocating, that was fine by me. I wanted to die. A slow painful asphyxiation would be better than my self-inflicted death by chronic embarrassment and terminal idiocy.

"I'm sorry. I guess I'm nervous."

"About what? You haven't called someone you're dating before?"

"Have you?" I asked, defensively.

"Charlie, it's not like you're my first boyfriend. I dated a guy at Phelps last year. We broke up when he graduated."

It was stupid, but I got a little jealous. Like part of me actually wished that Rob had never thought about liking guys until he met me.

"What about you?" Rob asked.

"Me. I've dated plenty of guys," I said, trying to sound so cocky and full of myself that Rob would know I was joking. "The Great Lakes Naval Academy . . . I dated everyone there. Broke all their hearts. When last year's class of graduates had to ship out, guys were throwing themselves off their boats to be with me. It was sad, really. I was on the dock and they'd be trying to climb out of the water, and I'd just have

72

to push their heads down with my foot and tell them, 'No, go back to your ship. Serve your country.'"

"Really?" Rob asked in mock disbelief. I started crushing hard on the sound of his voice. It was something I could imagine waking up to for the rest of my life, even if it was only to hear it nagging about where cheddar fell in the dinner lineup, dirty laundry, or Rosa Parks' bus route. "Well, Charlie, you're a regular Casanova."

"That's me, alright." I was feeling more comfortable, and so naturally my verbal diarrhea kicked in. "I saw this TV special on him . . . Casanova . . . and in it, they said one of the reasons he got so much action was 'cuz he'd tell hot women that they were smart, and smart women they were hot. Apparently, he figured the way you got a chick to pull up her skirt during the Renaissance was by giving her the compliment she didn't expect to hear."

"So, Casanova," Rob said, "how would you compliment me?"

I felt my central nervous system completely collapse. My nerves, spinal column, brain, they all went dead. No matter what I said, I'd be screwed. If I told Rob I thought he was hot, he'd think I thought he was too dumb to swallow his own drool; if I said he was smart, he'd think I thought his pants weren't worth getting into. I did the only thing I could do. I was honest.

"I'd say I just want to be in the same room as you."

Rob got quiet for a bit, so I figured I must've said the right thing. We talked for a while longer—about how he did on his auditions—awesome—school, the soccer team. Toward the end of the call, Rob said he used to think he'd miss New York, and he still kind of did, but he was glad he met me, 'cuz I made things easier.

"How?" I asked.

"Well, it's being with someone who's funny and cute."

That's when he noticed it was past ten and he said he had to get off the phone or his dad would kill him. We did the good-bye thing, saying how much we missed each other and couldn't wait to see each other at school tomorrow.

How awesome is it that Rob thinks I'm cute? At least I hope he really thinks I'm cute. What if he said that 'cuz he thinks I'm smart? I need to go to bed before I give myself an ulcer.

Wednesday, September 5

Today was incredible. Kyle Weir totally got busted for calling Mr. B a fucking Jew. Even more awesome, Rob and I traded hand jobs. I still can't believe it. I got a hand job. A real one. With somebody else's hand. I came all over the place—Rob's hand, my chest, neck, face—which was kind of gross, but really cool. I used to think that when it came to sex, I did my best work alone, but now I'm all about the teamwork.

It happened in choir, but only 'cuz Mrs. Reed was out sick and we had this substitute teacher who didn't know music. We were supposed to fend for ourselves while she read *Woman's World* or *Better Homes & Gardens*. Choir kids don't exactly have a reputation for being hell-raisers, so it's not like she had to worry about us going all *The Lord of the Flies* and shouting "die, Piggy, die" as we chased Tom Benson around the practice room.

Everyone spread out across the room and cracked their books, but I grabbed Rob and dragged him to the sub. I asked if the two of us could go to one of the private practice rooms and rehearse. She must've been totally oblivious, 'cuz when I said "rehearse," my voice didn't just put air quotes around the word, it spelled out what I really meant. *Gee, can Rob and I go to a practice room so we can, like, roll around together and maybe play with each other's knobs?* The sub didn't bother looking up from her celebrity recipe for a no-fuss-no-muss-no-bake tuna casserole and nodded.

When Rob grabbed some sheet music, I got worried that he thought I was serious about practicing. Rob winked at me. "For cover," he said, smiling ear-to-ear. Once we were in a practice room, Rob dropped the music, grabbed my ears, pulled my face to his, and kissed me. I guess jug ears aren't so bad when a cute boy's using them for handles.

"Hi, boyfriend," he said as he broke away. We'd been frenching for so long my jaw was numb. He stroked my hair and cupped my face in his hands. He smelled like Polo—the real stuff.

"Hi," I whispered into his mouth. Rob lay on his side and I got next to him and closed my eyes. We made out—light, quick kisses on each other's ears, lips, eyes, hair, and noses (he half-nipped, half-sucked mine, which sounds weird, but felt *way* cool). We were both in shorts. Today's high was supposed to hit, like, 87 degrees and we kept rubbing our bare legs together like crickets.

I didn't think anything could feel better and then Rob rolled on top of me, his legs at my sides. He pulled my shorts past my hips and snaked his hand into my underwear. He eased the waistband down, trapping it under my balls. I squirmed and tried to flip to my stomach, worried that when Rob saw how small my dick was, he'd make fun of me. Thank God, I was hard. I didn't look like a total inchworm. Rob stroked me slowly—his hand was warm—and massaged a pearl of pre-come from the tip of my dick. I shivered goose bumps from my toes to my shoulders. Rob leaned in to kiss me and I got nervous. Sure, I'd been wanting to do this since, like, forever, but I was scared. What if I screwed up and he found out I was a virgin? I scooted back.

"What?" he asked, all blue eyes and concern.

"I'm still a . . . I . . . I haven't done anything like this." My chest was pounding.

"It's okay," he said, nuzzling his lips where my neck met the back of my ear. "We'll go slowly."

I nodded. But then it dawned on me—I didn't want to go slow. I wanted this—wanted Rob touching me. I tore off my shirt like it was on fire and yanked open Rob's shorts.

"Easy, pup," Rob said, laughing and pulling his shirt over his head.

I felt him—wow!—he had a big blue vein running along the shaft. It seemed bigger than it looked in the locker room shower. Really wide, too, with a big mushroom-shaped tip that wouldn't fit through the center of a toilet paper roll. Okay, so I've tried with mine and I can. *It's not like I'm a horse.* His pubes were really soft, too. The best part was him smiling and saying it was really cool that I was so excited.

Side by side, we jacked each other off, watching what made the other feel good. Sometimes, he'd buck his hips, pumping his dick in my hand. Other times, he'd gasp, sucking air through his teeth. Right before he shot, his lips got all red and he pulled my face against his pecs so my mouth was over his nipple. He begged me to suck it, which seemed weird, 'cuz I didn't think guys could be sensitive there. I flicked it with my tongue and it got hard and pointy. He told me to bite it and when I did, Rob arched onto the balls of his feet. He was almost hyperventilating, but I kept stroking. He gushed, spilling over my knuckles and into his pubic hair.

Even while he was coming, Rob didn't stop pumping me. When I was about to pop, Rob did something I didn't expect. He swung around, facing me, and sucked the index finger of his free hand. Cradling my legs in the crook of his arms, he slipped a finger inside me. My butt grabbed Rob's finger with the strength of a baby's grip and I shot everywhere. He collapsed on top of me, both of us slick with sweat and come. Rob kissed me real softly and stuff.

I wiped what I could from my chin and chest, rubbed it on the carpet, and searched the room for something better to mop up with.

"Here," Rob said. He grabbed his socks, wiped his chest, and then tossed his socks to me. "Who's gonna know?"

We'd just finished drying off and getting dressed when there was a knock on the door. The substitute teacher poked her head inside and wanted to know why we weren't singing.

"Breathing exercises," Rob said. I tried not to crack up.

She looked at him and scowled. "In your bare feet?" Rob nodded. "Then how come you're in your shoes and socks?" she asked.

"Because he's a baritone and it's easier to hit the low notes barefoot."

"Well, get your shoes and socks back on," she told Rob, clucking her tongue. "The period's almost over."

Rob looked at me, making a sure-it's-kinda-gross-but-watcha-gonna-do shrug, and pulled them on. I felt bad for him, but at least it wasn't me. The bell rang and we ran out of the practice room, snickering.

I didn't see Rob again until seventh-hour passing period. He smiled, pulled me against a wall, and then glanced at his feet. He was still wearing the socks. I shook my head and smiled.

"Next time, pup, you're cleaning up your own mess," he said. He pinched my butt as we passed and I *sooo* got hard.

And just when I thought the day couldn't get better, it did. In seventh hour, Kyle got busted.

I don't know how Mr. Binkmeyer does it. If I was him, and I had to deal with Kyle, Joan, and me in class, I'd've skipped flatworms altogether and started dissecting students. For some reason, Mr. B calls everyone by their last names when he's in class, but gives you the first-name treatment if you are on the wrestling or girls' softball team. *As you'll see here, class, it's exactly as I suspected. Miss Hawkings is indeed an invertebrate, as noted by her complete and total lack of a spine. What's that, Mr. Marshall? Your lab partner, Mr. Stewart, is also spineless? Well, I can't say I'm shocked.*

Mr. B hadn't finished setting a stainless steel tray with two flatworms on Joan's table and she was already pushing it away.

"No." She shook her head and tucked her hands under her armpits. "I'm not killing anything."

"Well, Miss Hawkings," Mr. B sighed. He slid the tray back to Joan. "You don't have to. They died at dawn." Mr. B's hand flicked to his forehead in mock salute.

"Dude, that's awesome," Weir said, slapping his lab table. "How'd ya do it?"

"I shot them, Mr. Weir. With a very, very small pistol."

Before Kyle could ask, "Really?" Joan had started in on Mr. B again.

"You *killed* them? Why?"

"Because, Miss Hawkings, they knew too much." Mr. B grinned like a B-movie villain and rubbed his hands together. "Ze flatworms today. Tomorrow, ze world. Muwahahahaha!" The class laughed. Joan glared at Mr. B.

Normally, I'd've laughed, too, but it didn't feel right. I

78

could see Joan's point. Sure, the flatworms were dead and all, but that didn't make cutting them apart right. I mean, what was the point? So a bunch of high school dumbasses could see that the stupid things didn't have bones? That was already in our textbooks.

I raised my hand.

"Yes, Mr. Stewart?"

"Mr. B, do we really have to do this? It's not like we're gonna discover anything new about flatworms. It's kinda inhumane, isn't it?"

Mr. B balled his hands into fists. "Mr. Stewart," he said, "it's not '*kinda* inhumane.' It's completely inhumane. Flatworms aren't—gasp—human. Besides, Mr. Stewart, not everything worth knowing can be found between the covers of a book. I would have thought that you already learned that."

The rebellion was squashed and, like it or not, we were gonna dissect the damn bugs. Yeah, I know, they aren't bugs. *Big whoop.*

Kyle came up to Steve and me as we were cutting our worm open. He was holding his against the bulge in his crotch.

"Jealous of it, Charlie? It's bigger than yours."

"How would you know, Kyle?" Marshall asked, laughing. "Been checking him out?" Kyle's eyes narrowed.

"You're a dead man, Marshall," Kyle said. He flicked the worm at Steve. The worm smacked Steve's cheek. "A dead man," Kyle repeated, turning right into Mr. B, who was right behind him.

"If you wanted to spend time cleaning my lab after school, Mr. Weir," Mr. B said, handing Kyle a pink detention slip, "you could have asked."

"But I'll miss football practice!" Kyle protested.

"Two fifty-five, be here. I'll have a mop waiting."

Mr. B walked toward the blackboard and Kyle said, louder than he'd meant, "Goddamn Jew."

The class got so quiet I could hear the lab's fluorescent lights humming. Mr. B stepped toward Kyle, looking like he wanted to squeeze Kyle's head like a zit. Kyle scurried backward, slamming into a chair and scraping its metal legs across the linoleum. He was shaking so badly I expected to see piss gushing down his pant leg. Mr. B reached forward and Kyle winced.

Mr. B took in the classroom with his eyes. "Seats. Now." We couldn't move fast enough. Kids were practically crawling over each other. Kyle stood there, his lower lip quivering. Mr. B pushed up his shirtsleeves, and said, "Mr. Weir, follow me."

They left, Kyle blathering about how sorry he was, how his parents were gonna kill him, how he didn't mean it. Mr. B wasn't a Jew; well, he was—just not a goddamned one. "He's *sooo* dead," someone said as Mrs. Dover, an earth science teacher, walked into the classroom and told us to shut up and read chapter three in our texts. Nobody saw Kyle or Mr. B for the rest of the day.

As soon as I got home tonight, I called Bink to find out what happened. Principal Michael called in Weir's parents and Kyle supposedly bawled through the whole meeting. Principal Michael pushed for an expulsion, not caring if that meant Kyle couldn't get into a decent college. He didn't want filth like Kyle at *his* school. According to Bink, Mr. Weir said he understood, but there were better ways of punishing Kyle: Kyle takes a three-day suspension, he's off the football team, he has to write a 30-page paper on the Holocaust to be graded by Mr. B and Principal Michael, and for the rest of the semester, he's gotta wear a yarmulke and Star of David pinned to his chest. If he takes them off or causes any problems, he's expelled.

Bink's pissed about it, though. Not 'cuz Kyle's off the team—*C'mon, Charlie, it's not like it'd make any difference, we'll still lose*—but because it's Bink's yarmulke Kyle'll be wearing.

I can't stop thinking about the choir practice room. Wouldn't it be awesome if Rob and I went all the way?

Thursday, September 6

Everybody at school's heard about Kyle. All day, people've been asking Bink how to say "asshole," "dickweed," and "go fuck yourself" in Hebrew and Yiddish. At first, it pissed Bink off, 'cuz when Andy Moore wanted to know the Hebrew for "tampon," Bink sent him scurrying off, shouting, "What do I look like, a rabbi?" But by lunch, Bink was really getting into it, even though he admitted he was just making stuff up.

"I can't believe it. I just told someone that *l'chaim* is 'blow me' in Yiddish."

After practice today, Rob and I drove to Mister A's on Dole Avenue. It's a total pit, the kind of place that puts its hamburger patties in the deep fryer before slapping 'em on the grill, but it's got great Italian beef and really good cheese fries. I got a beef with cheese, sweet and hot, no dip, an order of fries, and a lemonade. Rob ordered two hot dogs with everything, a diet Coke, a cup of coffee with cream and sugar, and a glass of water.

"What?" he asked. "I like being hydrated."

I had him get the napkins and straws and grab a picnic

table outside. I waited for our order, watching him through the window. He was using the picnic table like a keyboard, fingers banging out something that looked really complicated. It was cute.

"These are hot dogs?" Rob asked as I handed him his plastic basket.

I nodded, swallowing a bite of my beef and wiping my mouth. "Chicago-style, with mustard, onions, relish, pickle, tomato slices, hot pepper, and celery salt."

"No lettuce?" Rob grinned, struggling to take a bite.

"Where would it fit?"

"Dork." He kicked my shoe. I kicked his back.

When we were done, Rob leaned across the table with a napkin to dab something from my face. I freaked a little. He stopped.

"I'm sorry," I said, "it's just—"

"You weren't kidding yesterday. You've never been with a guy." His eyes were wide. I shook my head. "Seriously?"

"Yeah." He squeezed my knee under the table. "I don't know crap about sex," I said. "You're the first guy I've ever, you know . . . But you've done stuff, right?"

"Yeah." Rob lowered his eyes.

"So, what'd you do with that guy from your old school? Blow jobs?" I asked, way too eagerly. Rob chuckled.

"You're a total horndog."

"You did, didn't you?"

He threw a crumpled napkin at me.

"What else? Like up the butt?"

Rob flashed a smile and said we should get going.

Back in Rob's room, he made me strip to my underwear. He did the same. He said he wanted to try something he'd never done with another guy.

82

"Lie down here," he said, pulling his desk chair toward him. "Face down and close your eyes."

I got on the bed with my arms at my sides and scooched to the edge. Rob sat next to me and smoothed his hand over my eyes. *"No peeking."* I heard him stretch, and then his fingertips tickled my back—quick flicks along my spine. His hands moved fast. I wriggled and tried not to get a woodie.

"Ticklish much?" Rob laughed.

"What are you doing?" I clenched my eyes and grabbed the bedsheets.

"Teaching you classical music," Rob said. "Guess what I'm playing."

"'Chopsticks'?"

"No. 'Flight of the Bumblebee.' Rimsky-Korsakov.' He hummed the notes his fingers would've made on the keyboard. "Okay, now guess what this is."

His hands moved slowly. It seemed like they were playing different songs, the right making all these flourishes between my shoulder blades, the left tapping the small of my back. I practically melted into the mattress. It took a while before I realized it wasn't two songs. It was point and counterpoint.

"That's Bach. Part of the Goldberg Variations," whispered Rob.

"Then what's Mozart feel like?" I rolled my head to the side and opened my eyes. Rob was smiling.

"Hey, pup, who's doing the teaching here?" He rubbed my hair. "Okay, even though Mozart's super-famous now, he still had competition."

"Yeah? Like in the movie *Amadeus?*"

"Well, that was Salieri. Salieri's better known for operas,

not piano stuff. The guy who gave Mozart a run for his money on the piano was a different Italian—Clementi.

"Some emperor guy threw this big Christmas party. To show off for all his friends, he had Clementi and Mozart compete in a musical duel. Clementi played this sonata."

Rob's fingers dashed across my back and I squirmed from under him, laughing and tucking my knees into my stomach.

"Get back here," Rob said as I rolled to the edge of the bed. "After Clementi was done, Mozart improvised something and then did a set of variations. The emperor called it a tie. Since what Mozart did wasn't written down, I'll just do Mozart's eleventh piano sonata."

He did, then he played Beethoven, then a guy named Liszt whose music gets used a lot in Bugs Bunny cartoons, then some Russians like Rachmaninoff, and then someone who composed a piece for just the left hand. Then he got to the Americans—ragtime and jazz. Rob said Scott Joplin, the guy who wrote "The Entertainer," stole stuff from French composers, but twisted it all up. His favorite American composer was Zez Confrey, some guy from here in Illinois who played a song called "Kitten on the Keys" at Gershwin's debut of *Rhapsody in Blue*. The way Rob's hands pounced on my back, it was easy to see how it got its name. According to Rob, Confrey was big into making music for piano rolls—compositions that would take at least two people to perform them live.

Rob would've kept talking, too, but I pulled him out of the chair and onto the bed. We started making out. We probably would've gotten off if his Dad hadn't called upstairs, saying it was dinnertime and asked Rob if I was staying.

I just got off the phone with Bink. He was all panicked because homecoming's almost a week away and he still hasn't called the florist to order Dana's corsage.

"Just get her something edible. Hay would be good. You'll save money on dinner," I told him while we were on the phone.

"I should have known you wouldn't be any help," Bink said.

"Okay, Bink. I'll be serious. What color is her dress?"

"That's just it, Charlie. I don't know. She said something about it being moth. What the hell color is 'moth'? What do I look like, a box of crayons?"

"She must've told you mauve," I said.

"Mauve? That's not a real color. That sounds like a skin condition."

"Bink, mauve's a color. Just think of it as purple on an iron-poor diet. Lavender-ish."

"Mauve. Lavender-ish. I swear, you better not be making this crap up." I laughed, but Bink didn't think it was funny. "Listen, Charlie, you've got it so much easier. You can stop in a 7-Eleven, buy Rob a carnation and be done with it. Some of us actually have to think. Talk to you later."

I hadn't thought about Rob and homecoming. Should I ask him? Who'm I kidding? Guys don't ask each other to dances. Well, not at South, anyway. But what if Rob doesn't know that?

What if he asks *me* instead?

Friday, September 7

We won our soccer game tonight, but I didn't get to hang out with Rob afterward. He had to take care of his mom, 'cuz, I guess, his dad had to go into the city for work. It's just as well. First was waiting after the game. More driving lessons.

No, your other right, Einstein. That stop sign wasn't put there for a decoration. Just because they're called bumpers doesn't mean you have to test them against everything.

I didn't let First get to me. That's 'cuz today I learned that the most important person in the world is me—at least according to the lame-ass, inspirational multimedia presentation we had to suffer through this morning.

The whole thing was this flashy, over-the-top production with C-list celebrities who probably only appeared in it as part of their court-ordered community service. The presentation was so lame I just know that some guidance counselors and child psychologists totally creamed their pants thinking it up. *We've got to make it really "connect" with today's youth. It should be MTV, but with a message. We'll get 'N Sync to talk about date rape or something. They're popular, right? I saw one of them in the news not too long ago. He was going out or something. Remember, people, this is bigger than all of us. We're saving lives here. If we make just one skinny 13-year-old girl stop going at her wrists with a hacksaw long enough to eat a piece of celery, we've done our jobs.*

The idea was that we were supposed to "say no" to drinking, drugs, sex, racism, and picking on the chess club dorks. They wanted us to say "yes" to living a clean life, having friends who—as long as they weren't devil-worshipping socialists—celebrated our differences and used the products manufactured by the video's corporate sponsors.

Since we had to miss first hour for the assembly, Mrs. Bailey made us take notes so we could "journal" our responses. Well, it gave me something to do with my pen besides poke out my eyes.

Here's what I *won't* be turning in:

Apparently, I'm smarter than every goddamn adult on this planet.

What happens to people after they turn thirty? Do they suddenly get retarded? It's got to be that, 'cuz there's no other reason to explain why they become a bunch of hypocrites. For instance:

Just Say No—The Sex Edition: Did you actually think making our health class teacher show us slides of a guy's dick rotting away from syphilis would stop us from fucking? C'mon, it didn't stop *you*, did it? And all those slides on abortions—another brilliant idea. Click. *This is a dilation and curettage, also known as a D&C. Here the abortionist* (never a doctor, because only butchers do this) *inserts a loop-shaped knife inside the uterus and hacks apart the baby and the placenta, then scrapes them both out.* Okay, so the slides stopped a few girls from putting out—for two weeks—but moms, here's the deal: You didn't solve anything.

Sure, you convinced your daughters that abortions are gross, but you also got them believing that their vaginas have a solvent that's so powerful it can eat through anything—condoms, IUDs, diaphragms, sponges, the Pill. Everything except for sperm and disease. So instead of your girls letting Trey or Matt or Justin go in through the front door, they let 'em in the back. Abortion worries over, 'cuz butt babies don't live.

Peer Pressure—The "Do As We Say, Not As We Do" Edition: If all your friends jumped off a bridge (and just how often are they doing that, really?), would you? Yeah, probably. But so would you. You're the people who bought a camper we never used—not even once in our own goddamn driveway—because the neighbors had one. Of course,

87

ours had to be bigger and better, for all the good it did. You're the ones who bought laserdiscs in the late '80s, swore by the tech sector in the late '90s, and voted for Bush, 'cuz after 9/11 he was the only guy with balls big enough to take on the "evil-doers."

Seriously, I'm embarrassed for you.

Just Say No—The Drugs Edition: This is your brain. This is your brain on drugs. Any questions? Yeah. You did them, so why not us? Because you know better now, you learned your lesson, and except for the occasional cigarette, Valium, amphetamine-laced diet pill, scotch-on-the-rocks, or white wine spritzer to unwind, you'd never do them? Is it because the drugs you guys did were so much safer? Yeah, that's gotta be it, 'cuz I just know the farm hicks out in Harvard and McHenry spent the last twenty years growing some superbreed of pot that's so powerful that after one puff, I'll be all Lou-Reed-waiting-for-the-man in some Cabrini Green alley with a needle in my arm. That is, when I'm not mugging little old ladies, knocking over a gas station, or blowing truck drivers to score my next fix.

You made the War on Drugs go guerilla, dipshits. You're the ones who pushed it underground. We may not be smoking meth or pot, but now the whole cheerleading squad is sneaking off campus for Chloroseptic Slurpees. Your generation sent Tim Parker to rehab 'cuz you caught him sucking the nitrous out of his mom's Reddi-wip cans.

And who can forget Jim Corley?

After he simultaneously took himself out of the running for and won South's Most Likely to Be an Idiot for Life Award with his stupid stunt *(Hey, you know what'd make for a totally awesome high, man? Scotchguard!)*, the school administrators dragged in an earn-your-degree-in-locksmithing-online therapist for an all-school assembly on the five stages of grief. It didn't help. The whole school had pretty much worked through 'em five minutes after we heard Corley bit the big one.

Denial: *There's no way anybody could be that stupid. I mean, really. Scotchguard? That stuff'll waterproof your lungs. Seriously, dude, no one's that much of a retread. You're sooo making this up.*

Anger: *Great, 45 minutes of listening to this dumb-ass talk about "feelings" and "sadness." Corley, you jagoff. This totally blows. I wish the paramedics kept you alive so I coulda killed ya. This is sooo gay.*

Bargaining: *Please, God, if I'm gonna die let it be some cool way. You know, like, having sex on the kitchen table with a pair of, like, hot lesbian twins. Okay, how about just having sex? Okay. Okay. How about not dying a virgin? Just please, God, don't take me out like you did Corley. And God, please, please, just make sure my parents don't find that stash of porn under the bed. God, if you just give me this one thing, I swear I'll stop jerking off. Well, at least to the Japanese anime of underaged schoolgirls I downloaded.*

Depression: *This sucks. Jim-bo was my ride to that party in Lake in the Hills this weekend. What am I supposed to do now? Stay home and watch TV with my parents? I'd rather die.*

Acceptance: *What do I care? I didn't know him. So, yeah, anyway, Weir had me do the ice cube thing on him once. You're right, I should really try it with menthol cough drops.*

I know; you had to destroy your children to save them.

Sunday, September 9

Big fight with First today. After church, I made the mistake of not immediately harnessing my nose to the grindstone of homework, chores, college application essays, memorizing some motivational best-seller like *Who Moved My Highly Effective Parachute?*, or developing and presenting to Stockholm a successful unified field theory. Stupid me, I just had to open my mouth and ask First if, when I was done with everything he suggested—instead of relaxing, like, for a whole ten seconds—if he wanted me to strap on a yoke and go out and plow the back forty. First went off on me, saying that if I didn't grow up soon, there was going to come a day when my mouth wrote a check my ass couldn't cash. Mom said he was the one who needed to grow up and stop riding me so hard.

I think First was going to let Mom's jab slide, but when she closed the drapes and turned up the stereo, letting our neighbors know that Michael Stipe felt just peachy about the apocalypse, First readied himself for another verbal round of bobbing and weaving.

"Jesus, Charles," Mom said, sighing in a stage whisper. "Give us all a break for once and stop trying to be the benevolent dictator." *Benevolent dictator? What the hell did she mean by that? Was it supposed to be, like, a toddler-friendly Idi Amin? A Muppet Hitler? Hi, kids, today we're going to learn about sharing. Do you know what sharing is, little comrades? It's when we go out to the sandbox and dig a mass grave for the traitors to the cause who have betrayed our dear leader.*

First smiled, but I could tell he was pissed. "That's right, Laura. I'm always deciding what's best for everyone. It's always my way or the highway, right?" His voice was all self-righteous indignation. "Forget the fact that I'm working sixty hours a week so we can have enough money to pay off a few damn bills and maybe, just maybe, have something left to help get our kid into a good school."

"You have an excuse for everything, don't you, Charles?" Mom said in a voice that was as sharp and cold as frostbite. She shook her head. "I suppose I was the one who put the gun to your head and made you run for state's attorney." Mom turned her back to him, like she couldn't be bothered with his next excuse.

"Is *that* what this is about? Jesus, how many times do we have to go through this? Fine, Laura, I'll drop out of the race, hand in my resignation at the office, find a job at some Chicago law firm. I'll work partners' hours . . . nights, weekends, holidays, vacations, Charlie's graduation. Is that what you want? Me never being around? Because I sure as hell thought you wanted something different. I thought we both did."

For a moment, Mom stood with her back to First, saying nothing. Their silence was so bad that it almost had a physical pain. I turned in my seat at the kitchen table and looked at First. I don't know what I was expecting—maybe him to be looking at Mom with this smug, cocky, self-satisfied grin on his face—but that wasn't how he looked at all.

He looked weak, defeated, almost too small to be human. His face was somehow older—his cheeks slack, loose, jowly; a five o'clock shadow before noon. First's eyes were dull, and I think, if there had been even the slightest trace of hate in them, I could have spent the rest of my life despising the man. But looking at him then, it was like I was an intruder into life's backstage—the department store Santa dressing, the stroke victim struggling to clean herself on the toilet.

Mom never did say anything. Eventually, she walked away and locked herself in their bedroom upstairs. First, he grabbed a bottle and rocks glass from a cabinet, went out on the deck, and sat on a lawn chair, pouring himself shots until well after dusk.

I don't know what to think. It's almost nine now, and Mom's still in her room and First's still on the deck, spilling more scotch than he's slurping.

It'd be easy if I still thought of First as the heavy, but that doesn't seem right anymore. Not entirely.

Monday, September 10

First's still in the doghouse with Mom. That's hardly surprising. After yesterday, I wouldn't be surprised to see him gnawing on rawhide, chasing cars, or trying to sniff the ass of the neighbors' Jack Russell terrier.

When I got up this morning, First was standing at the kitchen counter, shoveling spoonfuls of Honey Smacks into his mouth and getting milk all over the sleeve of his suit. I guess I'd never noticed it before, but First's clothes, in their own way, were worse than mine. His suit pants had a too-often-pressed sheen that was missing from their coats; the cuffs on the coats looked a little frayed, and his dress shirts were yellowing and stiff at the armpits. Maybe there'd been some truth to what he'c said about money, about trying to make things better for the family.

I felt sad for him and almost told him I loved him, but part of me thought it'd just make him suspicious, like he'd think I was working an angle and trying to play him off of Mom. Even if I had wanted to say something to him, I wouldn't have gotten the chance. Mom came downstairs, looked at him, shook her head, and told me to get dressed. The two of us were going out for breakfast.

By the time I was ready for school, Mom was in the Jeep. The motor was running. She was blasting a Police CD while lighting one cigarette off the cherry of another. Her music choices were beginning to worry me. Nothing says angry-slash-angst-slash-artsy m.sunderstood, sensitive middle-aged, all-my-dreams-are-dead soccer mom like a blind devotion to Sting and REM.

I didn't ask where we were going. Hostages don't have that right. With Mom doing 50 through the subdivision and shouting her own lyrics to "King of Pain" (*There's an asshole lawyer I want to choke today/It's the same old shit as yesterday*), I figured she wasn't interested in hearing from me.

At the restaurant, we were greeted by an ancient hostess, Leona. She was one of the concerned-citizen types who basically hated First 'cuz he never wanted to support the referendums she drafted to bulldoze elementary schools (with or without the kids in em) and block low-income housing developments, even though First was supposed to be a Republican. And since First had decided to run as an Independent against John Fisk, his colleague and the McHenry County Republican Party's poster boy for gassing the homeless, waterboarding unbaptized atheists, and clubbing liberals, Leona hated him.

"Good to see you, Mrs. Stewart," she said, the insincere flash of her dentures giving new meaning to fake smile. She handed Mom two laminated menus tucked under her flabby grandma arm. "That John Fisk sure is soaring in the polls. He's got my vote."

"Well, he's got my vote too, Leona," Mom said. The hostess looked back at her, confused. "We'll have a table for two. Smoking."

At the table, Mom lit up and slid the pack of Virginia Slims to me. I shook my head.

"Suit yourself."

She slipped the pack back into her purse, snapped it shut, scanned the menu, and complained—way too loudly—that maybe this place wouldn't be such a dump if they had screwdrivers or Bloody Marys.

"God, Charlie," she said, staring at Leona across the room. "I wanted to tell that old gossip your father's cheating on me."

Her face was hard. She sucked her cigarette and then stabbed the whole thing out in a tin ashtray.

"Is he?" I asked.

First sleeping around wasn't something I could imagine. Thinking about old people having sex—all of that flabby and sagging skin, the skinny legs that nearly give out after climbing a flight of stairs, graying hair in places it shouldn't be, dirty old men coming dust—that made me wanna retch. But if First was cheating, it would explain a lot: the Ps constant fighting, him missing dinner 'cuz of some "fund-raiser" or "campaign event," First saying how great his campaign manager was, and what a shame it was she wasn't married.

"Is he what?"

"Cheating?"

"Please," Mom said. She laughed, pushing the ashtray to

the table's edge. "I'm not that lucky. There isn't another woman dumb enough to sleep with him."

After we'd finished eating, Mom gave me money to pay the tab—she didn't wanna deal with Leona—and waited by the front of the restaurant. I met her there. She was on her cell phone.

"Hello. This is Mrs. Stewart. I'm calling to say that my son Charlie won't be in today. We're both sick of his father." She snapped the phone shut, looking the happiest I'd seen her in forever. Her hand found mine and squeezed it.

"Come on, kiddo, you're not too old to play hooky with your mom."

We spent the day shopping. Believe it or not, it was actually cool. I thought Mom'd make me get the stuff she wanted—dorky store-brand generic crap—but she didn't. She handed me about three or four pairs of designer jeans, a couple of chest-raping sweaters—the kind that normally only Vespa-riding, waistless Italian guys with thick sultry lips and eyebrows for days could pull off—some ties and dress shirts, and a bunch of designer underwear (the kind with ripped, way hung and way obviously gay models on the package and not the scrawny, feathered-hair dorks on the front of the Sears brand). She insisted I try everything on and hubba hubba-ed me 'cuz the jeans really showed off my butt. Okay, Mom checking out my ass was creepy, but she was right. I actually had a butt and not an ironing board. I was measured and fitted for a new suit (for church, graduation, and maybe homecoming, if I didn't press my luck) and a new sports coat and slacks. We even went to Foot Locker for K-Swiss shoes, 'cuz it was the only place we could find that carried size sixteen.

We stepped up to the watch counter in another department store and Mom asked which one I wanted.

"We shouldn't be spending this kind of money," I said.

"Well, Charlie, we are."

I felt guilty. Even though Mom said she wanted me to have all this stuff, I couldn't help thinking she was only doing this to piss off First. Normally, I wouldn't mind a little credit card therapy, but I hated the idea that Mom might be setting herself up for more fights with First—fights that would come on a monthly basis with way too much interest.

As much as I'd like to pretend that the Ps getting divorced wouldn't be a big deal, the idea of that happening actually scared me. Sure, I hated their fighting, but I didn't want to see what would happen when it stopped. Spending weekends at First's new bachelor pad with the fridge that never had anything in it but condiments and a half-empty box of Arm and Hammer. It'd be worse with Mom, though. I could see her drinking herself to sleep for the first few months, then maybe getting a job as a waitress and a string of dates with construction workers, car salesmen, and fourth-grade teachers still living at home with their elderly mothers.

Anyhow, I saw this cool wristwatch I wanted to get Rob, but seventy-five bucks was more than I'd ever spent on anyone. I bought it and felt guilty, like I should've been thinking about Mom and not Rob. I offered to get her something, but she wouldn't let me buy her anything but lunch.

In the food court, I started fiddling with the watch box, wondering what it'd mean if I actually gave it to Rob. Naturally, Mom figured out what was up.

"You really like him, don't you?"

"Who?" I asked. I looked at the table so she couldn't see how embarrassed I was. This wasn't the kind of chat I wanted to have with her. Weren't there supposed to be some boundaries between parents and kids? I knew what lines I wasn't supposed to cross. I pretended she never had

sex with First and overlooked the maxi pad wrappers that'd
missed the trash can and ended up on the bathroom floor.
In return, she also ignored all of my bodily functions and
my love life.

"Does Rob like you?"

"I dunno." I tried answering, but my voice cracked.

"I mean, maybe . . . I think so." I jammed the straw in my
mouth and sucked my iced tea.

"He seems to. At least when the two of you are parked
in the driveway."

I spat, spraying tea all over the place.

"You've got to be more careful."

I couldn't tell if she meant spitting my tea or what Rob
and I had been up to. She handed me a wad of napkins.

"It just went down the wrong pipe," I said, cleaning up
the mess I'd made.

We didn't leave the mall until after school would've ended,
and Mom drove me to the Binkmeyers' house. She told me
to wait in the car while she discussed something with Bink's
mom. They chatted for, like, ten minutes, but I couldn't hear
them. They hugged and then Mrs. B waved for me. I got out
of the car.

"Charlie, it looks like you'll be staying here for a few days,"
Mrs. B said, giving Mom another squeeze. "Your mom and
dad need time to figure things out."

"Whaddja do now?" Bink asked as I stepped inside. "Tell
everyone you wanna be a girl?"

I laughed, but Mrs. B cuffed the back of Bink's head and
told him not to be such a schmuck. Just because someone's gay doesn't mean they want to be a woman, she said.
*Look at Truman Capote. He didn't want to be a woman,
though you wouldn't know it from the way he talked—
that lisp!—or the way he dressed sometimes. Still, he was*

very successful. At least until he started popping pills and telling outrageous stories about his friends. Then everyone hated him.

Mom came back later with my stuff—my new clothes, my book bag (*Thank God this was in it—holy crap, imagine if one of them read it!*), toothpaste, toothbrush, deodorant, zit pads, and shaving cream and razor (in case I miraculously needed to start shaving). She slipped some money into Mrs. B's hand, saying there was no sense in me eating the Binkmeyers out of house and home.

I followed Mom out to the car, telling Mrs. B that I wanted to say good-bye to my mom, you know, in private, and Mrs. B said she didn't understand why teenaged boys acted like they would die if anyone saw them kissing their mothers. In her day, sons . . . who knows, gave their mothers sponge baths, full body massages, and . . . I stopped listening.

I climbed into the car next to Mom.

"So, do I get to know what's going on?" I asked.

"Things between your dad and I aren't going so well."

"Really?" I said, arching my eyebrow. It was a lame joke, but we laughed anyhow.

"Sometimes, Charlie," she said, "when you're with someone for a while, you find out that they aren't who you thought they were. That you aren't who you thought you were. Without ever knowing when or how it happened, you realize one day that the two of you've grown so far apart that the two of you are practically strangers." She lit a cigarette and laughed softly to herself. The smoke curled at her lips. "Listen to me talking. What do I know? Whatever happens, Charlie, I don't want you to worry."

She tried to be upbeat, but the way "I don't want you to worry" sounded, she might have said something as equally uplifting and inspiring like, "we need to talk," "you may want to sit down for this," or "the doctor would like to schedule a time for you to come in and discuss your test results."

Mom squeezed my knee.

"So, what's gonna happen now?"

"We're going to talk. But whatever happens after that, I want you to remember that I love you very much and I'm doing what I think is best."

"C'mon, Mom," I said, my voice catching on the tears I was trying to fight. "You're making it sound like you're walking out on me."

"Charlie, I'm not going to leave you. I'd never do that. Neither would your father."

I snorted and wiped my eyes and nose across my shirtsleeve.

"Tell me about it. The guy's like quicksand." I was trying to sound tougher than I felt. "It's like he's always there. Always pressing in around me. It's like he won't let you breathe."

"I know," Mom said, patting my leg, "that's something we're going to talk about."

She kissed me good-bye, told me to call her if I needed anything, and promised to call. I watched her back the Jeep out, and I stood in the driveway waving to her until she rounded a corner and vanished.

I didn't want her going back to First without me. It wasn't 'cuz I thought he'd hurt her or anything. For all his faults, First wasn't that kind of guy.

I just didn't want to be alone.

It's almost midnight. I'm in the bathroom. It's the only time I've had peace for, like, the last five hours. I forgot what a madhouse this place is—a family of seven and me in a three-bedroom house with one bathroom. It's amazing no one's killed anyone.

I'm out of here. Someone's at the door.

Wednesday, September 12

If I don't get this down now, I'm not sure I'll get another chance. We're practically living on top of each other. I'm sharing Bink and Aaron's room, sleeping on a rollaway mattress we dragged up from the basement. Bink says Aaron'll be gone soon 'cuz he keeps talking about joining the Marine Corps, which has Mr. and Mrs. B less than thrilled. Neither of them is shy about showing it, either.

At dinner last night, Bink's parents double-teamed poor Aaron, saying no son of theirs—especially one they sacrificed for to put through college—was gonna throw away his degree and become part of the military-industrial complex, go overseas, and kill brown people's babies.

Don't get me wrong; I love the Binkmeyers to death, but I'll go out of my skull if I have to stay here much longer.

Have I mentioned that unless you're a total exhibitionist, it's impossible to find a place to choke the chicken? Wherever you go, somebody's always around. You can't walk, like, three feet without tripping over one of Bink's little sisters. If you manage to get to the bathroom and it's empty, someone's pounding on the door thirty seconds after you've locked it. And the basement? Forget it. Well, even if it didn't look like it'd been repeatedly shelled with mortar fire, if I went near it, Mrs. B'd think I scarfed the Swiss Army knife Aaron got back in Boy Scouts and was planning on using the corkscrew to disembowel myself. *But, Charlie, you have so much to*

live for. Look at Liberace . . . actually he's not a good ex-
ample, either. Completely tacky, a friend of Nancy Reagan,
and he had AIDS.

There wasn't even time to spank it in the shower. To save
time, Mrs. B basically has "her boys" on rotation—one in the
shower, one on deck, and the other brushing his teeth. When
Bink was showering and Aaron was brushing his teeth in his
boxers, I was between them, cupping my hands in front of
my crotch to hide an overeager Mr. Five-Incher.

"What're you so embarrassed about, Stewart?" Aaron said,
absently scratching his furry stomach. I couldn't let my eyes
wander. Not even when Bink stepped out of the shower naked
and dripping wet. Even a quick peek would've sent me over
the edge. It's already killing me to share a room with the
two of them. I've always thought Bink was hot, but honestly,
Aaron's better looking. He looks tougher, thicker, and not
as dopey as Bink. You'd date Bink; you'd beg Aaron to crush
your head between his thighs.

God, I hope there's a sub in choir today. Five-to-one I
end up dying of blue balls before Mom and First sort things
out.

Thursday, September 13

I wish I could say I wasn't a perv, but last night, just when I
thought the Brothers Hot were finally asleep and I could milk
one out in relative privacy, Aaron's mattress started squeak-
ing like crazy. The room was pretty dark, but I could still kinda

see him tossing off. Aaron started to come and Bink threw a pillow at him, telling him to cut it out. He was trying to sleep. Aaron wiped himself with a pair of boxers he swiped from the ground and then kicked 'em past the end of his bed, right near my face.

Okay, I grabbed the boxers. And, yeah, figure out the rest. Without going into too many details, let's just say when I woke up, Aaron was working the boxers from my fingers.

"I'll take those," he said.

I buried my head under the sheets, wishing I were dead. I hope Aaron thinks he kicked them onto the rollaway.

Whom am I kidding? We both know he knows I fell asleep with my nose buried in the cotton crotch like it was some kind of security blanket. I should've taken it as a sign.

Come stains are a poor substitute for a good old-fashioned Oracle at Delphi.

I say this because, according to Mrs. Lardner, my ancient civilizations teacher, prior to the invention of hygiene, industrial pig farms, and assembly-line slaughterhouses, the entire western world functioned on the basis of superstition. If you wanted it to rain, you sacrificed a pigeon, goat, bull, nubile young virgin—whatever happened to be lying around—to the god of thunder. If you wanted to stop a torrential downpour that threatened to destroy nearly every living thing on the planet, you prayed to whatever anthropomorphized ADD-suffering autistic in the sky that was currently in vogue, built a really big boat, and promised not to look at your naked father, spill your seed upon the ground (*Do socks count?*), worship golden idols, or have hot man-on-man sex. If you were a citizen of the whackin' big Roman Empire and you wanted to know if you should cross the Rubicon or just spend the day shooting craps (*Iacta alea est*, Cicero, and you got snake-eyes), you found a cute little chicken, gutted it and stared at its entrails for your answer.

Anyhow, Aaron's dirty boxers proved to be about as effective at predicting my day as a Magic Eight Ball. They did a really crappy job of predicting just how shitty today's been. Things started going to hell in choir today and didn't end until I got off the phone with Mom just now.

When third period ended this morning and I was leaving the choir room, Rob grabbed the back of my neck and smiled so big that his dimples were practically the size of golf divots.

"Hey, pup," he said. "Follow me."

I might've asked where we were going, but it wouldn't have mattered. Rob was all I've-got-the-world-by-the-short-hairs-and-I'm-gonna-pull determination. Most of the time, he's only like that when he's trying to talk me out of my Jockeys and into his bed, and even then, it's not like I'd object. If I tried, even before I got the chance to open my mouth, Rob'd have my pants around my ankles, a hand cupping my bare ass, a tongue in my ear, and then I'd pretty much be begging him to push me down on all fours and ride me like a Preakness filly. Okay, so I'm horny right now. Crucify me. I haven't gotten off since before breakfast Monday morning. If my nut sack gets put under any more pressure, my sperm'll start dying of the bends.

Anyhow, Rob kept his hand on my neck, his thumb tracing these really small, intricate circles along the skin there, and he led me to the stupid little closet of a room in the cafeteria where work-study students (AKA future early release reprobates) sold "everything bright young minds need to grow and blossom," which apparently consists of green-and-gold-folders, graph paper, protractors, used copies of *The*

Grapes of Wrath, and gator-emblazoned stadium seat cushions. They also sold homecoming tickets.

Rob and I stepped up to the counter.

"Yeah?" said the cult of personality whose ass was fusing osmosis-wise to the stool she was sitting on behind the counter. She barely looked up from the copy of *People* that had her gums jawing as she sounded out the really hard words like "totally" and "cute" and "handbag." I couldn't remember the chick's name, but I'd heard that back in junior high, the school shrink had her sent to reform school 'cuz she'd sewn her own fingers together during home ec out of boredom, and then, still feeling her eighth-grade ennui, haphazardly got the thread out with a stitch ripper.

"Two tickets for homecoming," Rob said, sliding a twenty on the counter's faux laminate countertop.

Little Miss Self-Seamstress made this overly inconvenienced sigh that sounded like a blimp emptying its airbag. She looked at the money, at Rob, at me, back at the money.

"You're ten bucks short," she said. "Twenty for couples, fifteen each for stag tickets." Yves Self-Mutilation Laurent plopped her ass down on the stool, slurped her thumb, and flipped a magazine page to what was probably some hardhitting expose on how it was all the rage among celbutante heiresses to surgically implant tapeworms for maximum weight loss.

"We're a couple," Rob said, making sure she saw his hand slip from my neck to the small of my back.

"Rules say you aren't," she said with a shrug.

"What do you mean 'rules'? Like, 'You must be this tall,'" Rob raised his hand to just above his waist, "'to ride this ride?' Rules like 'No use of cell phones, flash photography or videotaping during the performance'? You gotta be kidding me. Just give me the tickets, alright."

Yves demonstrated her exceptional customer service skills by showing absolutely ro concern of flexibility. "Guy and a girl. Twenty bucks. Two guys, fifteen bucks each. Two girls, fifteen bucks each. That's how it is."

"That's bullshit," Rob said. His face was so red it looked like someone'd tied his jockstrap in double knots while he was still in it.

Stupid me, I made the mistake of giving the chick the extra ten-spot instead of all Martin Luther Queen, Junior, on her by telling her it didn't matter if Rob and I wanted to stretch each other's sphincters, we still had the right to save a Hamilton on going to some lame school dance.

When I got handed the tickets, Rob stormed off, shaking his head.

Rob avoided me the rest of the day, and after practice tonight he brushed past me. I shouted for him to wait, but he blew me off. I ran after him as he beelined through the parking lot to his BMW. When I finally caught up with him, I grabbed his shoulder and yelled, "What the hell's wrong with you?"

"Just leave me alone Charlie," he said, dropping his chin to his chest as he massaged his neck.

"No. Not until you tell me why you've been treating me like shit." I spat my words at him. "Is this about the tickets this morning? Jesus."

"Great," Rob said, leaning against the side of his car. He threw his head back and laughed—practically cackling at the sky. He looked unhinged, like he was one smart-ass remark from me away from completely losing it. "Just great. Now I've got to worry about your feelings, too. I'm so tired of making sure everyone in my goddamn life is perfectly comfortable."

Rob sank, his back sliding down the side of the car until

105

he was squatting along the wheel well, his face shielded behind his arms and knees. He started talking again, only the anger—the madness—in his voice was softer, strained. I couldn't tell if he was raging or crying. I sat beside him, trying hard not to set him off.

"Rob, what's wrong? Talk to me." He turned to face me and his eyes were as wet and runny as raw egg, his shoulders shook. He looked small, breakable.

"My mom," he said, smearing the back of his hand along his nose. "She's dying." He leaned into my shoulder, and I felt hollow and tense all at once. I wanted to say something, but my lips were dumb, so I just pulled him into me and pressed my face to his hair.

"I'm sick of nothing being fair. I want to be normal for once, you know?" Rob hugged my chest, curling against me. "I'm sick of everything being a fight."

"You don't have to fight," I said, holding him more tightly. "I'm here."

"But you're not going to fight," Rob said, matter-of-factly. It hurt, mostly 'cuz it was true. After this morning, I knew I had to be a better boyfriend. Rob deserved that much.

"We'll get through this. Everything will be okay." We both knew I was lying, but it was the only thing that sounded right.

We sat outside his car—Rob weeping against my chest, and me holding him hard and tight, wishing I could draw the hurt from his body. After a while, Rob stopped crying and said he was fine. He unlocked his car door and we kissed good-bye.

"I'm sorry for being a shit," I said.

"I know you are."

"Know I'm what?" I asked, smiling. "Know I'm sorry or know I'm a shit?"

"I'll never tell," Rob said, laughing. We kissed again and I walked to the Binkmeyers, hoping the worst was over. It wasn't. Mom called after dinner.

In my family, bad news doesn't get front-stoop delivery; it gets left in the gutter, we all pretend like we don't know it's there, and then finally, someone gets tired of ignoring it and goes out to get it. That's why my conversation with Mom tonight went the way it did.

After Mrs. B chatted with Mom for a bit, Mrs. B handed me the phone and shooed the rest of the Binkmeyer brood from the kitchen, saying I needed privacy. I wanted to tell her that if I ever got privacy, I wouldn't be on the phone, I'd be attending to certain, more urgent needs, but I didn't get the chance. Through the receiver, I could hear Mom asking, "So, how are things at the Binkmeyers'?"

She sounded upbeat enough, so I decided to joke around some.

"It's like spending summer camp on a hippie commune. Mrs. B's been making everyone listen to hairy-legged female folk singers so much that Bink's talking in his sleep about how he's woman, hear him roar. It got so bad that, yesterday, after he begged Mrs. B to lay off the Joan Baez stuff, Bink got all excited when Mrs. B said she'd play some Seeger. Poor Bink, he was hoping for some 'Night Moves' action, and Mrs. B's trying to get everyone to jam to 'Turn! Turn! Turn!'."

"And how's Mr. B?" Mom asked, playing it straight, but I knew she was trying not to laugh. I could tell she was having fun. So was I. She sounded like her old self, so I kept going.

"He's pretty good actually. He's really thrilled that he found the Charles Darwin *Evolution of the Species* edition of Barrel of Monkeys for Bink's sisters. The only problem is every time you walk around the house, you're stepping on a little red Australopithecus or Cro-Magnon."

"You're terrible," Mom said, laughing.

"I'm terrible? You don't even know the meaning of terrible until you've done a Binkmeyer family game night."

"And why's that?" Mom asked. I imagined her at the other end of the line, snaking a Virginia Slim out of her pack on the table and trying to hide a smirk.

"Well, being socialists and all, they've decided that they can't play *Monopoly* for fun. It's got to be a teachable moment, so Mr. and Mrs. B have been trying to invent *Marxist Monopoly*. Let me tell you what a blast that is.

"The state owns all the property, you don't get any cash for passing Go, there's no Free Parking 'cuz both of them have agreed that in a utopian society there'd be universal public transportation, and you can end up in the gulag if you draw a Fellow Comrade card that says you lost your signed copy of the *Little Red Book* or you were caught by the secret police trying to buy blue jeans that were smuggled into the country by some decadent Western capitalist. At least, that's what would happen if Mr. and Mrs. B could figure out how players move ahead."

"I'm afraid to ask," Mom said.

"Yeah. Mrs. B thinks that the players, acting as a collective, decide how far you get to move. Mr. B thinks players should advance, 'each according to his ability, each according to his needs.'"

"Well," Mom said, "it's good that you're having fun. One of us should." *Way to go, Mom. Suck all the life out of the room. Woo-hoo!* I pressed my ear harder against the phone like I expected the static on the line to tell me what Mom wasn't saying.

"Are you okay?"

There was a beat, and then Mom either blew a stream of smoke above her head or sighed, I couldn't tell.

"Your dad and I have agreed to a trial separation."

"What do you mean you're separating? I thought you were supposed to be working things out. Separating's like training wheels for divorce." My voice was wobbly and I saw I was frantically tapping my foot without even noticing it, I tried to make it stop in case Mrs. B walked past the kitchen, saw it, and freaked out (*Charlie, don't let a little bit of nerves get to you. Look at Marcel Proust . . . actually no, he's was a completely neurotic mama's boy. Not a good example . . . he was such a germaphobe he soaked his mail in formaldehyde, and died in a cork-lined room . . . but his writing always reminds me of madeleines. Oreo anyone?*), but I couldn't stop the tapping.

"Charlie, we're trying to work things out, but it's hard. Just because two people are in love—or were in love—that doesn't make things easier. Relationships take work. The longer you're with someone, the harder it gets. Love's hard."

Okay, even though it makes me seem like a fucking kid, I'll admit I was scared. I know it's pretty stupid, but I was thinking that if they could give up on each other over stupid stuff like bills and money and 'cuz they suddenly thought they wanted something more or different out of life, what was stopping them from giving up on me? I suppose I could joke and say, that, God knows, First's close enough to giving up on me already, but I don't feel like it.

"What about me?" I asked. And yeah, I blubbered like a baby. "Is loving me too much work?"

"Charlie," Mom said, her voice going soft. "You can't be serious. With you, it's not work. It's a calling. When it comes to you, I might as well be a nun." She laughed, trying to lighten the mood.

"Well, you look good in black," I said, smiling weakly.

"Listen, we'll be okay, kiddo."

"Yeah. We'll manage."

One of the Binkmeyer girls—Stacy? Tracy? Amanda? they all look the same—came into the kitchen, started tugging on my jeans, and asked me to play dolls with her.

"Mom, I gotta go. I love you."

"I love you, too, Charlie—even if it means not getting time-and-a-half for overtime. How about I swing by tomorrow and bring you home?"

I told her okay and said I loved her again, and we hung up.

What a day.

Friday, September 14

I'm home again, home again, jiggety jig. No more sharing a bedroom and imagining a totally hot Binkmeyer brother's incest porno. No more fighting with fourth-grade girls over a phone to call Rob. *Who's Rob? Is he your boyfriend? Then why don't you marry him?* No more sneaking around looking for places to jerk off. No more Mrs. B, God love her. *What about Tennessee Williams? No, he drank himself to death and those last plays of his . . . what was he thinking? Cannibalism? On Broadway?*

Home.

Today's pep rally was awesome. Well, not the pep rally, that pretty much sucked balls. We all knew Marian Central would completely trounce us. They always do. Of course, Weir was the only one who didn't see it that way. He'd been sitting next to me in the bleachers, a Star of David sewn to his shirt, ranting about how it wasn't fair that he wasn't part of the gridiron brain trust anymore. According to him, if he could play, South might actually stand a chance at winning. *Yeah, right. Marian Central could play their powder-puff team and we'd still lose.* What saved the pep rally was when they announced the homecoming king and queen (*who elects a monarch?*) and Dana Flannigan totally wigged out. That was classic.

After the school fight song, Principal Michael strutted to the center of the gym with Mrs. Bailey, who was holding two sashes, a tiara, and a scepter. Principal Michael cleared his throat, as if naming the homecoming king and queen was this big deal we were actually supposed to get excited about and wasn't just another exercise in high school Darwinism— survival of the coolest.

One of the band geeks—some total putz—did a drum roll as Principal Michael opened the envelope and announced that the homecoming queen was—here's a shocker—Kim Green. Kim rushed over to get her sash and tiara, tears of over-rehearsed surprise cutting channels through her bottle tan. I groaned and rolled my eyes, which ticked Weir off.

"Don't worry, Stewart, everyone knows you're still the biggest queen at South," he said, slamming my bicep so hard the left side of my body went numb. I couldn't come up with a snappy comeback and that pissed me off.

Anyhow, when Principal Michael said, in his best game-show-announcer voice, that Neil'd been elected king, things really got good. Bink was just about to have his sash clumsily draped over his shoulder by Mrs. Bailey when, out of nowhere, Dana marched across the floor in calf-high Doc Martens, plucked the microphone from a stunned Principal Michael, and said into the mike, "This is ridiculous." She walked over to Kim, wrapped both of her fists around the sash, and tore it in half.

Nobody said or did anything. They just sat there like the whole thing'd been staged and they were waiting for whatever was supposed to happen next.

It wasn't until Kim started wailing, all prom-night-Carrie-covered-in-pig's-blood, that people realized something was wrong. I laughed.

Deans Fuller and Warnoski charged Dana from behind, and in one motion grabbed the microphone from her hand, swept her up by her feet and armpits, and "escorted" her from the floor. The gym booed.

Dana was actually at the game tonight, but only 'cuz when she was in the principal's office after school, she'd threatened to file assault charges against the deans, take her case to the school board, and, if need be, the Supreme Court. She had a constitutional right to free speech, a right upheld in *Tinker v. Des Moines*, and blah, blah, blah. I'd stopped listening by that point, and the only thing that actually stopped Dana's jabbering was seeing Bink getting tackled—for the second time—in our own end zone.

Saturday, September 15

Today has been the worst day of my life and it's only three in the afternoon. Seriously, I wish someone killed me in my sleep last night. If the homecoming dance tonight is anything like today . . .

This morning, Mom caught me. Not in a my-back-to-the-door-only-the-fly-unbuttoned, me-making-little-hand-jive-jerking-motion incident that could be ignored with a polite oops-I-should've-knocked-let's-never-speak-of-this-again apology.

No, she saw it all—the underwear and jeans at the ankles, the little red dick strangled in a fist, a metal cigar tube from First's humidor wedged up my butt. She barged in when I was too far along to stop. I already had that Jerry's Kids look on my face—the twitchy, stupid, vacant eyes, the drool pooling at the corner of my mouth, the scrunched-up nose.

I was *unnnhhh-unnnhhh-unnnhhh*-ing to the finish line when Mom pushed open the door and stepped into the bathroom. I freaked. I tried covering my crotch and jumping out of sight, but I tripped over my pants. (*Where exactly did I think I was going to hide? Behind a hand towel?*) My chest hit the floor. The cigar tube popped out and skidded across the tile. The tube rolled against her shoe, trailing baby lotion, and Mom shrieked, shielding her eyes. The spill didn't stop Mr. Five-Incher. He kept right on going—throbbing one last time before spitting up his junk. Mom couldn't get away fast enough. She backed out, eyes buried in the crook of one arm, the other flailing as she said, "Ewww . . . sorry . . . sorry . . . ewww . . ."

When my heart finally started beating again and I was sure Mom was safely barricaded far away, I made sure that the bathroom door was locked—like a thousand times—and took my shower. Christ, why couldn't I have spanked it there in the first place? Afterward, I hacked my face apart while shaving. I practically had an entire roll of toilet paper pinned to all the bloody little cuts. That's when I noticed the whackin' big zit on my chin. I don't think I could've popped it using a pair of pliers. Trust me, I almost tried.

After getting caught jerking off, I didn't think things could get worse. I was wrong. I got a haircut.

The old guy who cut my hair was a real winner. His hands

smelled like ass, and while he butchered my hair, he'd shift to one leg, hitch his sagging butt into the air, and let one rip. Half the time, he acted like nothing happened, but the rest of the time, he'd grimace at me like I was the one with some rotting thing inside me.

And if the hands that smelled like crap, the farting, and the Alfalfa cowlick (an Eiffel Tower of hair jutting from the back of my head) weren't bad enough, the bastard practically cut my ear off. *Snip . . . snip . . . "Ouch, Goddamn it!" . . . snip . . . snip . . . "Oh, sorry, is that the top of your ear on the floor?"*

I look like a lopsided Doberman.

Homecoming's in two hours and everyone's *sooo* going to think I'm hot. The whole zit, cowlick, and gauze pad taped to the ear—they're showing that look on all the fashion runways. Screw being cool or popular. Just once in my life, I'd like to be human wallpaper.

Fat chance of that happening tonight. Rob and I are triple-dating with Bink and Dana and Steve and Joan. Bink's supposed to pick me up and then we'll drive over to Dana's. While he's making goo-goo eyes at Dana and her mom and dad are snapping even more pictures for the Flannigan family *foy-yay,* I'll go next door and grab Rob. Then we're supposed to pick up Joan and Steve.

All of us will then be crammed into Bink's station wagon. Shoot me now. It was Dana's idea. She's on one of her Save the Earth kicks. She thinks that by taking one car we'll stop the rain forests from killing the baby seals or something. It'd be a helluva lot easier if we drove separately. I guess if it gets too crowded we can fold Steve in half and tuck him away in the glove compartment.

I should get ready. I'm leaving my bedroom door open, though. I don't need Mom thinking I'm abusing myself again. *God, when will the humiliation end?*

Sunday, September 16

It wouldn't be homecoming without confessions of love; blow jobs in the school parking lot; crappy music and ugly dresses; bullying, boozing, and bleeding; the cops; more blow jobs; and still more confessions of true love.

Bink got here a little early on Saturday, which thrilled Mom. I couldn't blame her. His arrival made it easier for us to forget the Incident Which Must Never Be Spoken Of. We're both pretending like that one moment in time never existed. It's better this way. It means the Stewart family is just like everyone else. Denial—it's the glue barely holding millions of American families together.

Bink was a huge relief, 'cuz the usual Stewart denial tactics (thinking happy thoughts, discussing the weather, avoidance) had failed. It's scary how often you can bump into someone you're trying to avoid, even when it's just the two of you in a four-bedroom house. Once Bink got here, Mom stopped worrying about what other household items I might've experimented with—pens, candles, pop bottles, hot dogs, flashlights. (During lunch, she'd stopped making a salad after eyeballing the cucumber and carrots suspiciously. She trashed them, claiming they were spoiled. I knew better. *Produce died for my sins.*)

Mom dragged out a disposable camera and made Bink and I pose. Big dopey smiles. *You're growing up so fast.* Side by side and looking serious. *So handsome in your coats and ties. Neil, let me see the corsage you got for Dana. I can't be-*

lieve it, seniors in high school already. Bink holding me in a headlock. *Seems like it was yesterday when you were taking swimming lessons together.* The final shot—us sliding through the front windows of the station wagon. *Careful, you'll ruin your clothes.*

As we drove past mailboxes, whisking lawn sprinklers, and a dad helping his kid learn to ride a bike, Bink asked about my ear, pretending to be all sympathetic-like so he wouldn't come across as that big of a jagoff when he told me not to piss off Dana. I wasn't supposed to say anything about her hair, dress, corsage, the boutonniere she got him, or her freak-out during Friday's pep rally. Basically, I'd need a court-appointed attorney or U.N. peacekeeping force if I wanted to open my mouth.

The whole Flannigan brood—five generations of Irish Republican Army baby factories—met us in their driveway, *ooohhh*ing and *aaahhh*ing about how nice Bink looked in his sports coat. Bink *aww-shucks*-ed and kidded about not spilling anything on it 'cuz it was getting returned in the morning. The Flannigans laughed, but I'm not sure Bink was joking. Dana actually looked really good. I complimented her, and everyone—*I mean everyone*—stared at me. They wouldn't have believed me if I was strapped to a polygraph and doped up on sodium Pennzoil or whatever that truth serum stuff is. That was all I needed to exit stage right and head over to Rob's.

I didn't get a chance to knock. Rob swung the door open like he'd been waiting for me for hours. As soon as he saw the bandage on my ear, he started acting like I was dying from an open, sucking chest wound.

"Charlie, are you okay?"

"It's nothing. I'm fine."

"What happened?"

"I got cut by the stupid barber. Seriously, it's nothing. I'm fine."

When he was convinced I wasn't gonna collapse into his arms, dying from blood loss, Rob dragged me to the kitchen, practically skipping, and showed me the boutonnieres he'd gotten us. Mr. Hunt stood next to Rob's mom, holding an expensive-looking digital camera, and smiled at us. Mrs. Hunt looked really tired and worn down. Her skin was way pale and cracked. It seemed to sweat out that chemical-sweet, hospital-death smell. There was this brace thing-y around her neck that went from her breastbone to just under her chin. Besides the oxygen mask, there were all these tubes running in and out of her—one of 'em snaking alongside her wheelchair to a bag filled with piss.

"Here," Rob said, bouncing up to me with a boutonniere. He was beaming. I did my best to smile. I didn't want him thinking I was worried about his mom's condition. "Let me put it on you."

Teeth clenched, Rob fumbled with the pin and my lapel. I blushed, then to stop, I twisted my face up like Rob'd stuck me with the pin and I was in agony. Rob's dad laughed and snapped a picture.

There were more photos—me pinning on Rob's boutonniere, Rob's arm around my waist, mine around his shoulders, the two of us at the piano, holding hands. It felt weird—not bad, just different. I wasn't used to being in photos like that with another guy. It was pretty cool, but a little awkward.

I debated giving Rob the watch I'd slipped into my coat pocket, but decided not to. That would've made Rob and his dad totally geek out. We never would have made it to the dance. They'd be too busy picking out china patterns and drapes.

Leave it to Marshall to be a dick. When we picked him and Johanna up, Steve noticed right away that Rob and I had the same boutonnieres—white roses and baby's breath.

"Aww, how sweet. Matching corsages. You two gonna play kissy-face tonight?" Steve asked, lisping and flouncing his wrists.

"That's the plan," Rob said.

Rob frenched me like he was flossing my teeth with his tongue. When he stopped, he became this total hard ass, reached over his seat, and slugged Steve square in the chest. It was awesome. The punch was hard—a brick dropped on a timpani drum—but I didn't feel sorry for Marshall. It served him right.

"Any other problems you need help with?" Wheezing, Steve shook his head and sucked a hit from his asthma inhaler. "Good."

We drove to the Olive Garden in silence. Everyone was scared of saying something that'd give Rob a reason to put 'em in traction. The whole drive, we listened to morbid, easy-listening crap on the radio. By the time we pulled into the parking lot, the twenty-nine crewmembers of the *Edmund Fitzgerald* were at the bottom of Lake Superior; Buddy Holly, Ritchie Valens, and The Big Bopper's charred bodies smoldered in a snowy Iowa cornfield; *rigor mortis* was setting in on Marilyn Monroe's naked corpse; and some gambler on a train bit the dust. Cheery stuff. It fit the mood.

At dinner, Steve acted like if he so much as breathed funny, Rob'd tear his arms off and beat him to a bloody pulp. Steve would start to say something and Rob would pick up his bread knife, trace its edge with a finger, and watch Steve clam up. Nobody seemed to mind. Honestly, I think they liked it. It was nice having one meal without hearing Marshall brag about how he could swallow a string of spaghetti and rope it out his nostril.

Homecoming, as always, was in South's cafeteria, the same crappy crepe paper streamers in the school's green and gold colors, a lame disco ball lighting the makeshift dance floor, standard community college DJ spinning '80s pop (it was the junior class's idea to do a retro theme), girls in too much makeup, guys in their dads' cologne, chaperones swiping Coke bottles spiked with Jack Daniel's. The fat, the ugly, the date-less, and the dorks lining up against the lockers.

I'd never danced with a guy before and I was, like, totally nervous. I was sweating like I had some kind of skin disease. Rob squeezed my hand in his and pulled me past couples who jerked into motion with each flash of the strobe light. A couple of Rot-See Nazis shouted, "Hey motherfucker, get laid, get fucked," to Billy Idol's version of "Mony Mony." Rob smiled, tugging me along. He found the DJ, whispered something to him, and slipped him a bill. *Who tips the DJ at a high school dance?*

The speakers opened wide with the sound of a twangy electric guitar and hammering drums—Adam Ant's "Goody Two Shoes." I was caught in a stampede of suit coats and corsages. Some linebacker's foot crushed my toes and it was all I could do not to yelp. He thundered off, leaving me with a sock full of shattered bones. Shannon *yoo-hoo*-ed her date, waving at him. If it hadn't been for Rob twirling me away from Shannon, she'd'd've knocked the carnation on her wrist and half my teeth down my throat. Rob reeled me back in and we were jitterbugging like old people at a family wedding. He sang along, mouthing the words like a taunt, and slipped his arm around my waist. I was almost out of breath. People watched, probably wondering if the two of us were really gay or if us dancing together was a soccer team dare.

Someone behind me tapped my shoulder. Rob nodded with a big smile. It was Dana. I didn't want her cutting in, but it's not like I had much of a choice. Before I could say no, she shoehorned her way between Rob and me. Shannon stepped in, grabbed Rob's arm, and wrapped it around her waist. He took her free hand and rocked her to the left, their hands dipped low; he kicked, and rocked her to the right. I wanted to break 'em up, but Dana had me in a death grip. I felt like a fox caught in one of those steel-jawed traps and I finally understood why they chewed off their legs. I'd've done the same, only Dana would've sent the hounds after me. Dana led—more like dragged—and smashed her hips into mine. Her tits flattened against my chest and her hair was in my nose and mouth. I felt like Poland in 1939—invaded. A blitzkrieg of boobs and barrettes. *Javol, mein Führer!*

I hoped to squirm away when the song ended, but the DJ mixed in the Stray Cats' "(She's) Sexy and 17," and I was stuck. It was the stoners and the grease monkeys who finally saved me. Some stoner chick started arguing with little Miss National Honor Society about Tom Sawyer being a song, not a book, and that was the start of what turned out to be this huge catfight. Apparently, Stoner Chick had had it with the crap the DJ was spinning and wanted music she could slow dance to with her brother-slash-husband—Metallica or Ozzy. Mood music for climbing into the bed of a pickup truck and making more pinhead babies.

Miss National Honor Society made some crack about cashing welfare checks and drinking strawberry wine from screw-top bottles. Big mistake. Press-on nails flew, and before anyone could shout "catfight!" little Miss National Honor Society was nursing a bloody nose. Stoner Chick waved a bloody clump of blonde hair in her fist. She probably would've gone back for more if the deans hadn't stopped her.

A hand slid across my butt and pinched it. I turned. It

was Rob. He was sweating. I brushed the bangs from his eyes.

"Let's get some air," I said, grabbing his hand and walking to the cafeteria entrance.

Some nosy PTA mom stamped our hands and said how nice it was to see two brothers goofing off and dancing together. We should remember our girlfriends, though, and not hog the spotlight. I expected Rob to haul off and smack her one in the chest like he'd done to Marshall, but he told her he'd pay attention to girls once he started dating them.

We made our way to a concrete bench in front of the school, sat, legs touching, and watched the latecomers straggling from the parking lot to the dance.

"Hi," Rob laughed.

"Hi."

He slugged my arm, dimples flashing. "This school's really messed up."

"You think?" I asked, squeezing his hand. He leaned in and gave me an Eskimo kiss, our noses brushing. "Careful." I tapped the side of my nose. "This thing can put an eye out."

"So can something else." He reached down and grabbed me through my dress pants.

"Cut it out."

I swatted at him, but he dodged my hand, and then squeezed me.

"Let me see it," he said, licking my good ear. "I wanna touch it."

"Now? Here?"

"Sure."

Rob fumbled with my zipper and worked his hand through the fly of my boxers. We were skin to skin, him holding me at the base. I leaked over the knuckle of his thumb.

"Nice, pup," he said, fishing me out.

I scooched away, worried somebody'd see. Rob didn't care. His mouth was at my neck, hot and wet. I tried tucking myself back in.

"Un-unh," I said.

"Uh-huh."

"Un-unh. Not 'til I'm done."

Rob moved my hands away and lowered his head into my lap. My dick bounced and Rob's tongue flicked its head. A car horn blasted. I jumped and—thank God—Rob did, too. If he hadn't, my knees would've slammed his jaw and I'd have to do the Heimlich maneuver on him so he'd cough my crank from the back of his throat.

"What the hell?" Rob said.

I crammed my dick back into my pants and tugged the zipper. The horn was still whining. I scanned the lot. In a car about ten yards ahead of us I saw the outline of someone in the driver's seat, forehead slumped against the steering wheel, hands yanking his hair.

Rob smiled, crouched, and motioned for me to do the same.

"What?" I asked.

Rob put a finger to his lips, then crept commando-like across the bus lane and the small patch of grass at the edge of the parking lot.

"What?"

"You'll see." He duck-walked to the car, waving for me to follow.

We slipped around the passenger side, past the trunk, and squatted at the driver's side. Rob gestured for me to stay low and pointed at the mirror.

Kyle Weir. He had some girl's ponytail in one fist and his

other hand was wrapped around the back of her neck, pushing her face deeper into his crotch. She was gagging, but he didn't care. He looked frustrated. Whoever she was, she apparently was an amateur as far as Kyle was concerned. He rolled his eyes, grit his teeth, and forced her head down even farther.

When I bit my forearm to keep from laughing, I lost my balance. My dress shoes scraped against gravel on the asphalt. Panicked, Rob shushed me and waved at me to keep still.

"Damn it, bitch," Kyle said. "Why'd you stop? Jesus, I was close."

"I heard something," Kim Green said, bobbing up from Kyle's lap. I saw her reflection in the mirror. Her lips were smeared with spit and lipstick.

"Just pay attention, okay?" Kyle said, flinging Kim's tiara against the windshield.

"But there's somebody outside—"

"Yeah. You if you don't start sucking." Kim wiped her mouth, sniffling and looking like she was going to cry. "Screw it. I should get some chick who doesn't use teeth."

Yeah, Weir's a real charmer, but it's not like Kim was some wide-eyed innocent he'd ruined. She knew Weir was a dick but put up with him 'cuz his folks were loaded and she could make him buy her crap. She stared at the car's ceiling like she was debating losing her gravy train to one of her friends. Her tongue pressed the corner of her mouth and her button nose scrunched up. She wasn't ready for competition.

Her face vanished from the mirror and the slurping started again. Kyle moaned and his body slid against the driver's side door, leaning against it hard. Rob carefully hooked the door handle. When Kyle's face twisted, I grinned and nodded. Rob popped the door's handle, stepping back as it burst open. Kyle spilled out ass over elbows. Kim's bra was wrapped around his nuts and his come pumped past his chest and onto his face. Kim tumbled out after him, her tits dangling above Kyle's face like upside-down teepees.

Rob and I took one last look and bolted, cutting through backyards. We didn't stop until we reached the White Hen on Virginia Avenue. The place was dead.

"That," I said, "was classic."

Rob bent over, resting his hands on his knees, and caught his breath.

"Wanna go back to the dance?" I asked.

He shook his head, undid his tie, and folded his jacket over his arm. I found a spot on the curb next to him and draped my jacket across my lap. After the little stunt we pulled on Kyle and Kim, I wasn't gonna risk Rob going down on me in public. I figured I'd pretty much cashed in all my good karma. I felt the watch's weight in my jacket pocket. I still needed to give it to him, but wasn't sure how to do it without making a big production. I rested my head on his shoulder. Rob tussled my hair and kissed the top of my head.

"I could call my mom . . . have her pick us up."

"No. This is nice."

I wrapped my arm around his waist, my fingers counting the knuckles of his spine.

"Yeah. It is."

I started falling asleep, so I sat up and took the watch from my sports coat. I sorta dropped it in Rob's hands, trying not to make it seem like a big deal.

"What's this?"

He opened the case and slid off the watch he'd been wearing and held the one I'd given him to his wrist. "What do you think?" he asked.

I thought I was an idiot for never noticing he had a watch that was a lot more expensive than what I bought. And I thought he was just being polite until he whispered, "Thank you," and kissed me.

"I saw it and . . . I dunno . . . I wanted to get it for you. I guess I love you."

Even though I was totally mumbling, my voice cracked. It was the first time I told someone I wasn't related to that I loved them. After I said it, I worried I shouldn't have.

"You *guess* you love me?" Rob asked, hooking my neck in his elbow and giving me a noogie. "You *guess?* You don't know?"

"I know . . . I know . . ."

"You know what, pup?"

"I know I love you. I love you. Just watch the ear."

Rob quickly let go. "I'm sorry . . . you okay?" He grabbed my chin and tilted my head to examine the bandage. I nodded.

A county squad car crept alongside us. The officer rolled down his window.

"Evening, guys. What's going on?" he asked in one of those don't-I-sound-like-I-know-more-than-I'm-letting-on tones they probably teach everyone at the police academy. All over McHenry County doughnut shops went unprotected, intersections went without crossing guards, and little old ladies had huckleberry pies snatched from their windowsills 'cuz this total Barney Fife apparently got his rocks off on hassling overdressed high school kids for sitting on a sidewalk. I almost told Officer Overly Friendly that Rob and I were gonna knock over the store—we had the nylons and everything, but we didn't know what we were supposed to do with the blue plastic eggs the pantyhose came in.

"Nothing much," I answered, smiling way more than necessary—like I expected Officer OF to imagine a little gold halo above my head. I didn't want to let him off the hook too easily. He was county bacon, which meant that he worked with First, and that was reason enough to screw with him.

"The homecoming dance was lame. So here we are."

I watched him eyeballing me. He couldn't tell if I was trying to pull a fast one, if I was slightly brain damaged, or both. Officer OF leaned out the window and looked at Rob. Even though he was still sitting on the curb, Rob followed my lead and smiled back at the cop. Officer OF shook his head. Aggravation creased his face. His eyes narrowed on my ear.

"Get into a fight, son?"

"No, sir," I said, flashing a smile that showed all my teeth at once. "It's the barber on Williams Street." And then in a stage-whisper, I added, "I think he, you know . . ." I pantomimed taking a few slugs from a bottle. "But don't say anything. I don't want my dad making any trouble for him."

"And who's your dad, kid?" Officer OF said. He was halfway to pissed.

"Charles Stewart. He's assistant state's attorney."

"Christ." Officer OF squeezed the bridge of his nose. "You're the Stewart brat? The swimming pool kid? Shit, why'd I have to stop?"

"Something wrong, sir?" I asked, sounding positively bubbly.

"Just shut up and get in." Officer Now Less Than Friendly stepped out of his car and opened the back door. "You two are going home. Who's your friend and where's he live?"

I lied about Rob being our foreign exchange student from Liechtenstein so Officer NLTF wouldn't drive Rob back to his house. Officer NLTF raised an eyebrow. He wasn't buying it, so I made up a bunch of crap about Liechtenstein being this backwater European country that was so poor it couldn't af-

126

ford money; how Rob learned to speak English by listening to Doobie Brothers' records at the village church (Rob chimed in with a vaguely European accent, "*Ja*, Old Bleck Vater. I vant honky-tonk"); how he'd never seen indoor plumbing, silverware, or women without armpit or facial hair before he came to America; and then, when Rob finally got to our house, he couldn't sleep for the first few weeks. He missed curling up under the covers with his pet goat on the family's communal mattress, which doubled as the dinner table. Officer NLTF told me to shut the hell up. I was giving him a headache. After he pulled into my driveway, Officer NLTF couldn't get rid of us fast enough. As soon as we were out, he flipped on the siren and tore away.

There was a note for me on the kitchen table—Mom saying she was out, hoped I had fun at the dance, she might not be back home until very late, XOXOXO. That was it. I flipped it over. Nothing on the other side.

Well, it's not hard to figure out what happened next. We were alone in my house with no parental supervision. So of course, Rob wanted the grand tour. *Yeah, so this is the kitchen. There's the family room, bathroom, the dining room we barely use, the living room we never use, the stairs.* Rob complimented my mother's excellent taste in beige carpeting, ivory-colored paint, and lame-ass Hummel figurines.

Right. That's exactly what happened.

When we got to my bedroom, Rob's eyes zeroed in on the life-sized paintings of Flash and Dale, Superman and Lois, and Buck and Wilma.

"Not much of a comic book geek, are you?" Rob said.

"More of a space dork. Here we've got Superman," I said, pointing at the Man of Steel thrusting out his chest as tommy gun bullets ricocheted from it.

"So *that's* what Superman looks like. I always wondered."

"Smart-ass. There's Flash Gordon. The movie changed him into a quarterback, but in the comics he was a world-famous polo player. TV didn't get Buck Rogers right, either. He wasn't on a NASA mission. Some mysterious gas froze him in a cave for five hundred years."

"Why outer space?" he asked, sitting on my bed.

"I dunno. It's kinda stupid."

I felt dumb for geeking out on him. I must've seemed like a total schmuck.

"What?"

"Well, sometimes, it's just easier to think I'm not the freak. I'm just in an alien world."

"That's cool," Rob said, nodding. I wasn't sure if he understood. He spotted a come stain on the top of my comforter.

"Gee," he said, pointing at it and really hamming it up. "I wonder what you were doing here?"

"Shut up." I blushed.

Rob pulled the tie from my neck, unbuttoned my shirt, and slipped it from my shoulders. It fell to the floor. He kissed my shoulder and unbuckled my belt, pushing my pants to my ankles. I stepped free of them and used my toes to work off my socks. Rob reached through the front of my boxers and eased my dick out. I was hard. The room was sauna hot. I felt like I would pass out.

We kissed—openmouthed, careless, whisker-burn along the jaw, throat. I nuzzled his neck, shoulders. My dick pressed against his shirt. Rob held the back of my neck. His fingers teased my scalp. I licked his forehead, eyebrow, the tip of his nose. He tongued my ear, sucking at the lobe, lips brushing my neck. Bangs across his face, body forced into mine. He kissed his way down my chest and then kneeled.

His breath puffed soft against my dick. The backs of his

128

hands brushed the inside of my thighs. My throat tightened. Everywhere he touched burned. I moaned. My knees buckled and Rob steadied my legs, laying me on the bed and sliding my boxers off. He crawled between my legs.

"No fair."

"What?" Rob asked.

"You've still got your clothes on."

"Too bad." Rob shrugged, the dimple on his cheek growing.

He wrapped a hand around my dick, lifted it from my stomach, and watched my eyes as he licked it. It was amazing. My head fell into the pillows. I was halfway down his throat. It was wet, tight. I was going nuts. I couldn't touch him enough. His mouth felt incredible—soft and alive. I rubbed his shoulders and neck. Stroked his hair. My toes, like almost-hands, grabbed the blankets. As Rob worked his lips up and down, my back kept arching from the bed. My hips pumped. I had no control over them. I panted softly, my head lolling from side to side.

I grunted that I was about to come. I thought Rob would stop and maybe jerk me off, but he didn't. My toes clawed the bed and lifted my sweaty body from the blankets, pushing me deeper inside Rob's mouth. My body twisted. One of my legs was in the air, ankle practically at my ear. The entire weight of my body rested on my shoulders. The tendons in my neck and legs tightened. I couldn't hold back. It was like I'd been underwater holding my breath for too long, and then surfaced. My come rushed into Rob's mouth. I gulped for air and watched Rob swallow.

I collapsed and Rob crawled on top of me. We frenched and I could taste my spunk on his tongue.

When it was my turn, Rob was patient. I may not be a natural-born talent, but I wasn't completely awful. I know I scraped him a couple of times because he tensed up and gasped, "Teeth, teeth." Still, Rob wasn't rushed to the emergency room where a whole surgical team had to sew him back together. He's not even wearing a Band-Aid. I tried getting all of him in my mouth like he did with me, but it didn't work. My eyes watered, my nose got all runny, and I felt like a bulimic chick cramming her fist in her mouth to retch. There were other ways we were different, too. Like, every five minutes I had to stop and pick a pube off my tongue. And my jaw got totally sore. I don't think Rob's did. Still, he got off. I even swallowed. It tasted like baking soda and salt.

Afterward, we spooned and talked. I kept apologizing for being too skinny, not covering my teeth with my lips, gagging, bending him in the wrong direction once—*Okay, pup, not like that*—and Rob told me to relax. Then he did most of the talking, my head against his chest.

"You know the real reason I went to boarding school?" Rob asked. I nodded, running my finger along his treasure trail and hoping that he'd get hard again. I already was. Rob rolled me to my side, pulling my back into his chest and wrapping his arms around me. "They wanted to keep Mom's ALS a secret from me. At least, at first they did."

"When did they find out she had it?"

"I'm not sure when they knew . . . when I was a freshman or sophomore, I think. I remember that she seemed to be getting clumsy. She had trouble holding things and would trip over the carpet all the time. Then during Christmas break my sophomore year, something happened."

"What?"

"I didn't know until this year, when my dad told me why we were moving from Manhattan. One night, there was some big holiday benefit that they were supposed to go to. Dad was running late, and when he got home, he raced up to their room to put on his tux. Mom was sitting at her dressing table. He told her he was sorry that he was late, he'd been having trouble on one of his big accounts, but that they both needed to hurry. That's when he looked over at her and Mom was crying. Dad said she told him she'd spent the entire afternoon struggling to fix the seam of her stockings, clasp her necklace, and put on the earrings he'd given her for their anniversary. Simple tasks. Ones she'd done thousands of times, but couldn't manage anymore.

"They didn't end up going to the benefit. Dad says they spent the night talking about what would happen. About me. Mom said she didn't want me to see her getting worse. Part of me thinks she was right, but another part of me hated her for it."

"How come?" I asked softly, drawing his arms more tightly around my chest.

"Seeing her the way she is now is hard sometimes. I feel that maybe it would be easier for me to deal with it if I'd seen all of it happening—the cane, the slurred speech, the wheelchair. Dad says he doesn't think it would have made things easier for me and it wouldn't have made them easier for Mom. It would have broken her heart.

"The only reason we moved is because this is where she wants to die," Rob said into my shoulder blade. He might've been trying not to cry, but it was too hard to tell. "She wants to die where she grew up."

"Yeah, but there could be worse places to die," I said.

"Okay," Rob said, "name a worse place to die."

"At a convention for necrophiliacs." When things get serious or uncomfortable, I make jokes. It's my way of dealing with things. There was this one time when one of my great-uncles died and we'd all gone back to my great-aunt's house after the funeral, and Mom's sister pulled out this box of old-time family photographs—feathered hair, my great-uncle putting a black comb to his nose and pretending like he was Adolf

Hitler, and old tintype ones. I made some smart-ass remark about our family tree not sprouting branches until sometime in the 20th century. It got a laugh.

"Gross."

"Or being found electrocuted in your bedroom after an accident with a plug-in vibrator."

Rob chuckled.

We were hungry, so we got dressed and went downstairs. I made grilled cheese sandwiches with real butter, Velveeta, and Wonder Bread in an electric skillet—*anything less would be uncivilized*—and asked Rob if he wanted to watch a movie or something. He said sure, so I put in *Flash Gordon*. Sure, it's totally cheesy, but you can't go wrong with Max von Sydow as Ming the Merciless and an awesome soundtrack by Queen. It freaked out Rob that I could mouth all the actors' lines before they spoke them.

Mom came home just as the war rocket *Ajax* was impaling Ming. I wanted to know where she'd been, but she wouldn't say. She just told me I needed to clean up the mess I'd made in the kitchen. I asked if Rob could spend the night. Actually, I begged. She glanced at the watch on Rob's wrist and then stared at me like she was insulted I thought she was too dumb to figure out what was going on. I folded my hands like I was praying, mouthed the word "please," and gave her my best desperate I-swear-I'll-never-ask-you-for-anything-ever-again-just-let-me-spend-the-night-with-this-cute-boy look. She relented, saying it was okay if, one, Rob's parents said it was; and two, we cleaned up the kitchen; three, we slept in the family room (*Not your bedroom, Charlie, understood?*); and four, I basically promised to be her indentured servant for the rest of my natural life. Rob said his parents would let him, but he'd call to make sure.

While Rob called his dad, Mom made me help her get the quilts, afghans, pillows, and blankets for me and Rob to camp out downstairs.

"The watch looks good on him," Mom said, but her voice was really saying don't-think-I-don't-know-what-you've-got-planned-buster-and-don't-even-think-about-trying-it. "Let's make sure it stays on him tonight, okay?"

"It's not what you're thinking." Mom rolled her eyes and helped me carry the bedding back to the family room just as Ming picked up his ring at the end of the movie. Mom shook her head, said her good nights, and then went upstairs.

After I thought Rob was asleep, he surprised me by reaching over and wrapping an arm around my chest.

"Remember on the sidewalk at the White Hen?" he asked.

I nodded, but wasn't sure what he was talking about.

"When you said you loved me. I didn't say anything. I'm saying it now, pup. I love you."

"I love you, too."

We kissed and went to sleep.

Monday, September 17

School was pretty bad today. I figured it would be. You can't fag out at homecoming and expect nothing to happen.

It's got me thinking that I probably need to rework my college essay.

I'm the prince of public scorn. Sure, it may sound like a cushy title, but it carries with it a certain noblesse oblige, "nobility obligates," which in ancient civ we learned means that, every so often, those of us who've got it all—charm, wit, dashing good looks, country estates—should throw a bone to the inbred, dirt-under-the-fingernails crowd of little people.

There was this morning's de-pantsing in the Pit, which drew a larger crowd than the changing of the guard (please, no flash photography). That was followed by an audience with the ranking dignitaries— the math class jagoffs gleeking spit on the back of my neck and the Rot-See Nazis demonstrating the latest ass-whipping techniques. Then I had the investitures, where I presented pieces of my underwear—post-grundy—to the honor's list.

Of course, I had my public engagements, too, such as the installation of a new toilet in the boy's locker room. A bunch of the jocks decided I just had to be there for its christening by swirly. The day ended with a report from one of the government whips (imagine, they actually prefer to be called "deans"—how quaint) delivering messages of state. Look, Charles, we're not saying it's your fault, but if you toned it down you'd be less of a target.

Rob didn't catch any crap, though. Since his family's rich, he can get away with anything. At least at South. Even though Rob's not a totally blatant, lettered-in-three-sports varsity pussy-hound, he didn't catch shit. Hell, if he got caught sucking me off, everyone'd say I'd tricked him into doing it, saying how I tried screwing a rattlesnake, got bitten, and Rob, being a hero, was just sucking the venom out.

134

Tuesday, September 18

I think First's been driving by the house the last couple of nights. If he catches either of us looking at him from a window, he speeds off. I know he's been the one calling the house and hanging up if I answer. It's like he's in sixth grade. If Mom answers, she tells him she needs her space and his calls aren't helping any.

Mom's still going out and not saying what she's doing.

Thursday, September 20

Around three this morning, I woke up to hear Mom coming in the front door. She wasn't alone. First was with her. I couldn't make out what he was saying, but I could tell he was pissed. I got out of bed and kneeled next to one of the heating vents to try to hear them better.

Mom was telling First to keep his voice down. He was going to wake me.

"Well at least tell me where you've been," First said. He didn't sound demanding, just concerned. It was surprising. "I just want to know that you and Chip are all right."

"Look, Charles, I'm just walking in the door. It's late, and I'm tired from work . . ."

"Work?" First asked. "What are you doing?" I wanted to know the same thing.

"Do we have to do this now? Can't this wait until morning?"

"Work?" First asked again, all dog with a bone. "Who's watching Chip when you're at work?"

"Charles, he can look after himself. He's almost eighteen. How much trouble can he get into?"

There was a pause, and then they both laughed. *Ha ha ha. The two of them oughta go into stand-up together.*

"Can I come in?" First asked. "Just for a few minutes."

"I don't think that would be such a good idea."

"Laura, how are we supposed to work things out if we aren't talking? I want us to work through this together."

"Charles, it hasn't even been a week. I need time."

"The last time you said that we almost got divorced."

The last time? Divorced? It didn't make sense. I couldn't remember them ever being separated or even talking about throwing in the towel before now.

"The last time was different," Mom said. Her voice started to crack. "And I don't want to talk about it."

"I'm sorry, Laura. It's just that this . . . what's going on between us . . . for me, it's like another loss."

Mom started sobbing, and I heard the floorboards creak, like First had stepped inside to hold her. I pushed my ear closer to the heating vent to hear something—anything—but got nothing. I wanted to go downstairs and see if she was okay, but something told me I wouldn't get a straight answer from either of them.

After awhile, I heard First's shoes and him saying, "I should go."

Mom didn't speak, but I imagined her nodding.

Finally she said, "We'll talk in the morning," and closed

136

the front door. From my window, I watched First pull out of the driveway. I went back to bed, but couldn't sleep. I was dying to know what they *weren't* talking about, but I sure-as-shit know there's no way Mom'll tell me. Besides, it's not like there was an easy way to even bring it up. *Hey, Mom, while I was eavesdropping on you last night, it sounded like you were separated before? Wanna tell me about that?*

Ugh.

Friday, September 21

After our game today, Rob came over and we hung out in my room listening to music and stuff.

Rob took the Nestea plunge onto my bed. One of his socks had practically fallen off his foot and as soon as I saw his ankle, I wanted to lick it. I started getting a stiffy. By the time the second track was playing, our socks and shirts were at the end of my bed.

I'm supposed to take the Metra into Chicago with Rob to-morrow when he goes downtown for his piano lesson. We're going to hang out in the city afterward. It should be fun.

Saturday, September 22

Rob and I got thrown out of the Art Institute today. According to the security guard, you're not supposed to play tag around priceless pieces of art. They really ought to have a sign or something. Anyhow, I did manage to get postcards with pictures of some of the paintings Rob liked—*The Rock*, Warhol's *Mao*, some splattered thing by a guy named Pollock, and a couple of others.

Tomorrow's our three-week anniversary. Weird, huh? And to think, at first, I practically hated him; now I'm in love.

God, that seems stupid to write. I mean, really. I don't know anything about love.

I realized that this week. In creative writing, we've been reading from Elie Wiesel's *Night*, this book about surviving the Holocaust. We're reading it 'cuz Mrs. Bailey wants us to write an essay on The Most Important Thing We've Learned. For some reason, she got it in her dumb New Age-y head that our short little suburban lives are, get this, *rife with the same meaning and insights of someone who survived a concentration* camp and that *we just absolutely must commit our wisdom to paper, because forgetting is the gravest of sins.* What's worse, she's got the class believing her.

To piss Bailey off, I almost wrote that the most important thing I've learned is how to masturbate. It's given me hours of entertainment and lets me have sex—imaginary, of course—with just about everyone I could ever want: Rob, most of the guys on the soccer team, the entire swim team (they'd asked me to help them shave their legs so they were faster in the water, and well, soon we're all naked and shaving cream and spooge is flying everywhere), Neil and Aaron Binkmeyer (together and separately), just about every guy under the age of twenty-five who's appeared shirtless in *People*, the two barbecuing blond guys in First's old *Hustler*, and even Steve Marshall (gross, I know, but it worked when I pretended I had him tied up).

I didn't write my "How I Learned the Art of Self-Love" essay and worked on some stupid thing about reading being the most important thing I'd learned. The teacher's pet, some junior girl who writes all these crappy things about unicorns prancing around on rainbows and babies turning their heads to smile at their mothers like sunflowers meeting the sun, wrote how the most important thing she'd learned was How to Love. Not the hot-and-sweaty-jump-someone's-bones porno love, but the big syrupy Gandhi kind. Bailey wet her panties over it. She thinks it should be included in the school's literary magazine.

Here's what I know about love: It's not something anybody should bother writing about, especially songwriters, poets, and teenaged gay boys in the Midwest. Love is a many-splendored thing, love will keep us together, your love keeps lifting me higher. None of it means anything. All I know is it's not something you can explain.

Tuesday, September 25

Rob's decided that he's teaching me to drive. We started last night. I don't think he knows what he got himself into. He joked I couldn't be that bad. He was wrong.

Driving Test Failure Numero Uno: *The first time isn't supposed to count, right? It wasn't like it was my fault. That examiner woman kept scratching all this stuff about me on her clipboard. Can I help it if the Oldsmobile veered to the right and jumped a curb when I leaned over to see what she was writing? C'mon, she was writing about me. I had a right to know what she was saying.*

Driving Test Failure Number Two: *Okay, anybody could screw up and forget which pedal was for the gas and which was for the brake. And the woman with the baby stroller—no harm, no foul. I bet even she didn't know she could run that fast.*

The Hat Trick: *I can explain. This examiner was hot— big chest, thick arms, unbelievable eyes. He was wearing pants that were so tight they might as well've been carbon paper—I could've traced his dick through 'em. Keeping my eyes on the road would've totally been a problem—that is, if we'd ever made it out of the parking lot. When I told him that I'd sooo totally kiss him if I passed, he flunked me right then and there. How's that for a self-esteem booster?*

140

Attempt Number Four: *Again, not my fault. That dog practically jumped in front of us. Sure, the* Illinois Rules of the Road *says I should've run the mutt over, but try telling Timmy that after he's seen you scrape bits of Lassie from the fender.* Yeah, yeah. *So what if a doctor said some bureaucrat had to wear a neck brace 'cuz of the whiplash. Memo to all Department of Motor Vehicles employees: screaming doesn't help I don't care if you're in pain, it's still more than a little unnerving.*

Driving Test Failure Number Five: *So I parallel park as well as an epileptic having a seizure plays* Operation. *Still, I did less than a hundred bucks worth of damage so they should've let it slide.*

Failure Number Six—Last But Not Least: *I don't care what anyone says. I sooo did not cut off that ambulance. And I most definitely did not run it off the road.*

Tonight, I didn't hit anything. With Rob sitting shotgun, I was more relaxed behind the wheel than I am with First. But even Rob says I drive like a blind Asian midget. I'm oblivious to everything around me. I'll sing along with the radio, forget to use turn signals, or I won't put the car in park if I'm stopping somewhere I didn't check the mirrors as often as I should've, and when I did, it was only to make sure I'd look hot for Rob. Still, Rob's been good about the whole thing, even though when we had dinner at his house, he joked about how bad I am.

Mrs. Hunt's not doing well. She looks like she's in a lot of pain, too. After dinner, I volunteered to do the dishes as Rob helped his mom to the living room. While I was drying the plates, I heard Mr. Hunt on the phone with some doctor, saying he needed more drugs for Mrs. Hunt. The bottle they had ordered got knocked into the toilet while he was trying

141

to bathe his wife. It seemed weird, 'cuz there were tons of prescription bottles of something called diazepam—the same thing he was asking about on the phone—from different pharmacies in New York, from around Crystal Lake, and even a few bottles from Canada. It didn't make sense, and I guess that's why I didn't say anything. I mean seriously, if Mr. Hunt was gonna go all Republican-hypocrite-let's-round-up-all-the-black-crackheads-in-America-and-shoot-'em-in-the-street-before-they-rape-our-women-and-steal-the-Vicodin-I-swallow-like-a-fat-man-gorging-on-an-Easter-ham, it's not like Mr. Hunt'd be having bottles of whatever he was jonesing for just lying around. And if they really were for Mrs. Hunt, wouldn't Rob's dad make sure that she was taking 'em in the first place and not stockpiling them like they were nukes and he was some crazed Russian from a Bond flick? Who knows why old people do what they do? If you ask me everyone my parents' age is crazy, an asshole, or both.

Thursday, September 27

Bink pulled up this morning driving a baby blue Volkswagen Bug that screamed "Tijuana-built death trap."

"Nice wheels," I said, walking over to him. "Get this thing from a box of Trix?"

"Lucky Charms. Get in."

I tugged at the door, getting a you-really-need-to-pull-because-it-kinda-sticks look from Bink, folded myself in half, and slipped in shotgun, crunching a McDonald's bag and kicking an empty bottle of YooHoo under my feet.

"When'd you get this piece of junk?"

"Last night," Bink said. "I got tired of constantly begging for the Volvo. Only six hundred bucks."

"You were robbed."

"Jealous? Anyhow, the stereo doesn't work," Bink explained, fumbling to get some CD he'd burned into the boombox he'd jerry-rigged to the dash with duct tape. I snagged the case from him and glanced at the tracks. The Ramones, Lou Reed, The Smoking Popes, 88 Fingers Louie, Iggy Pop. The Lawrence Arms. Music that Bink insisted was better than any of the crap on the radio.

"Most of the music from the last twenty years is crap," Bink said like he expected me to pick a fight with him or something. He cranked the volume dial. "Wanna know what blows? When we're in our fifties, there won't be a grocery store or elevator that isn't playing a Muzak version of shit like Celine Dion or some hip-hop diva."

"Well, with Celine, at least we won't be able to tell if it's Muzak or the original," I said.

He groaned. Bink's a dork. Cute, but a dork.

We ditched school and hit Full Cyrkle, this record shop on Route 31 that caters to old fogies looking for Guy Lombardo and His Royal Canadians' *The Sweetest Waltzes This Side of Heaven* and stoners selling near-mint copies of *Dark Side of the Moon* or *Tommy* to pay for weed. I hadn't been there since I was, like, eight and First needed a birthday present for his mom and thought she'd like some album by four New Jersey potential wifebeaters singing in these corn syrup falsettos.

Bink, on the other hand, has practically lived there since, like, the seventh grade. As soon as we walked in, Bink asked about some garage band he saw at a party in Naperville back in March or maybe it was at the Elmhurst VFW hall, and then, like a Vegas card dealer, flipped through the albums Dave'd set out for him—all stone-faced efficiency. Patti Smith's *Horses* (*C'mon, Dave, like I don't already have this.*), The Cramps' *A Date with Elvis* (*"Can Your Pussy Do the Dog?"—great track.*), Siouxsie and the Banshees (*Live versions of "Hong Kong Garden" and "Dear Prudence"? For a bootleg, this doesn't suck.*), The Modern Lovers (*Ever hear Johnny Rotten's cover of "Roadrunner"? Hilarious. He can't remember the lyrics.*).

Afterward, we drove around, not really talking. It was cool. Almost like when we were kids and nobody paid attention to what we were doing—trying to scratch records like the Beastie Boys, broomstick bicycle jousting, tormenting Aaron before his junior prom. Only, the thing is, we aren't kids anymore. I mean, it's like if I spend any time around Bink, Mr. Five-Incher starts acting like he's got the mental capacity of an Alzheimer's patient and conveniently forgets that I've got this super hot guy as a boyfriend. Put me around a guy that's slightly above average in the looks department and my little buddy's demanding so much of my body's blood that it's a wonder my brain's getting enough oxygen to support basic human functioning.

I guess I'd feel really bad if I thought it was just me, but I swear to Christ, it's a guy thing. This summer, when everyone was playing truth or dare at Dana's party, I remember someone asking Kyle Weir if he'd rather have really awful, might-as-well-just-jerk-off-with-Stephen-Hawking's-paralytic-hand sex with a chick who measured 42"-18"-33" or make toe-curling, ball-shuddering, universe-shattering, mind-evaporating monkey love with a chick he'd just as soon put on a leash and feed dog biscuits. Weir said he'd nail 'em both, just as long as no one ever knew he was packing the homunculus's box. Yeah, Weir's a pig, but part of me thinks he's right. It seems like most guys—and let's face it, it's not like I'm an exception—would do the nasty with just about anything if

144

they could get away with it. Am I proud of this? No. But, then again, I'm not exactly proud of the fact that I spend ninety percent of my life practicing genital origami on myself.

Saturday, September 29

I feel like shit. If I wasn't such a wuss, I'd find a gun and blow my brains out. Rob's not talking to me. It's my fault. I'm such a prick.

We lost our first game yesterday. The thing is, McHenry wasn't supposed to beat us. It wasn't supposed to be close. They're the second-worst team in the conference. I don't know if we just got too cocky or if McHenry was so bad they dragged us down to their level, but Christ, we sucked.

In the visiting locker room, everyone acted like we lost 'cuz the ref called the game on a slaughter rule. Guys were shoving each other into lockers, yelling, throwing jerseys, cleats, and shin guards. That's when Rob and I got into it. He stood near me as I pulled off my shoes and socks.

"Smooth move on that save," Rob said. I should've realized he was kidding, but I was pissed about costing us the game. I didn't need anyone rubbing it in—least of all him. And, in classic Stewart style, I took it too far.

"Yeah? Maybe we'd've done better if your mom was out there in her wheelchair instead of you, dweeb."

Rob stood there like I'd sucker punched him. His teeth were clenched. He balled his hands into fists. I wanted to take it back instantly.

"Rob, I'm sorry . . . I didn't mean it," I said, stammering.

145

I closed my eyes, hoping he'd haul off and slug me, break my nose, something. Hell, if having my jaw wired shut for a few weeks kept me from saying stupid crap, so much the better. My arms were shaking and covered in goose bumps.

Rob didn't hit me. He didn't tackle me or anything. He just called me a bastard, took off the watch I'd given him, dropped it into my bag, and walked away.

I've been phoning Rob pretty much on the hour since yesterday. He won't answer.

Sunday, September 30

Rob's still not talking to me. I tried apologizing at church today. He blew me off, acting like I didn't even exist.

It didn't help any having First at church. He tried sitting with me and Mom, only she wasn't having his let's-pretend-we're-the-perfect-family-and-everything's-fine crap. She got up and sat in the pew across the aisle. There wasn't room for me, so I got stuck with him.

Trust me, even I'm having a hard time believing it, but First actually treated me like a real live human being and not like some freakish lab specimen that needed to be slapped on a slide, doused with iodine, and scrutinized under a microscope for defects.

"Everything okay with you, Chip? I mean, Charlie?" he asked, whispering. The church organist fog-horned her way through "Now Thank We All Our God" like it was a funeral dirge for some ancient lederhosen-wearing Bavarian lard-ass.

"I guess," I said, trying to say as little as possible so I didn't end up getting the third degree on the music I was listening to (it wasn't that long ago when Queen, the Butthole Surfers, the Queers, and the Dickies were all cause for suspicion) or how if I didn't get at least a B in AP Bio or pass my driver's test, I'd end up going from living in public housing to being someone's toothless, Skoal-gumming, tattooed prison bitch.

"And your mom?"

"She's fine."

"That's good," he said, looking down at the hymnal. "Is there anything you need from me?"

"Nope."

"Well, let me know if you need anything. I'd be happy to help."

Granted, it's not like the conversation we had was exactly riveting, but at least it ended without either of us wanting to kill each other.

Monday, October 1

Scribbled notes in second hour . . .

—Dating sucks.

What'd you do now, Charlie?

–How do you know it's my fault, Bink?

When you walk into the kitchen, see the trash can knocked to the ground and the family dog in the mid-

dle of all the garbage, you don't go searching for some homeless guy gnawing on a greasy chicken bone.
–Quit trying to be cute.
I'm just saying.
—You're just being a dick.
So, what'd you do?
–Said something to Rob I shouldn't have.
Then apologize.
–He won't talk to me.
Then write to him.
–But . . .
Well, boo hoo, then, Charlie. Boo hoo. You're as bad as Dana.

Tuesday, October 2

I've been calling Rob and he's still not answering. It sucks.

Mom finally said where she's been going at night. She's taken an accounting job at The Cottage, closing out the bar and kitchen registers, tallying up the receipts, and doing the books. She figures it'll help if she needs a job if they get a divorce. She's even thinking about maybe going back to school to get her CPA.

Wednesday, October 3

Why do I get stuck being God's walking punch line? I say one fricking dumb-ass thing about Rob's mom and I'm doomed to never touch another guy's dick.

THIRD PERIOD: CHOIR

Rob came up to me during choir. I got all excited, thinking he'd forgiven me. *Yeah, right.*

"Quit calling me," he said in front of everyone. Half of the kids burst out laughing. "You're making a fool of yourself."

I wanted to make some big dramatic "screw you, Rob" gesture, but tripped on my shoelaces, which had me pretty much falling all over myself. Not an off-balanced stumble— a total silent-movie, whackin'-big, face-first collapse. My teeth clamped down on the tip of my tongue. I coughed some blood-tinged, pink spit onto the tiles. Everybody laughed— even Mrs. Reed, the choir director. When she stopped drying her eyes, Mrs. Reed said I'd've laughed, too, if I saw myself, straight as a beanpole one moment, a blur of flapping arms and kicking legs the next. Then she got around to asking if I was okay.

"Yettthhh," I said as best I could manage without the tip of my tongue.

"Are you sure?" Mrs. Reed asked. She looked a little panicked. "You're bleeding and lisping."

"He's always lisping," Rob said.

Mrs. Reed shot him a you're-one-to-talk look and sent me off to the school nurse, who stuffed my mouth full of cotton balls. She made me stay in her office for the rest of third hour. In her "professional" opinion (*If she was such a medical professional, why couldn't she give me a damn aspirin?*), I'd live. *Duh.*

BETWEEN SIXTH PERIOD & SEVENTH PERIOD: IN THE JOHN

I got pissed on—really—by Kyle Weir.

I was taking a leak before heading to AP Bio when Kyle walked in and stood at the urinal next to mine. Kyle unzipped, slowly pulled it out, and then did this over-exaggerated stretch-and-yawn gesture, pushing one of his arms so close to my face he nearly clipped my nose. It was like he was daring me to look.

So, I did, even though I should've known better. And, I gotta admit, it looked pretty good—until Kyle aimed it at my feet. He started laughing and pissing a big yellow stream that splattered just under my kneecaps, soaking through my jeans and shoes. Then he zipped up.

"You attthhhhole," I said right as Dean Fuller walked into the bathroom.

"Christ, Stewart." Kyle pointed at my shins. "If you can't hold it, you should wear a pair of diapers or something. Oh, hi, Mr. Fuller." Weir pushed past me on his way out, leaving me alone with the dean.

Fuller looked me in the face, at the puddle of piss I was standing in, then back to me.

"Care to explain?" he asked, folding his arms across his chest, the tails of his sports coat hitching above his waist.

I shook my head. "I don't ttthhhink I can." Even if I'd ratted out Weir, it'd be his word against mine. He'd say it was self-defense. I tried to rape him so he pissed on me.

"Me either. Not having a good day today, are we, Stewart?" I could tell he wasn't sure what to do with me—be disgusted, feel pity, or just ignore me.

"No, ttthhhir."

Fuller said he'd get a mop from one of the janitors. As soon as I cleaned up the mess, he'd call my mom and have her pick me up. He'd leave it to me to explain why my shoes and jeans were soaked in urine.

Saturday, October 6

Finally, Rob and I are talking again. It's weird, 'cuz it's like we never stopped in the first place.

I followed Bink's advice. If Rob wasn't gonna talk to me, I'd apologize on the postcards I got at the Art Institute.

Postcard One:
The Top Ten Reasons Rob Hunt Should Be Smart Enough to Not Date Charlie Stewart, but Hopefully He's Dumb Enough Not to Have Noticed:
10) C.S.'s annoying inability to pronounce the final g-sound in present participles and gerunds like cuddlin', huggin', and kissin'.
9) C.S.'s ears are the size of airplane wings. It's a miracle he doesn't take off with a heavy wind.
8) That huge nose—he picks it. In fact, a TV camera caught

him doing it on "The Bozo Show" when he was six. His mom's sister took a snapshot of her TV. Multiple prints were made. One found its way to the local paper's photo desk. Though grainy, it appeared with a caption saying I was rooting around my nasal cavity while the crowd rooted for some girl playing the Grand Prize Game. You can see one sometime if you'd like.

7) C.S.'s irrational gephydrophobia (I looked it up)—the fear of crossing bridges. It's not the bridge he's afraid of. He's terrified of bridge builders, convinced that they're all like McDonald's employees and have these excuses for being lazy like "if it got wet, it got clean" or "it's still okay to serve if it was only on the ground for thirty seconds."

Postcard Two:
More Reasons You Probably Shouldn't Date Me But I Still Hope You Will:

6) After seeing *Breakin' 2: Electric Boogaloo* on television in third grade, I wanted to be a breakdancer. I begged my mom for parachute pants. She pointed out, correctly, that nobody had made them since before I was born. I threw a temper tantrum in the middle of the boy's section of Carson Pirie Scott. My mother told me if I didn't stop acting like a four year old, she'd treat me like one. I didn't. She did. In front of God and everyone, she bent me over her knee and spanked me. The sales clerks laughed. Another mother applauded.

5) Until freshman year, I thought a sanitary napkin was just another name for those disposable moist towelettes. I learned the difference by asking for one in a restaurant.

4) Let's just say I'm not as far along down there as most guys.

3) I have a lot of annoying habits—I leave damp towels

on the bathroom floor, flush the toilet before I've finished pissing, bite my nails, and I act stupid when I'm around you.

2) I talk way too much, say stuff I shouldn't, and I make really dumb-looking faces and noises when I'm doing things with you in bedrooms, on parking lot benches, and in choir practice rooms. But you already knew that.

Postcard Three:
The Biggest Thing About Me I Hope You'll Overlook:
1) I really am a jackass. I said stuff, Rob, that I didn't mean and I'll probably end up screwing things up even more. Probably before the end of this postcard. I'm hoping there's still a chance you like me anyhow, and that you know how really sorry I am. I'm an idiot. But I'd like it if you'd still let me be your idiot.

I stuffed the postcards in Rob's locker before chorus yesterday. When we saw each other crossing the Pit after sixth period, Rob passed me a note, which was kinda junior-high girly of him. His note was southpaw-smeared and full of misspellings, but it made me smile.

Charlie,
Your such a dweeb. Apology excepted. Now weres my watch?
XOXOXO
Rob

As the soccer team was heading out to the field for the conference title, I pulled Rob aside and gave him a quick peck on the cheek. It was warm and I'd almost forgotten how good he smelled.

"I'm really sorry," I said. "It's just that—"

"Shut up already, Charlie," he said. "It's okay. I'm sorry, too."

"Shut up."

"No, you shut up, okay?" Rob laughed.

After the game—we won three to zip—we went to Colonial for its Kitchen Sink, this sundae with, like, ten scoops of ice cream, four whole bananas, whipped cream, cherries, and peanuts, served in this hokey stainless steel trough standing on top of a plumbing drain. Rob made me drive there, saying Route 14 wasn't as bad as it seemed, that most accidents occurred within a mile of home. It wasn't very likely that a class of preschoolers would dart into oncoming traffic at seven o'clock on a Friday night. Even if they did, Rob said, he was sure I could swerve and miss most of them.

Rob had a piano lesson today and was gonna spend time with his uncle in the city afterward, so we're supposed to hang out tomorrow and Monday, since there's no school. Columbus Day.

Monday, October 8

Rob's mom's getting worse. They've got her on a feeding tube and she's bedridden. Every few hours, Rob or his dad has to move her so she doesn't get bedsores. She's also having problems breathing, especially at night. Rob says there are times when she's sleeping and she just stops breathing. She's got all this mucus and crap that's building up in her lungs. Mr. Hunt has to prop her up and tap her back so he can break up all the stuff for her to cough up.

154

"It sucks, Charlie," Rob said, sweeping the bangs from his eyes.

We were in his room and he was sitting on the edge of his bed. I was sprawled out on my stomach, lying next to him, proofreading an essay he'd written for his remedial English class. (If he wasn't *sooo* damn cute, I think I would have killed him. I mean, it takes a special kind of guy to misspell "the.")

"What sucks?" I asked.

"She wouldn't want to live like this. She can't breathe. It's horrible at night. She's struggling and there's nothing I can do. I wish it was me. Jesus, I wish it was me instead."

"Don't say that."

"It should be me. I'm the one wishing she'd just die and get it over with."

I sat up and pulled Rob into me, locking my arms around his chest.

"It's okay, Rob. You just don't want to see her like this. That's normal."

"No, it isn't," he said as he lowered his head. "What I told her last night wasn't normal. She was really bad. Dad was asleep—he'd been up almost two days straight. He's practically killing himself making sure she's not in pain.

"So, I'm in the chair next to that stupid hospital bed and she starts gasping. She started panicking, which made it worse. You should've seen her eyes. She looked really scared. I raised the bed and that seemed to help.

"I was stroking her hand, trying to help her relax. Then, after a while, I heard what I was saying to her. 'It's okay. Just let go. It's okay.' I kept saying it even after I realized I was telling her to die."

"You weren't telling her to die," I said, nuzzling against his cheek. He didn't say anything.

I should be ashamed of this. While I was kissing Rob and smelling his hair, I popped a major boner. One of those obvious, awful ones that can't be "casually" adjusted 'cuz it had managed to get tangled in the Y-front of my tighty whities. And if that wasn't bad enough, it poked the small of Rob's back.

"What is this? A stickup?" Rob laughed, stretching his hands up like he was a bank teller and I was a masked gunman.

"Sorry."

Rob rocked backward into me, forcing me to the bed, swung around, and grabbed a pillow from the head of the bed, swiping it across my head. I tried to snatch it from him, but wasn't quick enough. He straddled my chest, laughing, and pressed the pillow over my face. I reached over to snag the other pillow and swatted Rob with it, rolling him off me.

Inside of two minutes, we were totally going at it on his bed. We'd pulled off each other's shirts and Rob was above me, my hands rubbing his chest and fingering his nipples. His tongue worked its way along my jaw to behind my earlobe. I pulled his face into mine and we frenched—hard, my nose banging his. It was like I couldn't get enough of him in my mouth. Rob's hands slid alongside my torso, outlining my ribcage, until they were at my waist, fumbling with my fly. He tugged my jeans, nearly pulling me off the bed as he stripped me. I stood, giggled, told him it was my turn, and slipped his pants from his legs. He didn't have any underwear on. His hard-on slapped against his stomach.

I craned my neck forward to lick him and nip at his thighs 'cuz I wanted to make him squirm. Before I could, Rob grabbed my wrists, shouldered my legs so my ankles were at his ears, and eased me down onto the mattress. Pinned.

"Can I?" Rob asked. He leaned down and kissed me. I wasn't sure what he was asking until he was practically chewing through a condom wrapper and his dick was skirting against my tailbone. I never figured two boys could do it, you know, like, facing each other. I got nervous. Really nervous.

My butt clamped tight. I thought about a '20s Irish cop hammering on the door of a speakeasy, the mobsters inside shouting to the cigarette girl, "Katy, bar the door!"; a cartoon cat trying to suck a stupid yellow canary through a straw; portcullises dropping and drawbridges raising; caves being blocked off by avalanches; that sort of thing.

Sure, I've read my share of *Penthouse* letters about middle-aged bus drivers dipping their wicks doggy-style in the poop chutes of an entire girls' gymnastic team. But I'd never stopped to really consider that taking it from behind was bound to really, really hurt some of those pert little gymnasts. Besides, a few of them probably wouldn't have been exactly *clean*. I mean, it's called fudge-packing for a reason.

I'll admit that when it came right down to it, I only imagined *actual* sex in two ways—the romance-novel kind and the locker-room-joke version.

According to Harlequin, there'd be swooning, throbbing manhoods, blond hairy chests, whispered sweet nothings, me *glowing* (not sweating), and then, somehow, it'd just slide in. Trains entering mountain tunnels, rockets launching, fireworks exploding, volcanoes erupting. I'd sing opera solos, and that'd be it.

The joke version was scary and gross. There was some guy sticking his hand up another guy's ass and finding his birthday present, a Rolex watch; bar stools turned upside-down and four mustached guys named Bruce sitting on each leg; guys wearing dresses and leather chaps; guys with buckets of Crisco doing each other in the butt.

So, I wigged out when Rob asked if he could turn me

into his personal shish kebab. I wasn't up for getting my kidneys skewered or my lungs punctured.

Rob chuckled and said I was overreacting. Rob said he wasn't that big and he'd go slowly. Still, when I said no, Rob gave up and climbed onto the bed next to me and I sucked him off. If he was pissed that we didn't do anything more, he didn't show it.

Tuesday, October 9

Joan and Mr. B really got into it during AP Bio—Joan basically calling Mr. B a monster, Mr. B saying she was a cretin who didn't deserve the benefits of modern medicine or technology. It started 'cuz the bio lab'd been transformed into a kitty morgue. The place reeked of formaldehyde and our workstations were lined with what turned out to be dead cats covered by little white sheets.

The passing period between sixth and seventh hours hadn't ended, and Joan and I'd gotten to class early. The smell was almost enough to make me retch, but that didn't stop Hawkings. She lifted a corner of one of the sheets. Just as Mr. B walked in, she let out this total cheerleader-with-nothing-but-her-training-bra-and-panties-to-protect-her-from-a-chainsaw-wielding-maniac horror-movie shriek and covered her eyes. The sheet fluttered to the floor. Joan spun around, clutching her mouth like she was about to blow chunks. Mr. B, smelling like a just-sneaked cigarette, walked over to her— all *no big deal*—and blocked my view.

I climbed on my chair to see why she'd freaked. It was a

dead cat, a little *rigor mortis*-ed arm sticking over the tray's edge, dried-up eyes still open, lips curled over tiny teeth, leathery tongue lolling to the side.

"Miss Hawkings," Mr. B said, sipping his coffee, "no matter how loudly you scream, you won't wake the dead. And Mr. Stewart, unless your next words are 'O Captain! My Captain!' I suggest you use your chair in the manner for which it was designed. Sit, Mr. Stewart."

I scrambled off my chair as more kids filed into the classroom.

Joan glared at him, arms folded across her chest. The way she stared at him, all flush-faced and flared nostrils, I'd've sworn she thought Mr. B'd personally, and gleefully, strangled the dozen or so Friskys, Mr. Whiskers, and Snowballs, humming "Whistle While You Work" as he snapped each of their necks.

"These are people's *pets*." Joan stepped toward Mr. B and pointed a finger back at the cat corpses behind her. It reminded me of First's over-the-top courtroom antics, staring in outrage at a defendant on the witness stand while sympathetically motioning back to the poor victim. Only, First had never worked a murder case and Joan clearly wanted to turn this into a feline Nuremberg with Mr. B facing a firing squad at dawn.

The bell rang, which should've had Joan back in her corner, spitting out her mouth guard, getting toweled off, and taking a few moments to—I don't know—*breathe*, before she came out swinging. But Joan fought through the bell.

"I can't believe you actually expect us to butcher cats. These aren't worms or frogs. Don't you get it? These are people's *pets*."

"Miss Hawkings, these are not people's pets. They're dead. They won't be chasing any balls of yarn, climbing into anyone's lap to get scratched behind the ear, or vomiting hair-balls on someone's down comforter. In point of fact, if any-one wanted them to begin with, they wouldn't be here."

Joan's face looked like a clenched asshole. She gritted her teeth and dropped into her seat. Mr. B started taking atten-dance.

"So, since nobody loved them that makes it okay for us to slash them apart, right? I guess we'll be dissecting people in nursing homes next. Or kids in orphanages?"

The class snickered. Mr. B's eye twitched.

"Miss Hawkings, if you can't tell the difference between a cat and a person, then it's clear you shouldn't be in my AP Bio class."

"Oooh, there's a loss. A cat killer doesn't think I should be in his class."

"Here's a suggestion, Joan," Mr. B said, closing his roster. "Why don't you shut the fuck up?"

It was a TKO. I'd never heard any teacher swear at a kid, much less an easygoing guy like Mr. B. Sure, he could be stodgy and distant, but he wasn't the type of guy you'd peg for telling a student to stuff it just 'cuz he didn't agree with what she said. The rest of the class seemed just as shocked. Nobody said anything. Joan sat at her desk, refusing to par-ticipate, until Steve Marshall decided he'd play class clown.

"Look, our cat still has a little collar," Marshall joked.

As soon as Mr. B was out of earshot, Joan told Marshall he'd better enjoy exploring the pussy on the lab counter, 'cuz he wasn't gonna get to do the same with hers.

Friday, October 12

More second-hour therapy sessions with Dr. Bink:

—Thanks, Bink.
For what?
—I wrote Rob. We're back together.
Cool.
—The other day, he wanted to . . .
What?
—Go all the way.
Did you?
—No. I chickened out. Have you ever?
Duh. I told you, Dana's on the pill.
—No. The other way.
You mean, like, anal?
—Yeah. Have you?
I'm not telling you, pervert.
—You totally have, you freak. Admit it.
No.
—Why?
Because if I did, you'd never leave me alone. You'd be all, "Oh, Bink, Bink. Do me—I'm so much better than Dana."
—You can be a real jerk, you know that?
Learned it from you.
—Thanks.

Saturday, October 13

Some Things I Learned From Having Sex with Rob Hunt Friday Night in a Downstate Motel Room:

Those don't-have-sex-until-you're-married-or-you'll-make-the-baby-Jesus-cry types need to stop saying sex is this beautiful thing. It isn't. Who knows? Maybe the first time's incredibly awkward for everyone. It didn't help me any that my first time was in a tacky motel in Pontiac, Illinois, the soccer team got stuck in 'cuz the school was too cheap to spend anything but *Monopoly* money for division playoffs.

If there's one thing I've learned from the one whackin' big time I've had sex, it's that people shouldn't do it in front of mirrors. It's not pretty. No matter how hard you try not to, you end up looking over and seeing how big of a dork you are.

After we won our game in overtime on Friday—it was a close four to three—the team had dinner at Godfather's Pizza, played a few arcade games, and then went back to the motel. When Josh McCullough found out that Rob and I were bunking together, he started bitching that if the two of us got to share a room, the school district oughta foot a motel bill for him and his girlfriend.

"What girlfriend?" I asked on the bus ride back.

"Shut up, fag," Josh said, smacking me in the back of the head. "If we lose tomorrow 'cause you and your butt boy were up all night trying on each other's dresses and doing other sick stuff, I swear to God I'll kill you both."

"Josh," Rob said, turning around in the seat to stare the

162

prick down, "if you don't shut your fucking mouth . . . now . . . I'm going to tell Coach that you want to bunk with us."

"Bullshit," Josh said, horrified. "You wouldn't."

"Try me," Rob said, looking back at a pouting McCullough.

"And just think what we could do to you in your sleep," I said, laughing and rubbing my hands together to make Josh freak out even more.

"Oh yeah, McCullough," Rob said, stabbing both his index fingers at each other. "You'll be getting it from both ends."

"Like a pig on a spit," I said. A few of the guys from the team laughed, and McCullough huffed, tugging the draw-strings of his hoodie so tight that his face vanished.

Since the motel was overbooked, we got stuck in the "honeymoon suite" complete with mirrors on three of the four Pepto-Bismol pink walls and even one on the ceiling. The only wall without a mirror had framed posters of those vapid, sunglasses- and glove-wearing chicks copping a feel of each other's breasts. The frames were glued to the wall, like the management was actually afraid someone would wanna steal "the art." The rest of the room wasn't much better— red shag carpeting that climbed halfway up the wall, a vibrating bed topped with a mock polar bearskin comforter, a minibar stocked with a bottle of generic sparkling wine and a six-pack of Pabst (Coach Mueller had the manager remove 'em.), and a mildewy aquarium filled with this giant, one-eyed diseased goldfish.

The room terrified me. Not because I thought Rob'd put the moves on me. That was pretty much a given. He'd been joking about popping my cherry all week. No, the room was scary 'cuz I figured even most hookers wouldn't be caught in a place that looked this cheap. *I'll do anything you want, Mister . . . let you come on my face, suck off your dog, whatever . . . just please, take me to another motel.*

163

I was nervous. Really nervous. When Rob and I were inside our room, we kicked off our sneakers, and Rob fell backward onto the bed. He grinned, arching his eyebrows and practically begging me to strip and throw myself on top of him.

"I gotta go to the can," I said and raced to the bathroom, locking the door.

I should've brought a paper bag. I was that close to hyperventilating. My armpits were like a faucet with a slow drip. I paced the bathroom, stubbing my toe. I sat on the toilet, twiddling my thumbs. I got up and stared into the mirror, trying to give myself a pep talk. *Go get 'im, tiger. How bad can it hurt, really? You can take it. You're not a wuss.* I tried taking a crap. Nothing. It sounds gross, but I did a finger check on myself, figuring my index finger'd be a sorta Paul Revere. *The penis is coming, the penis is coming.* The dipstick came back clean.

I paced the bathroom some more, this time, hobbling on my heels, figuring I couldn't stub anything that way, but still, I managed to slam my toes into the toilet. I washed my hands, slapped cold water on my face, and put on some of Rob's cologne—to get him in the mood, *natch*—only I splashed so much of the stuff on me that it practically dripped off.

I was all set to give myself another pep talk when Rob knocked on the door.

"Fall in or something?"

"Nah," I said. I flushed the toilet so Rob'd think I actually did something in the john besides make a fool of myself. I opened the door, glad Rob was still in most of his clothes and wasn't waiting for me there buck-naked, glistening hard-on in hand, licking his lips. He'd only taken off his shirt and socks.

Rob peeked past me, trying to see what had kept me for so long.

"Got enough cologne on, pup?" Rob laughed, leading me to the bed. I sat at the edge. Sweat streaked my ribcage. Rob climbed behind me, sitting Indian-style, and massaged my shoulders. The television was on VH1, some "I Hate the '90s" show, and Vanilla Ice and the Pips—his whole "VIP posse" in white shirts and black vests and pants—jumped around to some over-choreographed MC Hammer-lite dance.

"Would you do him?" Rob asked.

"Vanilla Ice?"

"Yeah."

"Nah," I lied. "The riff's a total rip-off of 'Under Pressure.' It was a single off of Queen's crappiest album, *Hot Space*. The guy's a total fake."

Rob wasn't asking 'cuz he cared if I wanted to force a washed-up white rapper to bite pillow. He just wanted me naked and biting a pillow.

"I'd do him," Rob said. "He looks tall."

"That's all it takes with you? Being tall?" I asked, pushing my back against him.

"Well, pup, it helps if they've got a big—"

"What?"

"A big nose and huge ears. And, I like them skinny." Rob pulled me backward so my head was in his lap. I'd've told him to quit lying, but he leaned in and kissed me, sucking my tongue into his mouth.

Somehow, without ever unlocking lips, we scooched from the foot of the bed to the head. I grabbed the remote and turned off the TV. There was no way I was gonna lose my virginity with Vanilla Ice in the background. I couldn't've lived with myself.

Rob's fingers hooked the bottom of my T-shirt, turning it inside out as he tugged it over my chest. The collar caught my nose. Rob snickered and eased it loose. We struggled to get each other's jeans and underwear off, fingers not quite finding zippers, knees bumping, feet kicking denim and cotton to the floor. I cradled his head in my right arm, and traced his tongue with mine.

"I love you, Charlie," Rob said. He daubed his lips with the back of his hand and kissed both my eyelids.

"I love you, too."

Rob grabbed my face, pushed his lips against mine, and rolled on top of me. Licking me from my chin to my crotch, Rob slid down the bed. He cradled my dick and tongued it. I squirmed and bucked like crazy. Rob sucked one of my nuts almost to the back of his throat and then rolled it across his tongue. I arched on my toes and practically humped his face with my crotch. I felt hot, almost feverish. I scrambled down to Rob at the bed's edge, shoved my tongue into his mouth, and then tried to lick my way down to his dick.

"Don't," Rob whispered, bracing his hands on my shoulders and stopping me from kissing his inner thigh. "I'll come." He wrapped his arms around my neck and held my cheek to his chest.

"I really love you, pup," he said. He sounded sad, almost.

We held each other. My dick was throbbing and bumping Rob's. He pushed me back to the bed and reached into his bag for a rubber. The thing was red and when he got it on— *No, I didn't help; I'm not like those sluts who can slip a condom on their boyfriend's cock using just her mouth*—I almost laughed. Rob looked like he had an angry balloon animal taped to his crotch. He reached into the bag again, pulled out a bottle, and squeezed a stream of liquid into his hand.

"KY Jelly," he said. Rob slicked his dick with it, then mine—damn, it was cold—and then bent me over the bed. He reached around my waist, held my dick with one hand, and used the other to work one finger, then two, inside me.

It felt good, incredible even, but when Rob tried getting his dick up there, it hurt like hell. He wasn't even in a millimeter and I thought I was gonna die. My butt winced, pushing him out as I launched forward, yelping.

"Sorry, sorry," Rob repeated, planting little kisses along my knobby spine. "I'll go slowly."

Glacier slow, I wanted to say, but couldn't. In the mirror above the headboard, I saw why. I was biting my bottom lip so hard I was practically piercing it. My knuckles were bone white and grabbing the polar bear comforter so tightly it looked like I was trying to skin the thing with my bare hands. My head flopped to the side, melting into the bed, but I could still see myself sucking air through my teeth and Rob's second siege attempt.

"Should I stop?"

His reflection had this sincere, I'll-go-as-slow-as-you-need-me-to look, the kind a dad would hope the guy deflowering his only daughter would have. But I wasn't getting deflowered. Rob wanted to give me the full-on, gas-powered, Rototiller-tearing-up-the-garden treatment.

"Slowly," I said.

I looked to the mirror on the wall like I expected somebody to jump out and rescue me. Rob made a bit more headway, but I felt like I was being ripped apart. My face showed it. My teeth were grinding, I was making loud sucking noises. Out of instinct, I arched on my toes to get the leverage to push away, but Rob held my shoulders and kept easing himself inside.

"Does it hurt?"

Duh. Yeah. You couldn't tell by the way I was trying to slither out from under you?

"Yeah," I said, burying my face in a pillow and locking my fingers over the base of my neck in a grade school tornado-drill mode. Breathing heavily, Rob grabbed my hips and s-l-o-w-l-y slid the rest of his dick in. His pubes brushed my butt. He didn't start pumping right away, I guess letting me get used to the feeling.

We looked ridiculous. I could tell it was killing Rob not to just start screwing me. Even when he played a really hard piano piece, he didn't look like he was struggling as much as he did then. My face looked like a bad soap opera actor begging his director for some direction. The rest of me didn't look so hot, either—scarecrow torso pinned to the bed, toothpick arms with tiny biceps fanned out across the bearskin, my almost ass getting the pile driver treatment. I didn't remember losing my stiffy, and to be honest, I kinda prayed Rob would lose his, too.

"Maybe we should try a new position." *New position? Like what? The two of us finding girls and bringing them back to our hotel room to bang?* Rob pulled out and I expected to hear the sound of a champagne cork popping.

"Roll over."

I did and accidentally found my double in the ceiling. My mirror twin looked like an oversized baby getting his diaper changed—knees in the air, bony feet flapping around, toes splayed, an afterthought of dick across his stomach. I felt embarrassed for him and closed my eyes. Rob grabbed my ankles, wishboning my legs, and then hitched them onto his shoulders. He swabbed my butt with more KY Jelly, held the heels of my feet with his hand, and sawed into me.

I didn't shriek—*too much*—it actually felt good in a weird kinda way. I didn't exactly show any "star quality" in the bedroom mirrors. Part of the time, I looked retarded—hairless legs over Rob's shoulders, eyes rolling to the back of my head, and wide-open mouth making these dumb sex grunts. *Ah . . . ah . . . ouch! . . . unggh . . . ungggh . . . ouch! . . . ah . . . ah . . .* The rest of the time, I just grinned like an idiot, 'cuz we didn't look hot or romantic. We looked like two guys in a naked crab race. I laughed nervous, goofy laughter that threw off Rob's concentration. The motel room should've had some kinda sign above the bed.

WARNING: SEX IN FRONT OF THESE MIRRORS SHOULD ONLY BE ATTEMPTED BY PROFESSIONALS. OBJECTS IN MIRRORS APPEAR EXACTLY AS THEY DO IN REAL LIFE— YOU REALLY DO LOOK THAT STUPID; YOUR ASS REALLY IS THAT FAT; THAT IS GOING TO LEAVE A MARK; YEP, HE REALLY DID JUST CALL OUT SOMEONE ELSE'S NAME; YES, SHE'S ONLY DOING THIS SO YOU'LL STOP PES-TERING HER ABOUT IT; AND YES, BIG BOY, THAT RE-ALLY IS THE FACE YOU MAKE WHEN YOU COME.

ASHAMED OF YOURSELF YET? YOU SHOULD BE. ROLL OVER AND LET THE EMPTINESS, THE GUILT, AND THE SHAME SINK IN. ONLY, DON'T SIT AROUND FEELING SORRY FOR YOURSELF FOR TOO LONG. YOU RENTED THIS ROOM BY THE HOUR, BIG SPENDER.

—THE MANAGEMENT—

"Stop looking in the mirror," Rob said. We changed posi-tions again. This time I was on top of him. We were still face-to-face, but I was straddling him, kneeling. The bottoms of my thighs were on the top of his. My dick was trapped be-tween both our stomachs and each time Rob thrust, it felt like I was getting jacked off.

Now, for most guys in my position—well, guys who'd actually like being in my position—it probably would've been abso-*fricking*-lutely amazing. Rob'd found some secret, gay boy G-spot. But I had to bite my tongue to stop from laughing. It sounded like the fake farts kids make by cupping a hand under their armpits and squeezing the air out.

Rob's shoulders tensed and he wrapped an arm around my neck. I matched his rhythm. His hand slipped between our stomachs. I came as soon as he touched my dick, coating both our chests. Rob groaned and hugged me tighter, our chests practically cemented together. Somehow, he was getting deeper and faster than before. I shivered. Rob closed his eyes, hands locking my hips as he plunged. His Adam's apple seemed to bounce, flex. He shuddered, grunted. Still trembling, Rob rolled us over and collapsed on top of me.

"Hi," Rob said after he slipped out of me. He drew me into him.

"Hi."

"We need to do that again," he laughed, kissing my nose.

"I'm not in any rush," I said.

"Dork. I didn't mean right now."

More Things I Learned From Having Sex with Rob Hunt Friday Night in a Downstate Motel Room:

So, besides telling us that sex really isn't beautiful to look at, the people who've actually done it should tell us virgins what to expect afterward, too.

Sure, a total moron could figure out that after you take it up the ass, things are bound to be a little sore. Telling me that wouldn't've been helpful. A heads up about what to expect after getting my butt used like a butter churn would've been nice.

How was I supposed to know that Rob would find the only dry spot on the whole mattress, roll over, fall asleep, and leave me naked, wet, and shivering? And really, would it've been too hard to *casually* mention that the air and lube in me would be itching to get out?

We ended up winning two of the three games we had today, which meant the division title was ours, and we'll be playing for the state championship. Mom was waiting for me at school when we got back and she took me out to celebrate.

We pigged out on Cantonese—beef and broccoli, kung pao chicken, egg rolls, egg foo yung, lobster kow, and fortune and almond cookies. She kept pestering me about how I looked different, more mature. I didn't tell her about Rob and me. That'd have been too weird. She was already acting like she expected some Bar Mitzvah Today-I-Am-A-Man speech. An old man with hemorrhoids, maybe.

Sunday, October 14

Rob wasn't at church today and I was gonna call and see what was up, but when we got home, the phone was ringing. Mom answered.

"Ruth, settle down; what is it?" Ruth is Mrs. Binkmeyer. "Ruth, you're not making any sense. Just slow down."

Apparently, Aaron told the family he'd joined the Marines and was shipping out to boot camp on Monday. *Way to break it to 'em gently, Aaron.* Still, I think he was right for not telling Mrs. B sooner. If he had, he'd have spent weeks opening his bedroom door to find half-melted Cabbage Patch Kids at his feet. *This is what napalm does to children, Aaron. Is this what you want to do? Burn babies? Kill women and children?* Mom kept telling Mrs. B she shouldn't worry.

171

Nothing Mom said settled Mrs. B down, so we ended up spending the afternoon at their place. When we got there, Aaron and Mr. B were gone. Bink said Aaron had stormed out, yelling that it was his life, he'd do what he wanted, and no give-peace-a-chance guilt trip from a bunch of washed-up Jewish hippies was gonna stop him.

I made the mistake of saying I didn't see what all the fuss was about. Bink rolled his eyes, smacked me upside the head, and called me a dumb-ass, saying now everyone was gonna have to listen to one of Mrs. B's lectures—*again*. He was *sooo* right it was scary.

From the way Mrs. B reacted, practically spritzing Bink and me with patchouli oil and flashing the peace sign like it was the sign of the cross and she was a Catholic perform-ing an exorcism, you'd have thought I'd said I'd pay Aaron a nickel for every Sudanese baby he bayoneted. The next thing I knew, Mrs. B'd pulled out this giant cardboard box full of crap: tie-dyes and bell-bottoms; her yellowed and tear-stained front pages of the *Chicago Tribune* announcing the assassinations of Jack, Malcolm, Martin, and Bobby; her orig-inal Woodstock LP (signed by Sha Na Na and Arlo Guthrie—*Leave it to her*, Bink said, *to get it signed by the lamest people there.*); a snapshot of a naked, unwashed, and unshaved Mrs. B trying to give a flower to some frumpy lard-ass in glasses (Bink nearly got grounded for saying the guy looked like great-uncle Irving. *That's Kissinger. What a piece of work he was . . . told me to get my tits out of his way, go home to my bubbie, and stop embarrassing* our *people.*); a bunch of news-magazine clippings of murdered Vietnamese and Cambodian women and children; and her "Hey, Hey, LBJ, How Many Kids Did You Kill Today?" protest sign.

I couldn't've been more bored.

172

Apparently, Bink's not a big supporter of Aaron's whole Semper-Fi-defend-truth-justice-and-gay-porn-in-Abu-Ghraib thing, either. When we got to school yesterday morning, the Rot-See Nazis were all over him, shoving Dana to the side and telling Bink how frickin' awesome it was that his brother was in the Corps.

HOOAH!

Tripp, you're a dumb-ass. Hooah's *the Army. The Marines are OOH-RAH!*

Screw you, Paulson. Army, Marines—it doesn't matter. Binkmeyer's brother'll be picking off towel heads from fifteen hundred yards.

Earth to Tripp He'll have an M40A3. The range on that's, like, a little over a thousand, max.

Yeah, well, my cousin knows this guy who—

"You guys really need to get laid," Bink said, brushing past them.

"And since that's not going to happen," I said, "you better go home, pop in *Red Dawn*, and jerk each other off."

"Wolverines," Dana said, flashing a clenched fist at the Rot-See dorks before we walked away.

Thursday, October 18

Rob's mom is dead. She died late Tuesday night. When I called Rob—these last few days are all blending together—Mr. Hunt answered. He told me she'd passed away. He said I could come over if I wanted to. Rob could use a friend. Mom called me out of school yesterday so we could go over and help.

We were on the couch, Rob's head resting in my lap, when he told me how it happened. He wasn't crying, but his eyes were puffy and swollen, cheeks stained with dried tears. His mom had been having trouble breathing. It had been bad. Really bad. Rob's dad wanted him to play the piano for Mrs. Hunt while he got something to relax her. They were hoping music would make it easier for her to breathe until the medicine kicked in. Rob played "Morning Has Broken" as Mr. Hunt got the medicine ready. Rob said he couldn't concentrate and kept chipping notes—easy ones. He stopped and sat next to her, holding her hand, and kept apologizing, like, if he kept talking she'd get better. Whatever Mr. Hunt gave her, it helped for a while. She looked more peaceful than she had in months—almost like she could smile again.

"It's weird, Charlie." Rob's head was in my lap and I was stroking his hair, trying not to cry. I nodded, wiping my eyes on my shoulder. "I was holding her hand and just talking . . . not really saying anything . . . and that's when she was dying. I didn't notice it. Neither did Dad. You'd think if your mom was dying, you'd notice it. I didn't."

"Shhh," I said, pressing my fingers to his lips.

For the rest of the afternoon, Mom and I helped any way we could. Most of the funeral arrangements had been made in advance, so Mom and I cleaned, straightening the house and making up the guest bedrooms. Out-of-state relatives would call and Mom would give them directions from O'Hare or Midway to their hotels, from the hotel to Flagg and Son's Funeral Home.

Tonight was the wake. Mom said we shouldn't stay too long—that this was a time for Rob and his dad to be with family—but Rob didn't want me to go. Mom said it was okay, but I *had* to call her when the visitation was over so the Hunts could have some time alone.

Rob and his dad spent most of the night standing by the casket, hugging relatives, shaking hands with Mr. Hunt's co-workers and clients, chatting quietly with Rob's teachers and old friends of Mrs. Hunt who'd grown up with her in Crystal Lake. Coach Mueller and the guys from the soccer team came, looking out of place—like they'd all bought new dress shirts for the wake and had forgotten to take out the pins. The guys paid their respects with "Rob, dude, sorry, man," and slunk to the back of the funeral home, whispering about how creepy funeral homes are and wondering where they kept the bodies. Dana and the rest of the Flannigan horde showed up. I was surprised they didn't bring a camera—you know, another family portrait. The Flannigans in white robes, all harps and halos, gathered around Mrs. Hunt's casket as they waited for her bodily ascension into heaven.

I kept to myself and stayed out of the way mostly, but once, when there wasn't a stream of people offering Mr. Hunt casseroles and condolences, I asked him and Rob if they needed a break, something to eat. Mr. Hunt told Rob he should get out, have a bite, and maybe walk around.

175

"Where we going? I can't go far," Rob said when we stepped outside.

"We can head over to The Cottage if you want. I don't think anyone'd hassle you if you ordered a beer."

Rob kicked a plastic bottle cap from the sidewalk into the gutter.

"There's the Olympia down the street. Diner food. Good steak fries, though. We can stop by Pop's Corn Crib after. Get popcorn balls. Ever have one?"

Rob shook his head, his chin quivering. He was crying, only it wasn't crying, not exactly. It was something scarier. A silent movie howl. His eyes looked raw, pinched, and almost disappeared into his face. He was shaking all over. His shoulders trembled. I didn't know what to do. I was useless. It was like when Mrs. B got back from the hospital after having one of Bink's sisters and she'd asked if I wanted to hold the baby. Amanda started wailing and I freaked, thinking I broke her and they wouldn't be able to fix her. Mrs. B took Amanda from me, laughing. "Babies cry, Charlie. You didn't do anything wrong. Sometimes, they just need a good cry. We all do." But with Rob, I wasn't sure what to do. It's not like his pain and sadness were these things that someone older and wiser could take from him.

At the Olympia, I got us a spot in the back, away from the windows and the rest of the customers. Rob collapsed into the booth, elbows on the table, his face in his hands. I pulled a handkerchief out of my coat—the one with shoulder pads so large it made the suit look like it was still on the hanger—and handed it to Rob. He dried his eyes, blew his nose, and took a menu from the waitress.

Rob got a Monte Carlo that he didn't really eat, just picked at, stabbing it with his steak fries and pushing it through the rivers of ketchup on his plate. When he seemed bored with that, he dissected it with his butter knife and started dumping whatever he could find on the turkey and ham—Sweet 'N Low, half-and-half, sugar, salt, pepper, A1 Steak Sauce.

The waitress eyed us and I half-expected her to come over and bitch at us for acting like a couple of punks who wouldn't eat what they ordered like normal, decent people. Rob broke down before she could.

"That's not her in there, Charlie," he said, jabbing his butter knife in the direction of the funeral home. He sniffled and wiped his nose along the arm of his suit. "My mom's not in that fucking box. It's not her. She didn't wear makeup, not makeup like that." A tear dropped from his chin to the table.

"I hate this town, Charlie. I hate everything about it. This wouldn't have happened in Manhattan. This shitty little town."

Seeing him like that, raging, pissed beyond tears, one minute lashing at anything, too weak, too defeated the next—it was too much. I kept telling myself to do something, say something, but it was like my voice was trapped inside me. Here's this thing that's killing him, eating him from the inside, and I couldn't do or say anything that meant shit. All I had were the empty, funeral-home "sorry's" and "she's in a better place's." What the fuck good would those do him?

"She's dead." His body shook. "It hurts, Charlie. God, it hurts."

"Come on," I said. "Let's get you back."

I opened my wallet and threw money on the table, thanked the waitress—she'd overheard Rob and was tearing up—and took Rob back to the funeral home. Rob ran to his dad, threw his arms around him, and crumbled. Mr. Hunt held Rob close to his chest, buried his face in Rob's neck, and sobbed. "That's it, let it out. Let it all out." It was the first time I'd seen Mr. Hunt lose control.

It's probably terrible to say this, but there's something showy and selfish about grief. Everybody it touches gets this look-but-don't-touch, if-you-have-to-ask-you-can't-afford-it vibe. Like there's a rule that says whoever's suffering is one up on everyone else. It makes them different, special. Unreachable. No matter how many whispered is-there-anything-I-can-do-for-you offerings we make, there's nothing in our words that's strong enough to bridge the gap. Grief's an island.

Look at me—acting like I actually understand any of this crap.

About an hour after Rob and I got back to Flagg and Son's, I needed to take a leak. There was a first-floor bathroom, but a line of old men was waiting to get in. I figured they had to be at the funeral home window-shopping or hoping for some kind of morbid test drive. None of 'em had paid their respects, which was fine with me. Old people creep me out. They're always yammering about how the world's going to hell in a handbasket, how there hasn't been any decent music since the Andrews Sisters, and how if men are wearing earrings, they might as well wear bras, too. They smell, too—the half gallon of Old Spice that still doesn't cover the scent of mothballs, fifty years of smoking two packs a day, piss, iodine, and pending death. To get away from them, I pretended someone was calling me. I shouted, "Coming, Mom," and found the bathroom downstairs.

Nobody was there, which was great until Mr. Five-Incher decided not to cooperate. As soon as he was out of my fly, he decided to stretch out, so to speak. Even though we were in a funeral home, my little guy wasn't really in the mood to do the respectful thing and settle down.

What was I supposed to do? Wait until it went away? Like that'd happen. Go back upstairs, walk around, and, like a complete dweeb, pretend like I didn't have a hard-on? Yeah, and when it got spotted—there's no hiding 'em in suit pants—what would I say? *Oh, don't worry, I always get like this when I'm around dead people* That'd go over well.

So, I hate admitting this, but I did what needed to be done. I made sure the bathroom door was locked, pushed my suit pants and underwear below my knees, spit in my palm, and with no sense of decency or shame, I jerked off.

By the time I was done with my DNA dump, the visitation was almost over. The crowd in the viewing room had thinned out. I went past the floral sprays—crosses, hearts, and wreaths, the arrangements in baskets, floral pillows—and stood next to the casket for the first time.

Rob was right. It didn't look like her. Mrs. Hunt looked waxy and fake, like the mortician guessed at what she might've looked like once. I'd been trying to do the same thing since I met her. It was only when either Rob or Mr. Hunt was talking to her that I'd maybe see a glimpse of who she'd been. A twinkle in her eyes. Something in her hands, maybe. But that was it. Everything else is just what I imagined.

I felt a hand on my shoulder. It was Rob's dad.

"How are you, Mr. Hunt?"

"I'm fine. I've known this was coming for longer than Rob has."

"Can I get you something? Coffee? A Coke?"

"No, thanks," he said, folding his arms in front of him. "You would have liked her, Charlie, if you'd gotten a chance to really know her. The two of you were a lot alike. She could talk her way into or out of anything. Had a mouth on her that went a mile a minute, but she always meant well. She had a good heart and she loved Rob."

Mr. Hunt stopped talking and bowed his head, probably remembering stuff they'd done together. I did the same thing to look respectful and mature, you know, and that's when I noticed I should've shined my dress shoes. I got worried Mr. Hunt might notice, too, and think I was being disrespectful. People get weird about things like that. I did the poor man's polish and rubbed the tops against the back of my calves.

Actually, he was staring at my tie.

"Looks like you spilled something."

Sure enough—leave it to me to make an ass of myself—there was a glob of come, glistening smack dab in the center of the tie. Not only do I gotta strangle the weasel at somebody's wake, I've gotta show the evidence to her husband. *Hey, Mr. Hunt, look at my tie. Bet you can't guess what I was doing to myself in the bathroom, can ya?* I mumbled that I must've gotten something on me at the restaurant, rushed downstairs, tore the tie from my neck, rinsed it in the bathroom sink, and then stuffed it into the pocket of my suit.

When I got home, there was a message on the answering machine. Pastor Taylor said he didn't want to impose, but it would mean a lot to the Hunts if I served as a pallbearer at tomorrow's service. Mom called him back and said I'd be honored.

Saturday, October 20

Funeral directors are creepy. Being around dead people all the time must rub off on 'em—the pasty, ooohhh-doesn't-he-look-restful faces; suits just good enough to be buried in, but nothing too flashy or expensive; and the personalities of, well, corpses. Mr. Porter, the funeral director for Mrs. Hunt, was like that. If it weren't for the fact that I actually saw him blink, I'd've sworn somebody pulled *him* out of the box and propped him alongside his own casket.

We got to church early, so we stood in the narthex—which I learned in confirmation class is church-speak for *Jesus foy-yay*—until Mr. Porter stopped futzing with the flowers, walked toward us, and said we were welcome to wait in the fellow-ship room until just before the memorial. When he found out I was a pallbearer, he apologized and said some of the other pallbearers were already in the sanctuary (actually, it's called a nave—damn Pastor Taylor), offering their condo-lences to the family.

I walked in. The assistant pastor was lighting the altar can-dles and Pastor Taylor was speaking with Mr. Hunt and his mother, her arm clutching Mr. Hunt's waist. Rob was play-ing some "Come a Little Bit Closer" on the church organ and he was singing to some dark-haired guy with a mussed-up, longish haircut but with bangs along his forehead—the guy was Rob's kind of man. The grandmother shot Rob and the guy a dirty look. Rob got up and hugged the guy and they started laughing.

"Excuse me, Mr. Hunt," the funeral director said, cough-ing softly. The guy with Rob turned around. "I'm sorry to in-terrupt, but this is Charles Stewart. Your brother asked that he serve as one of your sister-in-law's pallbearers."

"Charlie," Rob said like he was surprised to see me. "This is my uncle, Chris. My dad's little brother."

Chris was anything but little. He was nearly as tall as me, and, Christ, he was built—huge shoulders and chest, thick neck, strong jaw, and a chin with a slight point. Chris's eye-brows were straight and so close to his eyes that it seemed like he was squinting. Chris had to be about thirty, but it was hard to tell. He looked much younger and *way* too hot for an old guy. I'd totally let him do me.

"Chris," Rob continued the introduction, "this is Charlie, my boyfriend."

"Hey, dude," Chris said, smiling a big Crest Kids' grin that showed his molars. He shook my hand—his practically swallowed mine.

"And you, Robby," Chris continued. I never dreamed anybody'd call him Robby. "Stop calling me 'uncle.' I'm not that old, dude."

"But you are, *Uncle* Chris," Rob teased. "It won't be long before we're putting you in a nursing home. I got one picked out for you already."

"Shut up, punk," Chris laughed, tossing his head back. "Is he this bad around you?" Chris grabbed Rob by the wrist, twisting Rob's arm behind his back and then slamming his hips into Rob's butt pretending to hump him. "Because if he is, Charlie, this'll shut him up."

"Christopher. Robert," Rob's grandmother scolded. "Cut that out. You two should be ashamed of yourselves. Acting like that in church." Grandma Hunt walked over to Chris and gave his ear a sharp jerk.

"Robby started it," said Chris, smirking and massaging his ear.

"I don't care if he started it or not, Christopher," she said, tugging his coat into place and straightening his tie. "You should be on a leash and a leather collar with metal studs."

"Left it at home, Ma," Chris smiled. "If I'd thought of it, dude, I *so* would've worn it."

"Mom would have loved it," Rob said, "but Dad would still have told you to at least wear a blazer."

Duh. That's why Rob's dad didn't freak about us dating,

and why Rob got pissed about getting two stag tickets to homecoming. Guys liking other guys was normal in his family—at least it wasn't something they got worked up over.

"A blazer to a funeral," Grandma Hunt said, tut-tutting. "Nearly thirty and can't afford a nice suit and tie. They don't have decent clothing stores in Chicago? Just Sears? If only you got yourself a real job. Acting, I swear if your father was alive—"

"He'd drop over dead. I know."

Pastor Taylor, Mr. Porter, and Mr. Hunt walked over to us.

"When shall we expect the other pallbearers?" Mr. Porter glanced at his watch. "There are a few things I'd like to go over with them."

Pallbearers should be allowed to wear cleats and work gloves. Carrying a casket may look easy, but even with five other guys, it ain't. Even though I only held one little section, it was still heavier than it looked. It wouldn't've been bad if everybody was the same height, but we weren't, so everybody struggled to keep the box level. Then there's the cemetery itself. The ground's not flat. I kept trying not to stumble over twigs and branches or slip on some dearly departed's headstone, and my dress shoes got zip for traction because of all the dew.

The graveside service was mostly okay. Mom and I stood in the back, where we really couldn't hear too much of what Pastor Taylor was saying. When Pastor Taylor was nearly finished, I'd noticed the nurse who Mr. Hunt had fired was next to us. Rob turned around, saw her, and waved. He whispered to his dad, then pointed her out. Mr. Hunt seemed pissed. He said something to Chris, who walked over to her.

"Julie," he said, "you're not welcome here. It's best if you left."

"Look, Chris," Julie said. Her voice was cold. "Paul kicked me out once. We both know what happened after that. I just want him to see me and remember what he did to her."

"Great timing," said Chris. "He's seen you. Now get the hell out of here."

Mr. Porter, seeing the commotion, broke away from the grave and came to Chris's side.

"Is there a problem, Mr. Hunt?" Porter asked. He placed a hand in the small of Chris's back, I guess to stop him from making a scene.

"No, dude," Chris said. "This lady's leaving."

Julie puffed her chest and acted like she planned on standing there until they dragged her away, but she finally sighed and stomped off. Chris and Mr. Porter returned to the rest of the family. Mom asked if I knew what that was about. I shrugged.

It did seem kind of weird, though. I mean, I remember Mr. Hunt and Julie getting into an argument, and yeah, it seemed serious at the time, but that was, like, weeks ago. I don't know. Maybe Mr. Hunt thought Julie was there to rub it in. Like he expected her to say that if he had just listened to her about the ventilator and the other stuff, then maybe Mrs. Hunt would still be alive.

I don't know. That'd be a pretty crappy thing to say to a guy at his wife's funeral.

Sunday, October 21

Almost as soon as we left the funeral luncheon, Mom and I started fighting. Christ, I didn't even have my seatbelt on yet. She'd asked me if I'd caught up on the schoolwork I'd missed. I guess I must've sighed or rolled my eyes, or just didn't see why she needed to be like First all of a sudden and act like the weight of the free world rested on my stupid pre-calc assignments.

"Look," I said, making this whackin' big, world-weary sigh that even I have to admit deserved me getting my ass slapped back into last week. "It's bad enough getting college brochures as stocking stuffers from one parent. I can't handle both of you breathing down my neck. Just lay off for, like, two seconds, okay?"

Mom didn't say anything at first, and that's when I knew I wasn't up the proverbial creek without the proverbial paddle. No, I was in an ocean of shit, in a piss-poor canoe with no life preservers, and I was sinking fast.

"You want me to leave you alone?" Mom asked, staring through the windshield and refusing to look at me. "Fine." Her voice had the flatness of a TV show's jury foreman reading a death sentence. "I get it, Charlie. We're horrible parents for having any expectations for you."

"That's not it," I said, groaning, stubbornly folding my arms across my chest, and rolling my eyes. For some reason, even though I knew I should, I couldn't put the emergency brakes on my clichéd, teenaged persecution complex. *Look at me, I'm poor pitiful Charlie. Watch my nobody-loves-me-everybody-hates-me-I'm-going-to-eat-some-worms pouty indignation.*

"Then what is it?" Mom said. The lines around her mouth tightened and the skin from her throat to her chest looked prickly and red. She drummed one thumb along the top of the steering wheel.

"It's just that you guys never fricking let up."

"Watch the mouth."

"Whatever . . ."

And that's when I got cracked across the chops. Mom hadn't hit me since, I dunno, I was a kid and she caught me trying to jam a bent-up paper clip in an electric socket. My lower lip started quivering like I was a toddler who'd taken a spill and was just waiting for someone to ask if I was okay before I started bawling.

"Charlie, I love you, but I will not allow you to talk to me that way."

"So, you haul off and smack me?"

"You know what? I can't deal with you. Not when you're like this. Maybe you'd be better off staying with your father for a few days."

"Mom," I whined, but she'd already stopped listening. When she pulled into our driveway, she got away from me so fast it was like she thought I was radioactive.

I chased after her, shouting that I was sorry, begging her not to send me off to First's. It didn't do any good. She went inside, closing the front door—even though I was right behind her—and called First.

Here's a shocker—when First picked me up, there weren't any lectures from him about being a snotty little ingrate or how if I had mouthed off to him like I did to Mom, he would've carved me into chum and fed me to the bottom-feeders in Lake Michigan All I got was, "Bad day, huh, kiddo?"

"Yeah," I said. "It's been a real winner. You?"

"About the same."

When we got to First's place, I dumped my stuff in the doorway.

"Here we are," First said.

"Yeah," I said, taking in the place. "Here we are."

First's apartment wasn't exactly a swinging bachelor pad, unless your idea of a swinging bachelor pad is a pre-fabricated, pre-furnished rental unit decorated by some overweight, middle-aged empty nester whose design aesthetics were driven by such postmodern concepts as "cozy," "homey," and "comfy." The place was all overstuffed couches, Ikea end tables, and painter-of-light-by-numbers English cottage drywall decorations. If it weren't for one of First's suit coats draped over a stool in the breakfast nook, the rental unit could have doubled for a model home or a chiropractor's waiting room. Rental plants, soft lights, muted colors, striving suburban middle-class bland-ness.

We ate dinner together in the kitchen. Between bites of microwaveable lasagna (*All the flavor of Italy! Now with twice the sodium!*), I watched him, wondering what his life would be like if he and Mom actually did get divorced. It wasn't pretty. I could picture him frying a gray, round eye steak, cutting his hand as he opened a can of French cut wax beans. Still, the idea of him eating was practically impossible to imagine.

Seriously, what was he gonna do? Go to a bar and hit on women half his age? Or would he just spend the rest of his life being *that* guy—the divorced dad who bitched about how his ex was breaking his balls, passed out every night from a six-pack stupor, and wasted whole weekends futzing around in the garage?

"Are you and Mom talking?" I asked, actually hoping, for his sake, that they were.

"A little," he said, sopping the sauce on his plate with a piece of garlic bread. "Why? What's on your mind?"

I shrugged, trying to make him think that I didn't care one way or the other. I wasn't up for any "very special episode" father-son bonding moments. That'd be like giving him an engraved invitation to micromanage my life all over again.

"Did you guys ever split up before now?"

"What did she tell you?" He sounded curious, not defensive.

"She didn't say anything. I just heard you guys talking one night and it sounded like this isn't the first time you guys wanted to get . . ." For some reason, I couldn't bring myself to say "divorced."

"Let's just say the last time was different."

"Different how?"

He pinched the bridge of his nose, his eyes narrowed, and his thumb and middle finger stroked his eyebrows against the grain. He looked like he was debating with himself about what to tell me. When he finally spoke, his voice was tentative, all stop-start, stop-start hesitation.

"I wanted kids," he said. "She . . . your mother . . . she said she wanted them, too. And we tried."

"What happened?"

"This is really something you should be asking her, Charlie." First carried his plate to the sink and rinsed it under the faucet. He started making coffee.

"What happened?" I asked again, somehow knowing whatever it was that he was afraid to talk about was something I'd never learn from Mom.

188

"We had a miscarriage. We'd just ended the second trimester with no problems. When it happened, it was a complete shock."

"I don't remember Mom being pregnant." Honestly, I didn't.

"You had to be about three or four years old, and you were really excited about having a baby brother or sister. Afterwards, you kept asking about the baby . . . when it was coming. At first, I thought that was the hardest part."

"What do you mean?"

"Well, after the miscarriage, it was like there was this rift separating me and your mother. It wasn't anyone's fault, and I'm not sure either of us knew it was happening at first, but somehow we started pulling apart. Probably when we needed each other the most. Your mother wanted to get pregnant again. The doctors said another miscarriage was likely, but she wanted to try anyway. I couldn't."

Dad—what's the point in trying to be cute by calling him First; Christ, even I'm not gonna be a smart-ass when someone's hurting like he was—Dad lowered his head as his hand worked the back of his neck. He sighed, poured himself a cup of coffee, then sat down at the table across from me. His face was slack and he looked weak, exhausted.

"I couldn't go through that again," Dad continued, "even though she wanted to. It was just too terrible."

I asked him what had stopped them from getting divorced back then.

"We found our way back to each other. It took time, but we did it. I couldn't risk losing either of you. I think it would've killed me. And now, in some ways, it feels like that all over again."

I didn't know what to say, so I just got up, squeezed Dad's shoulder, and found my way to the apartment's guest bedroom.

The more I think about it (and that's all I've been doing for the last couple of hours), I can kinda see how First—I mean, Dad—ended up such a control freak with me. Still, it'd have been nice if he maybe told me this shit before. Maybe I wouldn't have been such a jackass to him.

Monday, October 22

Soccer practice sucked tonight. The team's really crappy without Rob. If we can't get our act together, we're gonna lose state. It's less than two weeks away.

Rob's still not back at school yet. Since Dad says I'm still technically grounded for mouthing off to Mom and I'm not supposed to basically have a life, I called Rob tonight to see how he's holding up. He said he was fine, but I could tell he was lying.

He sounded okay. Exhausted and maybe a little pissed, but he wasn't crying. I was the one who ended up doing that.

We'd been struggling through small talk—me saying I liked his family, Rob joking that, no, I *liked* his uncle; me admitting that, yeah, Chris was hot, but who'd want to date a guy who was thirty? At that age, it's complaints about bad backs, root canals, how their metabolisms weren't what they used to be, and how the price of a box of Just for Men hair coloring had gone up a buck.

Rob laughed, then asked, "Why haven't you been over, Charlie? I miss you."

He didn't sound needy or upset, and I guess that's what

killed me. I told him that I wanted to be there, wanted to hug him until he didn't hurt anymore. It's just that I was grounded, and—

And that wasn't any excuse. The last few days, I've been such a shit.

After I got off the phone with Rob, Dad hollered for me, and wanted to know who I'd been talking to. For a split second, I was half-tempted to make some comment about how I was talking to my heroin dealer and seriously, why did he always have to act like he suspected anyone I talked to was a drunk-driving, date-raping, Swastika-on-the-side-of-a-synagogue-spray-painting, kiddie-porn-loving, terrorist-funding, granny mugger. Then it dawned on me, Mr. Not So Swift on the Uptake, that maybe, Dad was just genuinely curious.

When I told him that I'd called Rob to see how he was doing, Dad started drilling me with all these totally random questions about Mr. Hunt and Mrs. Hunt before she died. Like: *Were there a lot of pills—prescription bottles at the house?* I guess. Mrs. Hunt *was* sick. *How many?* I dunno. A lot. I didn't count. *Did you ever meet a nurse named Julie Carter at the Hunts?* I guess. *Did you talk to her?* No. *What was she like? Did she seem honest?* I only saw her like once at the house and then at Mrs. Hunt's funeral. *Did she get along with the family?* Yes. No. I dunno. I heard her arguing with Mr. Hunt once. And at the funeral, she seemed, like, I dunno, she wanted to make a scene or something.

Dad's face got this very serious look when I mentioned Julie arguing with Rob's dad. "What's this about?" I asked.

Dad ignored my question. "Do you remember what they were arguing about?"

"Sorta," I said. "I think they were talking about Mrs. Hunt's treatment."

"Do you remember what they said?"

"Not really. I don't think they agreed with each other is all." I was beginning to freak out, 'cuz Dad had slipped into his old First-as-grand-inquisitor role all over again. It was like he wanted me to tell him something—God only knows what—so he could use it, God only knows how.

"Seriously, you're wigging me out. What's going on, Dad?" I asked. My knee shook and I prayed Dad couldn't see it trembling through my pant leg.

"Don't worry," Dad said, smiling. "It looks like it's nothing. Mrs. Carter stopped by our office today looking to stir up trouble. Sounds like she's just got an axe to grind."

"About what?" I asked, my voice chipping like bone china.

"Who knows? She told me she thought Mrs. Hunt's death may have been an assisted suicide, but it sounds like she's just got a bug up her ass about the family."

"So what happened?"

"Mrs. Carter didn't think I was taking her seriously, so she asked to see Fisk, so I showed her to his office."

"And?" I asked, drawing the word out so I didn't sound nervous.

"I'm not sure. Fisk left before I could ask him what he thought. Why? Is there something you're not telling me?"

"No," I said, a little too quickly.

"Don't worry, kiddo. There are some people out there who just get off on stirring up a shit storm."

Don't worry. *Right*. Fuck, I don't know what to do. Dad's probably right; the whole thing's probably nothing. I mean, seriously, you'd have to be a total flaming bitch to try and ruin someone's funeral like Julie did.

Still, what if it's true? It's not like Mr. Hunt had a reason to be ordering all those prescriptions. Who am I kidding? It's probably true. Mr. Hunt fired Julie 'cuz he knew she'd never let him end her suffering. Christ, your *own* dad killing your mom. Like *actually* planning it, getting all those pills, forcing her to take them. That's *way* too fucking intense.

Fuck. This is my fault How could I have been so stupid? Shit. I should've said something about the pills to somebody. If I had, I dunno, maybe Mr. Hunt could've gotten help. Maybe someone could have talked him out of doing it and fucking things up for him and Rob. If I had, Mrs. Hunt would still be alive—at least for a little while longer.

Shit. I seriously don't know what to believe. Part of me wants to call Rob back right now, but if this blows over or it turns out to be nothing, I'll look like a total ass. Fuck Julie Carter.

Tuesday, October 23

The thing about guys my age I'll never understand is how they freak about two dudes messing around, but give them some kind of excuse—doesn't matter how lame it is—and they're practically elbowing each other to be first in line at the butt and balls buffet.

It starts with junior high sleepovers. No worries, it's only natural to check out who's got pubes. And jacking off with a bud—hey, just to see who shoots first. By high school, pretty much anything goes—towel snapping; grab-assing; wagging your dick in front of a teammate's face and joking how he's got better lips than any chick, as long it's clear that if a real fag looked at you, you'd *sooo* kick his ass; and getting wood during the football team's elephant walk only 'cuz you were imagining that it was Kim Green's hand on your crank.

Sure, it'd be easy to say these guys are a bunch of homos-in-training. But these are the guys who knock out knuckle babies any time a girl with a big pair of tits or a nice ass saunters through the Pit. It's not really a sex thing. To them, dicks are toys. They want to show 'em off.

I guess what got me thinking about this is the Crosstown Classic. It's this race a bunch of seniors started years ago. Guys form teams of three and in the middle of the night they run across town (*duh*), wearing only shoes, socks, a bandanna, and a jockstrap. The race starts at the Crystal Lake Country Club, goes along Route 14 with a check-in at Dollar Video, and it ends at Twin Ponds, the nine-hole public golf course in town.

Over crappy pizza and way-too-greasy fries, Bink asked me if I wanted to run with him Friday night. Bink was gung ho on doing it, mostly 'cuz it'd be something he could brag about thirty years from now, instead of having to explain what it was like being the QB for the world's worst high school football team ever.

"Dana doesn't know you're running, does she?" I asked.

The Crosstown Classic was the kinda thing that'd make Dana douse her bra in lighter fluid and race for the nearest blowtorch. Of course, she'd first have to lecture everybody about "male privilege" and how guys can run nearly naked through the streets and only get "boys-will-be-boys" shrugs. But, God forbid, if a woman makes a peep about how it's her body and she can do what she wants with it, they're burning her at the stake.

Bink mopped a blob of grease from his chin and stared at me, eyes narrowing. "No, and she's not gonna, is she, Charlie?"

"Who all's on your team?"

"Me and you. That's it so far," Bink said, stuffing his mouth with half his slice. He then asked if I thought Rob would be on our team. Rob, I said, probably wasn't at the stage in the grieving process where you run across Crystal Lake in a jock.

Bink wanted to know what guys I thought could join "our" team. I suggested Jon Bales (daydreaming about watching the muscles of his ass as I ran behind him). Bink said somebody already had him. Bink suggested Eric Degrassi. Too fat, I said. He'd get us busted. Lance Willford? "Back acne" is what I thought, but said he was too slow. Joan Hawkings, I offered. It's gotta be a guy, Bink said. She's close enough. Stuff a sock in her jock, no one'd know. Chan Lin? Bink closed his eyes and shook his head in disbelief. He was right. There was no way we'd convince a Laotian Mormon to give up his Jesus jammies.

I was about to give up and back out when Bink suggested Steve Marshall. I said no. Hell, I practically shouted it. There was no way I was running with that perverted little midget, but Bink wasn't having any of it.

So now, short of a terminal illness, I'm gonna spend Friday night freezing my ass off. I wonder how you catch malaria.

Wednesday, October 24

So I finally saw Rob today. I haven't talked much about what's going on there, not 'cuz I haven't been thinking about it—hell, I'm barely sleeping 'cuz it's the only thing I can think about. I guess the reason I haven't written anything here is 'cuz I dunno what the hell I'd say. It's like every time I try to sit down and figure things out, I just get more confused and end up tearing page after page out of this damn thing.

Then there's part of me that's completely paranoid—like I'm afraid I'll write something down, and then Dad, in one of his First-esque moods, will find this, read it, and it'll turn out that something I wrote will cause a frickin' damn universe of trouble.

Anyhow, the whole Nurse Julie thing really has been eating me up over the last few days, and I finally decided it was something I ought to tell Rob about. If nothing happens, well, Rob and I can just joke about what a crazy bitch Julie is; and if something does happen, well at least Rob can't accuse me of holding out on him. So, after school today, I lied to Coach Mueller about not feeling well, skipped practice and rode my ten-speed over to Rob's house. (And for the record, driving lessons with Dad have reached a *Rules of the Road* détente—hey, I know my Roger Moore-era Bond films. If I had to guess, I'm betting the main reason he's stopped riding my ass about tailgating school buses is because he's secretly mainlining Zoloft.)

When I got to Rob's house, he was in the front yard raking leaves. I was expecting him to look like crap, his eyes all puffy and bloodshot, huge bags under 'em. Actually, he looked kinda hot with his hair mussed and shaggier than I'd seen it, bangs drooping, a shadow of blue-black stubble along his jaw. I started getting a chubby, which was *sooo* wrong.

"You're late," Rob shouted at me. I dumped my bike along the driveway. Rob tossed the rake and I caught it by the handle. "It's time for my coffee break."

"Listen, Pedro," I said, hoping Rob'd catch on to the fact that he was the only white person on his block that was outside doing yard work. I think in Turnberry, it's practically illegal not to hire Mexicans to do the crap work. "Mr. Hunt's not paying you to take coffee breaks. He'll call immigration if he catches you slacking."

"I wouldn't if I were you," Rob said, grinning.

"And why's that, Pedro?"

"Well, if I get deported, you'll be doomed to a life of Internet porn."

"Hah," I said, playing along by trying to sound way too overconfident. "There's where you're wrong. My parents don't even let me on the Internet."

"So, why aren't you at soccer practice, pup?"

I told Rob everything—about Nurse Julie going to my dad, about her trying to make it sound like Rob's dad had something to do with Mrs. Hunt's death, how she must've said something about all the prescription drugs and about her getting fired by Mr. Hunt after the two of them got into an argument, how Julie got pissed that my dad thought she was just trying to cause problems; and most of all, I tried convincing Rob that my dad didn't think there was anything to what Julie was saying. Rob didn't say anything the whole time I was talking. He just stood there, with his hands tucked under his arms, shaking his head occasionally.

"What did you say to your dad?" Rob asked, barely breathing.

"I didn't really say anything. I mean, I told him I thought Julie was a bitch and that she tried crashing your mom's funeral, and when he asked about the prescriptions I just said there were a lot of them 'cuz your mom was sick."

"Well," Rob said. He straightened his back, took the rake from me, and started walking toward the garage. "I don't believe it. Julie's obviously lying, right?"

From the tone of his voice, I could tell he was asking for reassurance. It seemed like he was committing some new concept to memory. *The boiling point of water is 212 degrees Fahrenheit. A body in motion stays in motion unless acted upon by an outside force. Julie Carter is a liar.*

"That's what my dad thinks," I said.

"What did this other guy . . . Fisk . . . think?"

"I never heard. I just thought you should know what Julie's been saying."

"Yeah," Rob said, hanging the rake on a rack in the garage. "I should probably give my dad a call."

"Want me to stick around?"

"Nah," Rob said.

It wasn't until I was pedaling back to Dad's apartment that I realized Rob and I didn't really say good-bye. The two of us didn't even touch. Now I'm not sure if he's pissed at me or if he was just in shock. I probably need to stop worrying.

Friday, October 26

Dad was wrong—dead fucking wrong—about Julie. It's a front-page story in today's *Northwest Herald*.

Crystal Lake Man Arrested in Wife's Death

CRYSTAL LAKE—McHenry County sheriff's police arrested a 42-year-old man Wednesday evening on charges of second-degree murder, drug-induced homicide, and delivery of a controlled substance after his terminally ill wife, Katherine Hunt, died on October 16 of a drug overdose.

Paul Hunt of 4300 Partridge Lane in Turnberry entered a plea of not guilty to all charges and was released on $50,000 bond.

The McHenry County state's attorney's office alleges that Hunt administered a lethal dose of the drug diazepam to his wife, Katherine, who had been diagnosed with amyotrophic lateral sclerosis (ALS). ALS, commonly known as Lou Gehrig's disease, is a neuromuscular disease that causes the largest of the body's nerve cells to degenerate, leading to muscle weakness, paralysis, and eventually death.

"Based on the testimony of a star witness, the state's attorney's office believes that Paul Hunt is guilty of homicide," said John Fisk, assistant state's attorney, during a press conference outside the courthouse. "Paul Hunt wasn't a compassionate and loving husband dutifully carrying out the last wishes of his wife. Kathy Hunt's tragic illness stripped her of her ability to communicate those wishes. Her husband stripped her of her life."

The state's attorney's office alleges that Hunt deliberately dismissed his wife's primary caretaker when she objected to his plan to deliver a fatal dose of the sedative that had been prescribed to ease muscle spasms associated with his wife's ALS.

Hunt's attorney, Thomas Reiss, dismissed the state's charges as "baseless." Referring to Fisk's campaign for the position of state's attorney, Reiss stated, "My client is being railroaded so Fisk can grab headlines. He should be ashamed of himself for political gain and that's unconscionable."

"The state's attorney's office filed charges based on the evidence against the defendant," Fisk said. "We cannot become a culture of disposability in which anyone can determine the value of the lives of the terminally ill."

Hunt is scheduled to appear in court February 25.

I never thought I'd say this, but thank God for the Crosstown tonight. It's the only thing that's stopped most of the gossip at school. Since Rob's still not back, everyone's acting like I've got the inside dirt on what really happened.

Dude, how many pills did he have to give her? How long can they put Mr. Hunt away for? I heard he ground them up and put them in chocolate pudding. How come she didn't choke? No, bro, So-and-so says she totally choked. Puked even, so they, like, made her eat more. She kept telling them to stop. C'mon, that's crap. She did not. She was a vegetable before they killed her. How was she gonna fight back? By drooling? I heard Rob was in on it, too. Like he held her mouth open and stuff.

It made me sick. Thank God for Bink. Any time he heard someone asking me a question, he'd tell 'em to leave me alone. If they didn't lay off, Bink'd pull 'em aside and explain that if they didn't shut their damn mouths, he'd be forced to do it for them in a manner that'd require a trip to the emergency room, jaw wirings, and eating through a straw.

Anyhow, I'm two hours away from strapping on the jock, tying a bandanna around my face Lone Ranger–style, and trying to make it across town before my nuts climb into the back of my throat from the cold. If Marshall hadn't shot his mouth off this afternoon, I wouldn't be worried that Mr. Five-Incher was crawling into my abdomen and turning me into a human Ken doll.

We were supposed to be doing some AP Bio lab. Marshall was useless, as usual. He kept babbling about the Crosstown Classic.

"So, what are you doing with the socks?" Marshall asked, looking up from the microscope. He was only pretending to do something class related, 'cuz Mr. B'd walked past us.

"Make hand puppets. I thought I'd sew some button eyes on 'em, give 'em little yarn wigs." Steve looked at me like he thought I was serious. "I'm wearing 'em, dork. Why?"

Marshall looked at his crotch, then down at mine. I knew what he was getting at. Neither of us was packing like porn stars.

"Well," Steve said in a whisper. "I'm stuffing. I wanna look my best for the honeys, if you know what I'm saying. Half the school's gonna be at the finish line. Once all the babes check me out, they'll all want a piece of Steve-o."

"Yeah, 'cuz every girl wants an enormous sock cock. She can diddle herself with it and keep her feet warm."

"Screw you, Stewart. You're such a fag. The guys are freaked you're gonna try and get their dicks up your Hershey Highway."

"Nice," I said.

I should go. Maybe try calling Rob again. I'm supposed to meet Bink and Steve at Bink's place in about an hour. Marshall wants us to go over the course he's mapped out—what a dork.

Saturday, October 27

Christ, Rob didn't have to take it out on me. I wasn't the one who killed his stupid gimp mom—that was his dad. Get it fucking straight. The bastard should've beat the crap out of him, not me.

Anyhow, Rob didn't turn my face into hamburger until after I finished the Crosstown Classic. I should've known last night was gonna be awful when Marshall picked me up at Dad's place.

Even though he's shorter than me, Steve and I have similar builds, which means on a good day we look like human tapeworms. And yesterday wasn't a good day. It was, like, two hours before the race, and there was Marshall, *way* too ready. He looked like an anorexic chick pretending to be a Green Beret for Halloween—bandanna tied above the forehead, black body paint creasing his chest, arms, and legs.

"Close the door already," Marshall said, "I'm freezing my nuts off."

I couldn't tell from looking at his crotch. Marshall had stuffed like he'd said he would. He didn't look bigger. He looked sick. Freakishly sick. Eight-pound-tumor-in-the-'nads sick. I laughed.

"What?"

"Nothing." I looked out of the passenger side window 'cuz if I looked at the 16-inch softball between Marshall's toothpick thighs, I'd lose it.

Things got worse for Marshall when we pulled into Bink's driveway. Bink's Ps weren't home—they'd skipped temple to go to some washed-out, ex-hippie, antiwar rally. Bink's little sisters and an army of neighborhood girls were in the front yard, trying to put a tutu and tiara on a golden retriever. They probably would've tried lipstick, too, if they could've found any. When Marshall realized he'd have to walk past all these five-, six-, and seven-year-old girls wearing only his jock-turned-bowling-ball-bag, he had the same please-shoot-me-now-and-end-the-misery look as the dog.

"Give me your coat. I can wrap it around me."

"No."

"C'mon, give it to me. How am I gonna get inside?"

"Not my problem," I said, getting out of the minivan.

"Dickweed."

I left Marshall pouting and walked to the front door. Part of me wanted to tell the girls that Steve'd take them for ice cream if they got in. The only thing that stopped me was knowing Steve would freak, slam into reverse, and back over a few kids and the cross-dressing mutt before he made it to the end of the driveway.

In his kitchen, Bink couldn't stop ranting. And not 'cuz Marshall made Bink scrounge up a pair of sweatpants and an old T-shirt. No, Bink said, nails scraping his scalp, foam at the corner of his lips, he was pissed 'cuz Marshall'd been too worried about the size of his posing pouch to figure out how we'd get our frozen butts from the finish line at Twin Ponds back to the start of the course where the car was parked. If Marshall hadn't wasted so much time stuffing, Bink bitched, we could have parked his car at the finish line and been done with it. Marshall, Bink said, was forcing him to do the one thing he didn't want to. Call Dana.

Needless to say, that was a big mistake. Dana was about as supportive as a training bra on a four year old. She didn't even stop bitching when we got to the country club. *This is total crap, Neil. You didn't think I'd find out? What were you thinking? That's right, you weren't. Ooohhh, look at me, I'm Neil Binkmeyer and I'm in a jockstrap. I'm Mr. Big Man. Jesus Christ, why am I dating a guy who's running in the Crosstown Classic?* Blah, blah, blah.

Bink finally shut Dana up by shoving his tongue down her throat. I wanted to retch. They went at it like they were trying to chew each other's jaws off. They probably would've kept going, but Kyle Weir came up to the Bug, spread his ass cheeks against the driver's side window, puckered his rosebud, and in this girly voice, said, "Kiss me, Dana. It's my turn. Kiss me." Dana looked up and Weir farted. Dana gagged like she was about to puke. I jumped out of the car, trying not to piss myself laughing.

With the exception of the sweaty guys at the end, the

Crosstown Classic was lame. Dana was right—running through Crystal Lake in the middle of the night in a jock wasn't this earth-shattering rite of passage. It was pointless. It wasn't like scandalized citizens lit up the 911 line, demanding something be done to stop the teenaged boys streaking through the city's backyards. Sure, I saw some cop cars while we were running, but why they bothered was beyond me. If they'd had any sense—*I know, we're talking about Crystal Lake's finest here*—they'd just wait along Route 14 to pick up the lard-asses on the football team as they struggled to get their man-boobs across the finish line. Even if they busted nothing but stragglers, they'd make their quotas.

Still, the end of the race was way hot. I don't know who won, but it didn't matter. I've got enough spank-the-monkey material to last me until graduation. Bob Collins—*down, boy, down*—that butt, I swear, if it was a pillow, you'd wanna drool in your sleep. Weir—yeah, he pissed on me, but I'd be lying if I said I still wouldn't lick the sweat out of his armpits. Jon Bales's jock was so sweaty it was practically Saran Wrap—clingy and nearly transparent. He's got this incredible chest—a total V-shaped torso that tapers to a thin waist—and his legs are totally covered with reddish-blond hair that looks like wisps of cotton candy.

I didn't notice Rob right away, and it would've been better if I hadn't. He was leaning against his BMW, arms folded across his chest like he was waiting for me. Dana was next to him, trying to cheer him up. They seemed trashed, like they'd been doing keg stands all night. Bink didn't think that Dana should be driving and was yelling at her to give him the keys to the Volkswagen.

Rob rocked off the fender and I walked toward him, hoping we'd go somewhere and talk. He stepped into the Beamer's headlights. A silhouette. Everything went to hell.

My nose crunched. It felt like I'd been knocked blind and my head'd been split open. I staggered backward. Blood was everywhere—around my mouth, streaking down my neck, on my chest—hot and runny. I could taste it in the back of my throat. My eyes burned.

"You fucking *knew* he was going to kill her, didn't you, bitch?" Rob fanned his fingers and massaged his knuckles.

"I swear. I didn't."

"Bullshit."

Rob swung again, splitting my lip and knocking teeth loose. I fell, skidding bare-assed across the parking lot's gravel. The stones tore my skin. My head slammed against the ground. Something smelled like chlorine. My nose throbbed like a second heart. I couldn't breathe. I could barely see. Rob glared at me with dead eyes. A circle of kids closed around us. Vultures waiting for Rob to make the kill.

"Rob—"

"You fucking let him kill my mom!"

I tried not to cry, but it just happened. I cried so hard my ribs hurt and I gasped and gagged. Blood and snot, spit and tears were all over. Rob laughed, kicked me in the gut, called me a faggot, kicked me in the nuts. I almost puked. I didn't look up. I didn't want to see Rob staring at me like I was a sideshow freak. Like I was nothing.

He kicked the ground. I winced, trying to shield myself as gravel machine-gunned my chest and arm. Dust was everywhere—my nostrils, my face, my eyes. I coughed. Blood splattered my chin and my front teeth moved.

"Leave him alone," someone said. My eyes were swelling shut. My body ached. I wiped the dirt and crap from my face and curled into a ball, hiding my face. More pain. "Leave 'im alone, Hunt," the voice repeated. It was Bink. "Or I swear I'll—"

"Or you'll what?" Rob asked.

A squad car's siren blared close to Twin Ponds' entrance. I strained to open an eye. Bink and Rob stood toe-to-toe, eyes locked, daring each other to move. Red and blue lights cut across the treetops. Kids scrambled like a fire alarm had been pulled in a home for the permanently spastic. People shoved past each other to get to cars that weren't even theirs. A girl started bawling about how her mother was *sooo* going to kill her. A few guys bolted for the woods beyond the driving range. Steve Marshall, out to win the award for Best Achievement in Stating the Obvious, kept shouting "The cops! The cops!" before diving into Rob's car. Rob backed down and walked toward his car, Bink keeping a bead on each step.

Rob climbed into the BMW, shoving Marshall across the seat. Bob Collins claimed shotgun, scurrying in after them. Shannon Debold, Dana, and a pair of legs I didn't recognize crammed into Rob's backseat all asses-over-elbows. I ran to the Beamer. If I could stop him, make him understand, then maybe things could go back to normal. I grabbed for the door and Rob triggered the power lock, leaving me tugging a dead handle.

"Rob—"

I slapped the window, smearing it with blood and dirt. Marshall reached an arm across Bob and flipped me the bird. Rob peeled away, practically taking my arm off. Bink hurled a handful of rocks, shouting, "Asshole!" The rear window cracked, but Rob kept driving. Other cars screeched after him.

I stood there, numb. Maybe I blacked out. My chest wasn't moving. My body felt cut off from my brain. "Charlie, move it," Bink said, "we gotta go, 'less you wanna get busted."

Bink touched my shoulder and it was like I'd been jump-started with heart paddles.

A cop car pulled into the parking lot, blocking off the entrance. We weren't getting out until they were gone. Bink jerked my arm and dragged my ass, stubborn-puppy like, toward the mini-putt course. Cops' flashlights chased us past hokey mock-ups of European "culture"—a scaled-down Eiffel Tower; a Big Ben that chimed every time someone sank a putt; a matador whose red, sheet-metal cape swatted balls from the hole. We collapsed behind the Dutch windmill on the twelfth hole.

When the cops left—probably headed back to Country Donuts—Bink shouted, "Ollie ollie oxen free free free," shoulder-checked me, and helped me off my ass. I caught a whiff of him—grass stains on musky skin and Ivory soap that'd just about given up. He smelled humid, if that's even possible. I don't think I've ever wanted him to hold me more. We trudged back to his car.

I grabbed the passenger side door handle and found that the Bug was locked with my clothes inside because . . . 'cuz . . . why'd Dana have to go and lock the car? What the hell was she thinking? That the moment the Beetle was out of her sight, it'd be stripped and sold for parts by a gang of shop-class rejects? That some sophomore girl, hopped up on Dexatrim and Chloroseptic Slurpees would pry the glove box open with a crowbar, steal the Triple A road map of Lake Geneva, and sell it to score her next fix? *Stupid, stupid bitch.*

Bink pulled a key from his sock and unlocked and opened the door for me. I reached across the front seat and popped the lock for him. We grabbed the clothes from our bags, dressed, and then took off. Cheek resting on the window, I caught a glimpse of myself in the side mirror. I looked like hell—purple and black bruises, raccoon eyes, nose busted, cheeks caked with dirt and blood and sweat. Worst of all I was pouting. I sucked in my lip and stopped.

Bink dropped me off at Dad's, but I knew I couldn't stay. Call me a baby, but I wanted my mom. I grabbed some of my stuff and biked over to The Cottage to catch her.

She's been pretty cool so far. More on that later.

Sunday, October 28

So, the rest of Friday night.

When I sneaked into Dad's place, he was on the couch, dead to the world, head snapped back and snoring, fingers barely clutching the cable remote. His wristwatch rested on his stomach like he'd been waiting to bust me for breaking curfew. Some black and white movie with a bunch of bad actors from the '40s was on TV.

It felt strange watching Dad sleep. In a weird way, watching him snore made me kinda feel what parents have gotta feel when they check in at night on their kids. I wrote a quick note saying I was at Mom's. Since Dad had tried waiting up for me, I felt like I owed it to him to let him know I wasn't dying in a ditch somewhere. I headed out, leaving the boob tube on to camouflage my escape.

Why Mom decided to work at a bar like The Cottage is beyond me. The place is a joke. The only people who go there are really sad South graduates, the get-on-with-your-life-already-and-stop-showing-up-at-every-home-football-game-trying-to-convince-yourself-that-you-aren't-a-washed-up-loser types. There wasn't any "catching someone at a good time" at The Cottage. Friday night was no exception. The bar was packed, the usual rejects hammered, the waitresses with those pissed-off, constipated looking faces that made them seem like they could burp shit.

Looking for Mom, I pushed my way through a group of ex-JV jocks reliving the glory of getting off the bench (*And then Coach was, like, "Johnson get in there. Game's riding on you." So I'm, like, grabbing my helmet, and the field lights, bro, they were so damn bright, and . . . Dude, fuckin' watch it. That's my goddamn beer, asswipe.*), past a table of flabby-thighed skanks sucking down Capri Ultra Lights and dollar pulls of Pabst Blue Ribbon (*Puh-leaze, that's sooo gay, Abbie! Oh my God, ten o'clock. He's sooo hot. Where? Which one? Christ, Abby. Ten o'clock! Way awesome bod! Not you, you freak. Yeah, freak. Damn, Bridget, didja see that kid's face? Yeah, what's up with that?*). I finally shoehorned a spot between a drunk whose lips seemed like they were melting off his face and some broad French-inhaling a thin cigar. Drunk nodded at me. I smiled, even though it hurt to move my face, and returned the nod. The broad turned away like she couldn't be bothered.

"Charlie, what are you doing—Jesus, your face. Are you okay?"

Mom was behind the bar, changing out a register, but when she caught my reflection in the mirror behind the shelves of booze, she flipped. Her face lost its color. She dropped the drawer she'd been holding and, don't ask me how, managed to grab me by the armpits and nearly heaved me over the bar's side.

"What happened? Who did this?" I didn't get a chance to answer. Mom's hands cupped my head and she tilted my face into the light, rolling it from side to side. One of her fingers pulled my lip down, checking to see if I still had teeth.

209

She told her boss she needed to leave and hustled me out. What surprised me was once we were out of earshot, Mom didn't yell at me like I thought she would.

"Did you bike here?" she asked.

I nodded, pointing to where I'd dumped my ten-speed. Mom tossed me the car keys and had me open the back of the Jeep. We fought to get the bike far enough inside to close the hatch.

"We're going to the emergency room," Mom said, slipping her hand into the small of my back. I shook my head. "You sure?" she asked, raising an eyebrow. I nodded and my teeth felt like the flippers in a pinball machine. "Let's go home then."

In the car, Mom stabbed her key in the ignition and the speakers coughed to life, playing "Push It" by Salt-n-Pepa.

"God, I used to love this song." Mom turned the volume down and fished through her purse for her smokes. "Every time I hear it, it reminds me of the night your father and I—never mind. At least, Charlie, I kept you from being a cliché. Christ, your father wanted 'In-A-Gadda-Da-Vida.' The 18-minute version. Wishful thinking, if you ask me. I made him change CDs."

"Huh? I don't get it," I lied. Who wants to hear about their parents bumping uglies?

"I'll tell you when you're older."

I sighed, wondering if anybody's parents ever meant that. Like, did they keep a list somewhere? *This is where babies come from, the man from Nantucket had a dick so long he could suck it, Aunt Edna wasn't at Thanksgiving last year because she was in rehab, not 'cuz she was "tired."*

"So," Mom said, ignoring me as she slid the car into gear and backed out of her parking spot, "if we're not going to the emergency room, should we stop by the grocery store? Get a couple of steaks for those shiners?" I shook my head. *Tilt! Tilt!*

She didn't ask what happened until after we'd gotten home, I'd soaked in the tub (she went all out, using the fancy bath beads that looked like opals and smelled like lilacs), and I was wearing one of Dad's bathrobes. The whole thing made me feel a little girly, but it was nice. Mom came into my room, warm milk—I always thought it was kinda gross—and painkillers in tow.

"Don't tell your father." She shook a codeine-spiked Tylenol from its brown plastic bottle into my palm. "He'd probably accuse me of giving you heroin." I popped it in my mouth and I couldn't help thinking about Mrs. Hunt. I took a swig of milk, handed the glass back to Mom, and curled up on my bed.

"It's no steak," she said, folding a damp washcloth into a roll and resting it on my eyes, "but I suppose it'll do."

I ended up spilling my guts. Verbal diarrhea. How I knew about Mr. Hunt's fight with the nurse, the pills, how I felt like shit for not telling anyone, the Crosstown Classic, my fight with Rob. Mom didn't say anything and I kept babbling; then I guess I zonked out.

When I woke up a few hours later, I heard Mom downstairs talking to Dad. They weren't arguing or fighting and Dad wasn't pleading with her to take him back, so it took me a few minutes to realize I wasn't dreaming the whole thing. Mom must've called Dad shortly after I passed out, 'cuz from what I could barely hear of their conversation, they weren't talking about Rob's near-perfect attempt to beat the ever-living piss out of me. They were talking about the charges that Fisk had filed against Mr. Hunt.

I dropped my aching ass to the ground and dragged myself alongside the heating vent on my bedroom floor for a little quality eavesdropping.

Dad was in the middle of some thought I couldn't quite follow. ". . . it may be his show, but that doesn't mean it will wind up on stage."

"I'm not following you," Mom said.

"I might be able to stop the case from ever going to trial. Hunt's attorney's right. Fisk is just using Hunt for publicity."

"So if there really isn't a case, why did your office file charges?" Mom asked. I wanted to know, too. I pressed my ear against the vent's metal grate even harder, waiting for Dad's answer.

"I'm not saying Fisk doesn't have a case. He can make one. It's just not a strong one. Even if Paul Hunt turns out to be guilty, getting a conviction will be tough. His lawyers will push for a jury trial. They'll call a series of sympathetic witnesses that Fisk won't be able to get aggressive with on cross without running the risk of coming across as a monster. I can't imagine any jury that wouldn't have at least one juror who either hasn't gone through what Hunt did or at the very least can imagine being in his situation. Knowing that, Hunt's attorneys will play hardball. They will probably argue the only way that the state can get what it's after is to let Hunt plead to some minor charge with no time."

"So, Charles, how do you fit into this?"

"I'm going to the boss tomorrow. If I can lay it all out for Ed, show him just how much of a waste of time and money this is for our office, he may pull the plug. Since he's stepping down as state's attorney, Ed doesn't have a dog in this fight, at least not politically. If he sees it my way, maybe he'll work to get the charges dropped."

"You're not doing this because of tonight, are you? You

know, Charles, if you are, you can't keep protecting Charlie."

"It's not about Charlie," Dad said. My stomach soured, and for a split second, I was like *Charles James Stewart the First, he's my hero—not!* "If getting the case dropped helps Charlie with his . . . friend . . . that's neither here nor there. It's about doing what's right. Look, you and I know what a loss can do to a family. I don't see any reason for my office to step in and make someone else's loss worse."

I found myself nodding, and then decided I was too old to be listening in on the Ps' convos.

A few weeks ago—hell, at any point in my life as a teen—if someone told me I'd be proud of my dad, I would've told him he was more full of crap than a septic tank. But you know what? Little by little, it seems like he's turning out to be an almost-cool guy.

Mom and I just got back from church. I didn't want to go, but she insisted since it was Reformation Sunday, which is supposed to be a big deal for Lutherans when we celebrate Marty Luther pissing off a pope and getting himself some hot nun action. And what a celebration—the toneless "A Mighty Fortress Is Our God" garbage, Pastor Taylor's anti-Catholic tirade about cardinals and bishops turning St. Peter's into a wall-to-wall brothel of naked Catholic boys (*that got my attention*), and then Pastor T doling out the wafers like poker chips, waving his hand abracadabra and mumbling "Body of Christ, shed for you."

The wafer stuck to the roof of my mouth. I tried working it free with my tongue, but gave up when I started thinking about how the wafer was supposed to be Jesus. He was in my mouth and He didn't taste like chicken; He tasted like envelope paste.

Feeling better? You look like crap.
—Ever consider a job writing greeting cards, Bink?
I did. Hallmark didn't like the samples I sent. Outside:
Here's to your speedy recovery. *Inside:* Because we're tired
of you bitching about how it hurts.
—I'm surprised they weren't impressed.
What can I say? Some people don't have any taste. Speak-
ing of which, have you seen Rob yet? Word has it he still
wants to kill you. Dana says his uncle's staying with him
and that his dad's checked into a hotel to give him some
space.
—I'm surprised he didn't kill me Friday night.
Well, it wasn't for lack of trying.
—But you saved me. My hero.
Did you hear that?
—What?
The sound of my eyes rolling into the back of my head.
—Cute.
What will you do when you see him?
—Dunno, but I gotta think of something fast. Choir's next
period.

As for my big brilliant plan about seeing Rob in choir—the
one where I basically avoided getting shivved by him in a hallway by wandering into third period late—well, it didn't work.
As soon as study hall let out, I headed to the boy's bath-

room by the chorus room. And since Fickle Fate likes to keep me around as her personal chew toy, Rob was at a sink, washing his hands. Before I could hightail it out of there, Rob spotted me. For a second, I thought he was glad to see me—bluish eyes widening to a twinkle, his mouth nearly to its "hey, pup" beam, but that didn't last. It was like a switch in Rob's brain flipped and he now wanted to satisfy his taste for blood by going back to me for seconds.

"Nice face. Hope it hurts," he said. He stepped toward me, feinting a jab, and I jerked back. "Wuss."

"Yeah," I said, doing one of those tight-lipped, chin thrust things the jocks do when they're trying to act like they mean business. Only it didn't make me look tough. It just proved what a dork I was.

"Jesus, you're a pussy."

Rob body-checked me, making sure his elbow got me good and hard in the ribs, and pushed his way out of the bathroom.

"Rob, look. I'm sorry."

Rob stopped, the muscles of his back tensing. "Sorry? That's rich. Charlie's sorry. Big fucking deal. That's not going to bring my mom back. It doesn't make it easier to stop hating my dad because he may have killed her."

"Maybe he didn't want her to suffer—"

"That's your excuse? You don't know shit, asshole. Fuck you, Charlie. Seriously, fuck you."

The rest of the day was cold shoulders from everyone. I got treated like I was radioactive. In AP Bio, Marshall was his usual mix of complete wannabe and mouthy little bitch— *Friday night was awesome. I still can't believe we did the Crosstown and didn't get busted. We are sooo righteous. Stewart, man, Rob totally kicked your ass; you were bawling like a little girl.*

215

Soccer practice was a bust. State's this weekend and we don't have our crap together. Coach kept yelling that we needed to get our heads in the game, but the team was too busy waiting for the Stewart-Hunt rematch, where after one hit to my glass jaw, I'd get my lights permanently snuffed out.

Tuesday, October 30

Dirty looks from Rob in choir, during passing periods, in the locker room. It seems like the whole world is on his shit list, not just me. I wish I could do something to get off it. Mom and Mrs. B say to give it time. He'll come around. It'd be nice to believe that was true, but it's not gonna happen. If I were Rob, I'm not sure I'd know who to trust or if I could even trust anyone again.

I hung out again at Bink's house after practice. The team still sucks little green apples. Mrs. B was her usual tidings-of-comfort-and-joy self. *Maybe this is just a bump in the road for you and Rob, like the poets Paul Verlaine and Arthur Rimbaud. Well, not exactly like them. They were horrible to each other—knife fights, Verlaine shooting Rimbaud in the wrist. Still, Charlie, you look a little like Rimbaud, you know. How was it that Verlaine described him? An angel in exile.* Quit it, Ma, nobody wants to hear about two dead French fruits.

Mr. B wasn't much better. *Think about it this way, Charlie, you've got it easy. When it comes to mating and courtship, Mother Nature is ruthless.* And then Mr. B launched into lectures on brood parasitism—birds dumping their eggs into other birds' nests; sexual cannibalism—some male spider from Australia would be nailing his eight-legged hottie when he, *and here's a great idea*, does a somersault so she can sink her fangs into his abdomen; and filial cannibalism, which is when Mommy Hamster dines out at the all-you-can-eat baby hamster buffet. *Jesus, why can't I have parents who aren't freaks?* Bink's sisters were the only ones saying anything that made sense. *Boys are gross. Yeah, Neil's farts smell like burning matches. Yeah, boys are stoo-pid.*

But these last two days, it's been Bink and me out on his back porch, mostly. Him smoking and glancing at the kitchen's screen door every once in a while to make sure the Ps weren't watching. And me, I just griped, practically non-stop, about how things were over with Rob and how it hurt so much. Sure, Bink acted like he was listening. I knew he wasn't. He was imagining a million different ways to shut me up (gag, chloroform, cutting out my tongue, sewing my lips shut, frontal lobotomy, smothering me in my sleep).

Tonight, though, I was three-boxes-of-Kleenex, celebrity-tear-jerker-interview awful. Over everyone's plates of polish sausage, canned green beans, and Betty Crocker scalloped potatoes, I started in on my usual I-love-Rob-I-love-him-not-I-wanna-know-what-love-is-I-don't-know-how-to-love-him verbal circle-jerk.

"Some of us are trying to eat here," Bink said, gulping down the lime Jell-O (it goes with everything, according to Mrs. B) he'd been swishing and gargling through clenched teeth. With his eyes clamped shut, Bink nudged the sausage on his plate to the edge like he was worried that processed meat might turn him into a pole smoker.

"Quit playing with your food, Neil," Mrs. B said, shooting

Bink a look that could strip wallpaper. "Why do I even bother with plates? I should put out troughs or tie feedbags to your necks."

"I'm not playing with my food, Mommy," one of Bink's sisters bragged.

A glob of potatoes plopped from Bink's fork to his plate. It sounded like someone having a rough go of it on the toilet.

"All right, you two. Enough. Behave. We have company."

"C'mon, Mom," Bink said, crossing his arms. "Company? Charlie practically lives here. And, you wanna know what really sucks?" Bink's eyes darted from Mrs. B to his dad to see if either of them would smack the taste out of his mouth. "You treat him better than you do us.

"Charlie whines and you drop everything. Most of the time it's cool, since it means you stop harping on me about my grades or Dana. And, lately, it's stopped you from wigging out about Aaron getting his head blown off in Afghanistan. Which, let's face it, normal parents wouldn't talk about that in front of their kids."

Bink's sisters started bawling, snot greasing their lips like melted butter.

"But you know what?" Bink asked, continuing. "I'm sick of it now. Forget Charlie for once, okay? What about us?"

Red-faced and shaking, Bink stopped. Mrs. B glared at him like he'd wiped his ass on the Torah. Mr. B's hands were folded, thumbs pressed together so hard they'd gone white.

"Finished?" Mr. B asked. He leaned forward and Bink flinched.

"Yes," Bink said, trying to sound defiant.

"Then eat what's on your plate."

Nobody wanted to be at the table anymore, but we ate, staring at our plates and chewing like we'd forgotten how to swallow and were just going through the motions of mashing wads of wet cardboard between our gums. Mrs. B said there was chocolate cake for dessert, but I said I should be getting home. Mom would be expecting me. I think she nodded. Bink didn't say anything. He didn't even look at me.

Wednesday, October 31

Bink and I, we're cool again. During study hall today, he apologized for being a dick ast night. The only reason he got pissed was that I was sounding like Dana. *Ouch*. He just couldn't take it. Can't say that I blame him really. I should've kept my mouth shut.

Thursday, November 1

Believe it or not, Rob stopped by last night. Not for a hot grudge fuck that would've had my arms pinned to the green felt of a pool table (naturally, Rob'd hold the pockets for more leverage), 'cuz a half inch of slate's got no give. No, Rob and a bunch of guys from South were out front, egging and TPing our house. It was too dark to see who was piling out of Rob's Beamer, but I recognized the voices of a couple of guys on the soccer team—Bales, Collins, Weir. Dumbasses. I should've called the cops, not 'cuz I was ticked about getting TPed, but because they were begging to get caught.

They didn't care about slamming car doors, leaving the head-lights on, or that Weir was on his cell phone, telling some chick he had a bone he wanted to bury. They might as well've taken out a full-page, four-color ad in the paper announcing their plan, trained searchlights on our house, and invited the entire U.S. Marine Corps Band to march across the lawn play-ing "Stars and Stripes Forever" loudly enough to make the neighbors think they were double-timing it to Baghdad.

What I should've done is gone downstairs, taken their damn toilet paper, and trashed our place myself. A group of retarded quadriplegic fifth-grade Girl Scouts in wheelchairs could've done better. They really were that bad. It was just eggs and toilet paper—no boxes of Uncle Ben's Minute Rice emptied onto the grass (try cleaning that crap up after a thunderstorm), no smoked kippers tossed into the basket-ball net, no fertilizer burning misspelled obscenities in the lawn, no bags of flaming dog shit on the front porch, no pigs' feet in the mailbox. Amateurs.

I sat in the dark, wondering why they even bothered. It's not like Mom's yard was this wooded wonderland and I'd spend three months cleaning crap from tree limbs. There was just one skinny sapling in the middle of the yard, a two-foot-tall pine tree that'd been dying since Dad planted it last summer, and the basketball hoop I'd backed into during one of Dad's first "driving lessons." *You see this? It's a rearview mirror. It's there for a reason. Do you have any idea how many children are backed over each year by people who don't check the rearview mirror? Do you even know what they do in prison to people who kill children in vehicular homicide incidents?* Even though they wouldn't need more than a four-pack of Charmin to do the house up in style, Rob and his friends seemed to be having a riot. I went down, flipped the porch light switch, watched Rob and crew scatter, and then went to bed.

I can't be the only one this happens to (it's not one of those things I can ask other guys about), but when I woke up after a wet dream about Rob fucking Bob Collins (*way fricking hot*), I had a total zombie hard-on, the kind you beat and beat, and once you think you've finished off, it lurches back to life, piss-slit opening and closing like a tiny, undead mouth.

Even after making Mr. Five-Incher suffer through three rounds of getting sandpapered against my mattress and he couldn't cough up anything else, he still wouldn't stay down. I only got him under control after I'd shit, showered, and shaved (a once-a-week ritual—the shaving part). I dressed, then went downstairs and cleaned the yard.

Friday, November 2

Soccer finals are way the hell down state, deep in roadkill-eating, sister-fucking, redneck country, so we had to leave way too early—like three a.m. And, I swear to God, like, the whole damn bus ride, Rob was trying to piss me off.

But it's cool, 'cuz we sooo got a break at quarterfinals this morning. We totally dodged the Granite City Warriors and got the Brother Rice Crusaders out of Chicago. Slaughtered 'em three-one. Yeah, I missed one up in the first half—hell, the first five minutes of play. Guess that's what I get for paying more attention to Rob and Bob Collins' grab-assing than my own shit. (Rob and Bob . . . c'mon, it's like they're the perfect names for a gay retread couple.)

Like I said, Rob basically spent the morning giving me the *et-tu-Brute?*-let's-just-see-how-much-more–"as seen on TV"– cutlery-I-can-plunge-in-your-back treatment. On the bus ride down, he went out of his way to jerk my chain—making sure he got a seat next to Bob, whining to anyone who'd listen about how we weren't going to take state 'cuz our defense sucked (Coach Mueller eventually told him to zip it), conning Bob into giving him a back rub, and making sure to smirk at me as Bob's hands kneaded his shoulders.

It was worse in the locker room. The three of us ended up changing into our uniforms next to each other. Once Collins had his shirt off, Rob was all *You been working out, dude? Let's see who's got the bigger pecs, tighter abs, thicker calves, and biggest barely concealed boner.* The whole time, Rob kept glancing back at me to make sure I was taking it all in.

Out on the field, the two of them actually got gayer, even though I didn't think it was possible. After practically every one of our team's plays, the two of them would start man-hugging and patting each other's asses. It was so bad that if there'd been Clydesdales or college coeds with huge knockers on the field, I would've sworn I was trapped in a beer commercial. I had to look away. That's when one of Brother Rice's forwards nailed one to the back of the net. Dad winced, burying his eyes in his hands. He shook his head and then wiped his mouth.

"Yo, crotch rot," Josh McCullough said as he cuffed the back of my head. "You think you can, I dunno, tend the goddamn goal?"

McCullough was a total jagoff the rest of the game. I swear he let a few Crusaders slip by just to make me pay for missing a shot.

But what really sucked was that if it wasn't for Rob we'd've been shut out. He got all the goals. Our offense was so crappy that one of our forwards (*I don't wanna humiliate anyone— especially not Jon Bales—so I won't name names*) practically gave the Crusader halfbacks engraved invitations to steal the ball. Hell, he'd've played better if he sat in the middle of the field and picked dandelions. A Crusader might trip over him.

Just to frost my cake, Rob had to be diplomatic—mostly— about pulling our asses out of the fire. Despite the back-slapping and high-fiving in the locker room, Rob took it in stride—tucking his awww-quit-it-fellas-you're-embarrassing-me smile into his shoulder. It wasn't just him, he said, absently polishing the topside of his cleats on his calf, it was a team effort. If it weren't for everybody's help, Brother Rice would've beaten us one-zip. The guys ate it up. Of course, he looked at me when he made his one-zip dig. I grabbed my gear and headed out. I didn't wanna get in the way when they all hailed the conquering hero by dropping to their knees and sucking Rob off.

As I pushed my way through the door, Dad was hovering outside the locker room. He threw his arm around my back, "good game-ed" me, and tried to tousle my hair, but I dodged his hand like a skittish dog. I was still pissed about letting the Crusaders score and wasn't exactly up for celebrating— especially when I knew all the guys were still wondering why, if I wasn't a contortionist, I had my head up my ass during the first half of the game.

"What's wrong?" Dad asked.

"Lemme see . . . oh yeah, I missed the easiest shot in the history of soccer."

"Don't worry about it," Dad said. "Look, I asked your coach if I could take you to lunch for some father-son bonding. He said it's fine as long as I get you back in time for semifinals."

"Nice of you to ask me."

Even though the idea of being seen in public with the Ps would normally have me wanting to nurse on the business end of a service revolver—especially when Dad had come right out and said he was gung ho for some Harry-Chapin-we'll-have-a-good-time-then lovefests—lunch with Dad would be better than watching the team *me-first-me-first*-ing to see who'd get to bury their lips in Rob's ass.

We ended up at some Western-themed steakhouse. When we walked in, the bartender looked up from the beer glass he'd been spit-shining (I kid—*barely*) and scowled at us.

"All ya'll lost?"

"No, sir, I reckon we're hungry," Dad said, his voice slipping into a twang. It was more embarrassing than my summer sports physical when the doctor told me to turn my head and cough, and my dick saluted him. I wanted to silently crawl into a corner somewhere and die or make up some kind of excuse for him. *Sorry, my father hasn't been the same since his stroke.*

The five guys at the bar swiveled in their stools, pushed up the brims of their Stetsons and bills of their seed company hats, and eyed me like I was in lace panties instead of soccer shorts and a flimsy jersey. My face burned. Dad smiled like a brain-damaged chimpanzee. I half-expected someone to say Dad had a "real purdy mouth."

The bartender shouted to someone named Lurlene about having customers, and the guys went back to nursing their Coors. Can't say I blamed them for drinking in the middle of the day. How could you live in downstate Illinois and still be sober?

"How y'all doing today?" a woman—Lurlene, I guessed—asked. She was a short thing with straw-colored hair and a voice burnt raw by a three-pack-a-day smoking habit. "Y'all here for the soccer competition?" Clearly, Mensa hadn't rushed to beat down Lurlene's door.

"Yes'm," Dad said, hooking his thumbs in his belt loops and hitching up his parts, looking more Roy Rogers than John Wayne. I could've killed him. Lurlene didn't notice, though. She led us to a wagon wheel table and under a whackin' big cowbell bolted to the wall.

"What's that for?" asked Dad.

"Hon," Lurlene said, finger pointing at an item on Dad's menu, "we ring that bell anytime some fool with eyes bigger than his stomach orders our Biggest Toad in the Puddle special. Clean yer plate in two hours, and y'all eat for free."

Dad smiled, boasting he'd not only order it, but he reckoned he was fixin' ta finish it. *Go ahead*, I thought, *just make complete jackasses outta us. I mean, really, why stop now?*

I have no idea why Dad thought he'd be able to finish the Biggest Toad in the Puddle. The thing included the Dude Rancher, a 72-ounce porterhouse steak; a bowl of Blazing Saddles chili, which the menu bragged was "hotter than a burnin' stump and fiery enough ta scald yer rump"; a side of Kiss My Grits; two ears of buttered sweet corn; Bronco Bustin' red beans and rice; a baked potato, smothered in bacon-wrapped bacon, cheese, jalapeños, red onion, and sour cream; and a slice of Lurlene's own husband-pleasin' apple pie served *Remember the Alamo-de* (Dad actually thought that was clever) and topped with a slice of cheddar cheese. Lurlene asked what I wanted. I told her to give me what was left of the cow after they finished butchering it for Dad. She laughed like I'd been flirting. Her pencil made one last scratch on the pad, then she walked off to the kitchen, bumping the jukebox with her hip as she breezed past it. The thing sprang to life, playing some song that sounded like a semi's horn whine as it passed a car doing seventy. The music got fast—like there was a fiddler trapped in the jukebox trying to saw his way out—and without meaning to, I was bobbing my head along with the music. Dad smiled at me. And yeah, it shocked me, but I smiled back.

"Neat place, isn't it?" Dad asked. I glanced around—mechanical bull and souvenir shop *sooo* over-the-top you had to laugh. It was crammed with license-plate-sized belt buckles, Tony Lama boots, hideous plaid shirts with stepmother-of-pearl snaps, and tons of plastic crap: plastic tomahawks, baby dolls dressed like squaws, six-shooter cap guns. Have Gum Will Travel bubble gum. It wasn't neat, it was hokey. I didn't care.

"Yeah," I said. "I guess it is."

"You were really good this morning."

"Yeah, well, tell that to the guys on the team. I'm the moron who cost us a goal. According to them, Rob's the only reason we won."

"What do they know?" Dad slapped the table. I wasn't sure if I jumped from being startled or from an aftershock. "Christ, Charlie, how many saves did you make? Twenty? Twenty-five? If the other team got those goals could Rob make up the difference?"

"It doesn't work that way."

"Then you know what, Charlie? Screw them. Keep doing what you're supposed to. It doesn't matter what anybody thinks. If the rest of the team'd done their jobs, when would you have seen the ball?"

I nodded. He grinned like he knew something I didn't.

Another song came on and Dad chuckled. I asked what was funny.

"Back when I was in law school, your Mom and I'd dance to this at a bar we always went to—a real dive. Quarter pitchers of Schlitz. What was I saying?"

"Some dive bar you and Mom went to—"

"An absolute dive bar," he said, leaning forward. "Place was filthy—walls yellow from all the smoke, busted-up seats, floors so dirty your shoes stuck—but it had an amazing jukebox. We'd go with this other couple, and for some reason, the gal . . . what was her name? She'd always play this song, 'Don't Come Home a Drinkin' (With Lovin' on Your Mind).' Loretta Lynn. Your mom and I'd sing to each other, spinning around on the dance floor."

It was hard to picture Mom and Dad dancing together. I was about to ask about it when Lurlene brought the food, her wrist threatening to snap under the weight of Dad's plate. Not batting an eye, Dad draped a napkin across his lap, carved into his porterhouse, and asked what the team's chances were for the rest of the finals.

I said I wasn't worried about the semifinal game. We were up against Palatine. We'd played the Pirates during the regular season and sure, they had some really strong guys on the team, but that actually was good for us. Their forwards all thought they were better than each other. Even if someone else had a better chance to score, their forwards wouldn't pass. They just went for the shot. Dad nodded, hefting another forkful to his mouth. Beating the Pirates would depend on our halfbacks and fullbacks. They needed to pressure Palatine's forwards to play more aggressively than they should. If they did, we had a pretty good chance of winning.

The trick for us, though, was making sure our forwards didn't play too hard. If we beat the Pirates, we'd need all our energy. We'd probably face Granite City for the championship on Saturday.

Man, those guys know defense. They won state last year, went to semifinals the year before, and won state three years ago. It's still pretty much the same team—a bunch of seniors who've been playing together their whole lives. They play the field like music.

Dad raised an eyebrow. Yeah, I said, that sounds weird, but the way they move—it's amazing. But honestly, and I'm not being a pessimist, I don't think our chances of winning are so hot.

"But, I guess I just need to do what I'm supposed to," I said.

Dad had the kind of grin on his face I'd seen on Mr. B when Bink actually completed a pass (*to somebody actually on South's team*), which, let's face it, was kind of rare. Real pride. I felt blood rushing to my cheeks and looked down at my plate and my barely touched T-bone. Dad's was empty. *Ding, ding.*

After lunch, Dad asked if I had my learner's permit. I did, but only 'cuz I'd been too lazy to take it out of my wallet. He had me drive. He managed not to swear the whole drive, not even under his breath, and only stomped the imaginary brake twice (*a new record*).

Dad and I got to the field before the rest of the team, but not before the Pirates. They were running drills with military precision and playing a helluva lot better than they had during regular season. When the rest of the team showed up, they got nervous, too. During warm-ups, our passing was crap and the retreads from F-Hall could've played better defense. Hell, Jon Bales muffed dribbling, getting tangled up in his own footwork, his face going teeth to turf. It wasn't pretty.

Coach Mueller was ticked. He huddled us and, forgetting we weren't in one of his English lit classes, launched into

this eyes-glazing, yawn-hiding pep talk about how we few—
we happy few—needed to get in the game, 'cuz, the under-
classmen still abed in Crystal Lake (*huh? it was two in the
afternoon*) would be ticked they weren't here when we won.
We didn't know if we should shout "Go Gators!" or guess
what he'd been paraphrasing. Thirty empty eyes and fifteen
open mouths gawking at him was too much. Coach looked
away. He spotted Rob outside the huddle, staring at the side-
line.

I saw what was up. Mr. Hunt was there and Rob was glaring at him, any compassion dissolved from his eyes, like he
wanted to forcibly disconnect his dad's head from his neck.
Mr. Hunt stared back at Rob with this broken, defeated look,
almost like he was trying to apologize by telepathy. Part of
me wanted to say or do something that'd make it right between the two of them—I mean, hell, even Dad and I were
finally trying to work through our crap—but I knew that the
shit between the two of them didn't compare to my being
a smart-ass and Dad having been First.

"Plan on joining us, Hunt?" Coach said. "Or do you think
after winning the last game you're better than the rest of
us?" It was a lame joke, but a couple of halfbacks still laughed.

Rob walked to the huddle, looking back to make sure
nothing else happened, and managed a muffled, "Sorry, Coach."

Coach ran through the strategy. *Change of plans. The
Pirates'll expect us to run a standard 4-4-2 formation. We
could play that and still beat them, but I want you guys to
play 3-5-2. McCullough, you're moving to midfield. I'm counting on you fielders to share the work. I want fluid play out
there, got it? Stewart, can you handle being down a fullback?* I nodded, ignoring Josh's smug sighs and pissy looks.

We lost the coin toss, which left us royally shafted for the
first half. The Pirates' captain chose to put the sun behind

their goal and the wind against us. Our halfbacks struggled. Palatine almost never left our half of the field. I ended up blocking fourteen shots—two I had to dive for and one I was forced to tip over the crossbar. Bales bitched that I just set the Pirates up for a corner kick. It didn't do them any good though. I scooped the ball and bounced it to McCullough. Josh volleyed the ball out of the fray, sending it to Rob who was wide open. Rob was still too busy giving his dad dirty looks to realize what was happening on the field. I lost it.

"Pay attention, Hunt," I said, shouting so hard that the tendons in my neck felt like wire coat hangers. I wanted to run from the goal box and smack Rob back into reality. Rob snapped to and rushed a breakaway dribble down the side-line. Bales shrugged free from the thick of Palatine halfbacks, bolting full sprint, and pirouetted outside the six in front of the Pirates' goal. Rob kicked, punting hard and *way* too high. Bales leapt like he was gonna overhead volley like Pelé in *Victory*. Instead, he did a backward head flick and nabbed our first point.

By halftime, the team went from treating Rob like he was a god to practically asking for directions to the nearest lumber-yard so they could scrounge up two pine boards to nail Rob's ass to. McCullough was the worst. He wouldn't let up. When Mueller said he wanted us to keep looking for the shots, Josh said it'd be a helluva lot easier if Rob took his thumb out of his ass.

"Jesus, McCullough, lay off already," I said, not sure why I was in Rob's corner. "No one wants to hear your crap." I got a sickly looking smile from Rob and a gee-there's-a-surprise-one-butt-boy-sticking-up-for-another sneer from Josh.

The second half went better. Our halfbacks kept the play by Palatine down. McCullough nailed our second goal—

cherry-picking the ball from the Pirates' defense and nudging it past the goalie with an instep tap. He may be a prick, but it was an awesome play.

Still, I'd have been happy with a one-zip victory if it meant not having to room with McCullough.

When Coach Mueller said we were bunking together, Josh had a dump-the-milk-in-Canada, Chernobyl-sized meltdown, temper-tantrum-ing about how he wasn't sharing a bed with a queer and, if I so much as breathed my "gay" on him, he'd kill me in my sleep. I dealt with it like a ten year old. I pouted and hung out in the parking lot until it was too cold to be outside.

I unlocked the door and checked out our room. Complimentary copy of *USA Today* on the desk near the front window. Desk chair missing. Old color TV with aluminum foil wadded around its rabbit ears. Nightstand topped by an alarm clock and Gideon Bible. One king-sized bed with McCullough's stuff covering it like he had dibs. It's a miracle he hadn't pissed on the comforter to mark his territory. The shower was running, which explained where the chair was—wedged under the doorknob inside the bathroom.

I guess Josh was freaked he'd be trapped in a homo version of *Psycho*, where I'd sneak into the bathroom—*in a granny dress, of course*—jerk the shower curtain back, and then plunge Mr. Five-Incher in and out and in and out of Josh's tight little jock butt. *Like that was gonna happen.* He was probably showering in a pair of swimming trunks.

Since McCullough was being a dick, I decided to be one too. The only thing separating the bed's headboard in our room from the headboard next door was two pieces of quarter-inch drywall and some insulation. So, I climbed on the bed, kicked Josh's crap out of the way, and jumped up and down. With each crash of the headboard, I moaned things like, "Oh, yeah, McCullough, keep taking it. Oh, yeah. You know you like it. God, that's sweet."

It didn't work the way I'd hoped—the team thinking that I'd used Josh like a prison bitch. I'd been having too much fun shouting stuff—*Damn, that's hot, dude. Yeah, Josh, you're so tight. Charlie likes!*—that I didn't notice Bales, hands cupped around his eyes, peering through the window. I stopped jumping.

"Sad, man," Bales said, a laugh snorting through his nose. "Really sad." He walked away.

I got off the bed and pulled the blinds closed just as Josh came out of the bathroom, fully clothed—and I mean, fully clothed—socks, shoes, blue jeans, undershirt, T-shirt, sweater, bubble wrap, duct tape, mummification gauze, biohazard suit, deep sea diving helmet. He scowled at me, grabbed the newspaper and the Gideon from the desk, crumpling their pages and dropping them around the bed. I asked what he was doing.

"Protection, faggot. If I fall asleep and you try to jump me, I'll hear the paper move. And if I don't—"

I bit the inside of my cheek while Josh explained his Russian-nesting-doll theory of pajama armor from unwanted, pervert-making dick-on-dick swashbuckling. Under his jeans, he'd said, he was wearing a pair of boxers, under which were a pair of tighty whities, under which was a jockstrap, under which was a cup, under which, he said, I sure as hell was never gonna see.

"Christ, McCullough, I know I'm not going to see it. In the four years we've been on the soccer team together, I've never seen it once in the showers."

"Ha, ha," Josh said coldly.

"You think I'm joking? I'm not. During freshman year, a couple of guys on the team seriously asked me if there was something wrong with you, like, medically."

"Bullshit." McCullough threw a pillow at me and I batted it away. "I'm fucking bigger than you, pin dick."

"You been checking me out, Josh? Did you like what you saw?" I asked. I grabbed Mr. Five-Incher, gave Josh my best you-*sooo*-make-me-wet-down-there softcore porn look. and ran my tongue along my teeth. It killed me not to break out laughing.

"I'm telling Coach. You're fagging out."

"Yeah, McCullough, that's exactly what I'm doing. I want your cock, even though the thing is smaller than those mini ears of corn you get in Chinese food."

Josh's face went red. He gulped, practically swallowing his Adam's apple.

"The chicks don't think I'm small," he said, his voice cracking. He sounded like he was trying to convince himself it was true.

"What chicks?" I asked, laughing. "Midgets?"

"Lots of girls . . . you wouldn't know them. Ones up in Canada."

"How convenient."

"Whatever. When my family was in Montreal this past summer, this one chick couldn't stop playing with my dick."

"Did she think it was cute?" I asked, setting the bait for Josh's further indignities.

"Hell, yeah."

"Figures," I said, stroking my chin like I was contemplating some deep truth. Actually, I just wanted McCullough to bite so I could piss him off even more.

"Whaddja mean 'figures,' asshole?"

"McCullough, don't tell me you never noticed how girls are always saying little things are cute . . . kittens, puppies, babies."

Josh's eyes looked runny and he sniffed his nose. I was breaking him and it felt *good*.

"Well, even if your imaginary girlfriend in Canada thinks you've got a massive dick, that's not what the girls at South think."

"Shut up."

"It's true. One day, at lunch, a bunch of senior girls came up to me, wanting to know what all the guys were *really* like." I was lying, but it didn't matter. McCullough was eating it up. "They wanted to know all sorts of sex stuff. You know, did Binkmeyer have red pubes? Was Kyle as wide as a beer can? Did Piers, the foreign-exchange student, have a foreskin? If he did, did it really look all gross and stuff, like a turtleneck pulled over someone's head?"

Josh shifted nervously in the bed. His body tensed and he locked his arms across his chest for double-extra protection.

"They asked if it was true that you had an innie," I said. "And they weren't talking about your belly button."

McCullough chewed his lip. His forehead was pinpricked with sweat.

"Whaddja tell them?"

"It doesn't matter," I said, tugging the spare blanket around my shoulder and rolling over. "Good night."

"No. Whaddja say?"

"I said I didn't know."

The bedsprings creaked. I popped my head up. Josh's face was in the pillow and he was mumbling how it wasn't true.

It's been three hours and McCullough hasn't come up for

234

air. He keeps whimpering "I'm not an innie. I'm not an innie." About a half hour ago, I was feeling bad for him, so I told him that chicks know some guys are grow-ers, not show-ers, but that set off a crying jag. Now I just wish he'd shut up and go to sleep, 'cuz I'm tired and can't think of anything else to write.

Monday, November 5

They say Granite City trounced us four-to-one on Saturday. I don't know. Thanks to a skull-sloshing, Grade 3 concussion during the game, I don t remember Saturday at all. Sunday's a blur. Today's been fair-to-partly-cloudy at best. According to Dad, I checked out for about five minutes after diving head-first into a goalpost for a save. Mom says (she'd driven down-state once she got off work Friday night, I guess) she nearly flipped when the referee didn't notice that I wasn't getting up right away.

Supposedly, when I came to, I was completely out of it. My pupils were way huge, which I guess isn't a good thing. I couldn't count backward from ten without getting stuck at nine. Dad said that while I was arguing with the ref about how I could still play, I opened my mouth so wide I looked like a snake dislocating its jaw, and blew chunks—hosing the ref, shirt to shoes. After that, it was an ambulance to the emergency room and an overnight stay for observation.

The hospital absolutely sucked. They put me in one of those hospital gowns that barely covered my practically nonexistent butt. I felt like such a dork. Any time I had to piss, somebody—Mom, Dad, the nurse, but no, never the cute blond orderly with the freckles and forearms—had to walk me to the bathroom and wait outside in case, I don't know, I, like, keeled over dead. On top of that, it felt like spinal fluid was leaking from my ears. The doctor wouldn't give me anything but these orange-flavored, chewable non-aspirin painkillers, which made the headaches worse 'cuz I had to chew 'em. Then EVERY S-I-N-G-L-E HOUR Saturday night, some nurse with old-lady orthopedic shoes thundered into my room to wake me up.

Sleeping all right?

Not anymore.

Sorry, doctor's orders. We want to be sure you don't slip into a coma.

I should be so lucky.

You're such a pill, Charlie, you know that, don't you?

Yeah, you keep waking me up to tell me.

I don't care if this makes me seem like a baby, but I was glad Mom and Dad spent the night. No matter how tough I tried to act, I was scared. The nurses had me freaked out about comas and strokes; every time I drifted off to sleep, I had nightmares about everyone thinking I was dead when I really wasn't. (Okay, so I'm more than a little irrationally creeped out by the idea of being buried alive.) I don't care, go ahead, hand me a binkie, I didn't want the Ps to leave. I was in the hospital and, for as much as I rag on them, the Ps have been awesome when it comes to my "dire" health crises—real or imagined. It really takes a special class of people to ply you with dry toast and flat ginger ale, after they've spent God knows how many hours sitting on the edge of the bathtub, pressing a cold damp washcloth to the back of your neck as you vomit against a just-bleached toilet seat. Hell, back in first grade, I had my tonsils out, and I remember that Dad stayed home with me for a few days after my surgery, and the two of us gorged ourselves on mint chocolate chip ice cream for breakfast, lunch, and dinner. When I was nine, Bink and I managed to get both of my ankles sprained at the same time (don't ask), and Dad spent the week lugging my scrawny ass up and down the stairs in our house. And who can forget seventh grade, when Mom basically spent three days as my seeing-eye dog after I wound up getting both my corneas scratched and matching eye patches in gym class? Leave it to me to make square-dancing a full contact sport. I don't always like admitting it, but Mom and Dad have always been there for me—whether it's been me in a pair of footie pajamas hollering for a drink of water, or me in a T-shirt and a pair of Umbros shouting for them 'cuz I was convinced that the wood grain patterns on the back of my bedroom door looked like a hell-bent, knife-wielding psychopath ready to spring on me and carve my heart from my ribcage. I don't care how old you are, there's just times when you need your Ps.

On Sunday afternoon, when the neurologist was convinced I wasn't any more brain damaged than normal, he gave Mom and Dad a rundown of what to expect from me. *Keep in mind, he's probably going to feel nauseous and have headaches on and off for the next few days . . . no soccer, no gym, no exertion for two weeks. He may experience some disorientation, irritability, sleepiness, sensitivity to light.*

"I take it you don't have any teenagers of your own, doctor," Mom said with a laugh.

The only time Mom and Dad argued, if you could even call it that, was before the drive home. Mom wanted to take me in her car, but Dad said it'd be better if I was in the Olds because I could stretch out in the backseat. Dad even handed her the keys and said he'd drive the Jeep back to her place.

I spent the rest of Sunday and most of today at home resting, listening to Mom and Dad try to piece together as much of Saturday for me as they could. They seemed surprised I couldn't remember that the guys'd stopped by the hospital to tell me I'd been named MVP for the season— probably on a pity vote. Even still, that had to make Rob's ass chew gum. After dinner, when I was resting on the couch, the phone rang. Dad answered. He said it was Josh McCullough calling to see if I was okay, but when Dad asked him if he wanted to talk to me, he said no, he should probably let me rest.

"It's nice that your teammates care," Mom said. "That has to make you feel good."

"A new head would feel better."

Dad laughed and made like he was going to tousle my hair, but when I flinched, he thought better of it and chucked my shoulder.

Maybe I'm still out of it. The more I think about things, nothing makes any goddamn sense. Mom and Dad staying together under the same roof. Josh McCullough calling to see if I was okay.

Something doesn't add up. I'm too beat to figure it out.

Tuesday, November 6

Today was Election Day, which for the average American meant it was just another Tuesday.

For me it meant hauling my ass out of bed at five in the morning and joining Dad at the makeshift polling place at

238

West Beach's field house. While he was shaking hands and begging for last-minute votes, my job was to hand out dough-nuts, coffee, and pamphlets to the busloads of the Fixodent and fixed-income set who only skipped their breakfasts of tinned cat food with prune juice chasers to vote down a referendum to provide school kids with heated classrooms, text books, and running water. After Mom dropped me off, I expected her to vote and head home. But she actually stuck around, grabbed a stack of voter's guides from me, and helped pass them out before she had to take me to school.

"I don't get it," I said as we climbed into the Jeep. "Are you and Dad getting back together?"

The sun was coming up, which still bugged me a little, so I slipped on the Ray-Ban Wayfarers I'd been wearing since Sunday. There's something about sunglasses that lets you get away with stuff you normally wouldn't. Like people won't call your bluff when they can't see your eyes. I thought they made me look good in a geeky-cool kind of way. Mom didn't agree.

"You look like a drug addict wearing those," she said, looking over her hands as she lit a cigarette. She waved the pack at me, offering me one. I shook my head. "I know, I know. I should be the one telling you not to smoke. But if you smoked, I wouldn't feel guilty doing it."

"Yeah, Mom, that makes perfect sense. So are you?"

"Am I what?"

"Getting back together with Dad?"

Mom exhaled, smoke streaming from her nostrils like a cartoon bull. "Your father's worked hard for this. The least we can do is show him some support."

"So, are you letting him move back in?"

I wasn't sure I knew what I wanted her answer to be. I

actually kinda missed not having him constantly breathing down my neck—at least, a little bit.

"We'll see." Ending the conversation, Mom fiddled with the radio dial, searching for something other than WAIT's Iraq War–boosting broadcast ("Rock the Casbah" and "Midnight at the Oasis"). She'd almost breezed past what sounded like the Velvet Underground, but I grabbed her elbow and made her stop.

"This?" Mom asked, snickering. I nodded, and she threw her hands up in a what's-to-understand shrug as she pulled into the entrance of South's parking lot. Then Lou had to go and embarrass us, ordering Severin to taste the whip, kiss the leather boots. I couldn't have gotten out of the car faster if I'd been pushed.

Even before classes started, things were different at school. The guys from the soccer team wanted me to sit in the Pit with them, wondering why I hadn't been there all season. Funny, if I'd known a concussion'd get me entrance to South's *sanctum sanctorum* (who'da thunkit, nearly three-and-a-half years of Latin and I finally find a use for it), I'd still wanna sit in the cafeteria. Jon Bales kept telling anyone who'd listen about me Technicolor-yawning on the referee (*It was totally volcanic—we're talking Mount St. Helens. The ref actually stopped the game so he could shower and change.*) and how Josh went batshit-crazy on Bob, earning himself what had to be a one-of-a-kind state record—a red card and immediate ejection from the game for spitting, unsportsmanlike conduct, violence, and swearing—all directed at a teammate.

The way Bales tells it, Coach decided Bob should sub for me. After Bob blew our lead, giving up four shots back to back, Josh lost it. He got right up in Bob's face and started shoving him around, screaming about how much better the team was when it had a *real* fag for a goalie. The problem with guys like Bob was they let in anything and everything. I guess Bob, trying to be a team player, said something about showing the Crusaders that we came to play. Not missing a beat, McCullough mouthed off, "Oh, yeah, Collins, you asshole, you came to play all right—with yourself in the shower." Then Josh spit in Bob's face, snatched his red card from the ref, and stormed off the field, saying that he should've joined the golf team four years ago, 'cuz at least in golf all the queers are rug-munchers.

After Bales shut his mouth, Marshall wanted to know if it was true I couldn't remember anything from Saturday (*wow, just like amnesia*), and then Bink complained about his Mom wanting to bring me chicken soup. (*She's whining, Neil, it's Jewish penicillin, and I said, Mom, he's got a concussion, not pneumonia.*) And Dana—Dana was as humorless as always. She berated me for trusting the neurologist and thinking I *only* had a concussion, because for all I knew, it could be a contusion, a hematoma. I could go from being fine one moment to suddenly stroking out and bleeding out of my eyes.

Trying to get to third-hour choir during passing period wasn't easy. After years of being the dork who even preschoolers would point and laugh at, I was suddenly, maybe not popular, but at least not invisible. I got *What's up?*s and *Dude, how's it hanging?*s from guys on the varsity basketball team. Chicks—and not just the fat ones who asked me to school dances, but ones Bink said he'd like to bang—tugged me into their fog of hairspray, perfume, and Binaca, wanting to know if I was okay. They'd heard from Bales that I, *oh, my God*, went into a coma right there on the field and, *can you believe it, almost totally died* in the hospital. And then, this was way too weird—*Have you ever, like, you know, tried* *doing it with a girl? Dana says some people with head injuries, like, get whole new personalities, you know?*

I ended up getting to choir late, but I wasn't worried. I'd just tell Mrs. Reed I'd felt a little light-headed before class and needed to sit.

The problem with choir, though, was wearing sunglasses and trying to navigate the dark corridor separating the entrance from the rest of the room. It wasn't easy. I felt my way through the dark, groping for the walls and trying not to trip over my own feet.

"Jesus," someone said as I staggered into the room, "it's true. Charlie's blind."

Mrs. Reed covered her mouth, trapping a short gasp; the tenors reeled backward, blinking wildly; a high-strung soprano, looking too much like a horror-movie chick about to take an axe to the head, dug her fingernails into her cheeks; but it was Rob who actually shocked me.

I kinda expected him to throw his head back in maniacal *muwahahahaha* laughter and greedily rub his hands together. It didn't happen. Rob's mouth was slack and his face went dead-people white, like some plug inside him had been pulled to drain his color. He dropped his sheet music. He gulped, his Adam's apple vanishing then barely reappearing. Rob seemed to be saying something, but his lips tripped on the words.

So it was one of those stupid, split-second daydreams, but how's this for a disconnect with reality:

Rob has one of those mom-with-her-kid-trapped-under-an-18-wheeler adrenaline rushes. He lets out this rafter-shaking, animal-dying howl, flails through the altos and sopranos crowded on the risers below him, his arms thrashing wildly, and rushes to me. He throws himself into me, a hand wrapping around my waist, the other gently cupping the base of

242

my head. He's crying, his face in my neck, whispering how sorry he is. He never meant to hurt me. Everything will be okay. We'll be together always, he promises between the sobs and gasps. We'll drop out of South, and hand-in-hand, we'll run from the chorus room to his car.

We'll move to Chicago. Find a cheap studio apartment. If he has to, he'll take some money from a trust left to him by some dead rich family member, maybe he can't get all the money, but he figures what he can get will be enough for a year's rent. The place—our place—won't be much. We won't be able to afford electricity at first, but we'll steal candles from churches and fancy nightclubs. The shower won't work and we'll sponge each other clean from the bathroom sink, playing this game where each of us kisses the spot on the other we like best.

Each night, we'll sit together on the queen-sized mattress on the kitchen floor, in nothing but our skivvies, eating from the carton of ham-fried rice we'll splurge on with what Rob will always say is the last of our cash. Miraculously, it never is. And feeling frisky, Rob will crawl over to me, and with chopsticks I've never figured out how to use, he'll grab the elastic band of my underwear, and tug it past my hipbone. I'll get hard and he'll ask if it's for him. I'll blush and nod, and then he'll roll on top of me, the two of us nipping at each other like puppies. Then, shy and tender all of a sudden, Rob'll ask if he can—and I'll kiss him, wrap my legs around him, my ankles in the small of his back. Afterward, he'll smooth my eyebrow with his thumb. I'll smile up at him and we'll laugh like we were drunk.

It wasn't until Mrs. Reed tapped her baton against the metal sheet music holder, ordering everyone to settle down, that I stopped daydreaming. The best thing, though, was Rob was looking at me like he still cared. But I gotta face it, he only seemed like he cared 'cuz that's what I wanted from him. Once he found out I wasn't blind and I wasn't gonna die, Rob didn't look at me again. I tried telling myself it didn't matter, but it pissed me off.

I wish I could just grow up and get over him, but I can't.

I gotta run. Mom's saying we need to meet up with Dad to see if there's anything we can do before the polls close.

Wednesday, November 7

Well, the big news, I guess, is that Dad won with a margin so wide that, even if he'd been running as a Democrat and not an Independent, the McHenry County Republican party can't whine that their rightful, ordained-by-God ascension to power was stolen from them by a vast left-wing conspiracy involving class warfare, race baiting, and entire cemeteries of registered voters magically punching ballots.

This morning there were a bunch of articles in the *Herald*, talking about how Dad's victory as an Independent was an "upset," which makes sense. It seems like adults are always bitching at election time about how there's no viable third-party candidates, but if they saw Dad's campaign headquarters last night, it'd be pretty clear why.

The restaurant where everyone had gathered to watch the returns—which, let's face it, were practically a footnote as far as Chicago TV producers and political reporters were concerned—was, without a doubt, an ecumenical clusterfuck. The Binkmeyers—Crystal Lake's self-appointed last bastion

244

of liberalism—were there, pushing petitions for McHenry County to make reparations to virtually every minority group that ever had a hangnail and thought they could pin the blame on the federal government; referendums on a woman's right to choose the nail polish for her mani and pedi while getting an abortion and microderm abrasion facial; and, of course, they were soliciting donations—AKA begging—to build a center for radical feminist, vegan, Wiccan house pets.

Believe it or not, Mr. and Mrs. B were tame compared to everyone else. There were the libertarians who—as best I can figure—were a bunch of self-employed, middle-aged, hydroponics and *High Times*, toke-'em-if-you've-got-'em white guys who couldn't stop bitching about how The Man kept them down; how the Constitution gave them the right to personally own more nukes than were banned in either SALT Treaty, but it didn't give the government the right to tax them—even if no taxes meant the local police force would basically be the equivalent of a group of lard-asses who couldn't qualify for the mall's rent-a-cop position. Another part of the crowd seemed to be either a) lost; b) looking for a place to keep warm; c) under the mistaken impression that there was a bus stop nearby; or d) looking for a more attractive place to die than their local assisted-living senior center. And last, there were the county's "don't ask, don't tell" closet case Democrats—the L.L. Bean-wearing, Republican-acting/-appearing liberals—who spent the night praying that if Dad won the election he wouldn't go mad with power and try to ban National Public Radio.

After being elbow-to-elbow with so many freaks for ten minutes, I was looking for any excuse to get the hell out of there, which is why I was glad when Dad's campaign manager—a short, severe woman who was all pearls and nylons—thrust a clipboard at me and "suggested" my time would be better spent drumming up votes at the train station.

Dad stared at her like she was one of those retreads who can recite the first thousand digits of pi, but can't work a knife and fork without stabbing herself in the forehead. Dad patted her head—actually, patted it—and "suggested" she take the rest of the night off.

"She's right," Mom said. "Somebody should be at the station. Charlie and I'll go hand out voter's guides."

"For what, Laura?" Dad asked, his hand circling Mom's waist. "So you can get frostbite? Look at him." Dad thrust his chin at me. "The kid doesn't want to stand outside freezing his nuts off, do you, Charlie?"

I didn't, but I was smart. I glanced at Dad's campaign manager. Her eyebrows double-stitched together and her bullfrogging gullet strained her necklace, threatening to machine-gun the room with cultured pearls. "Say 'yes,'" she mouthed silently, nose scrunched, razor teeth chewing the air. "Tell him you'll do it."

"I'll do it," I said, hands in my coat pockets. Dad's manager exhaled and her neck shrank from its DEFCON 1 proportions. I wouldn't be picking imitation-Tiffany's shrapnel out of my spleen.

"No one's doing anything. Whatever happens, happens."

"What?" the campaign manager asked. Her look was priceless—she was like a little kindergartener and Dad was this big bad man who'd come along, snatched the cocker spaniel puppy from her arms, squeezed it by the neck 'til its soft brown eyes popped out of its little puppy skull, and then handed her its limp and lifeless body. She blubbered.

Dad spent the next few hours "working" the room, which meant dragging me from table to table and alternating bragging about his family with hand kissing, baby shaking, and puckering-up-and-planting-a-big-wet-one on his donors' sphincters. Around eight, when the polls showed he was a shoe-in for state's attorney, Dad disappeared. A few minutes later, he came back, plucked a water glass from the nearest table, and rang its edge with a spoon.

"May I have your attention, please," Dad said. "I have an announcement."

The crowd turned, looking at Dad with smug smiles and wet-eyed expectancy. Arthritic fingers crossed, the gummy ends of cigars were pulled from thick lips. Some young no-girl's-gonna-make-me-put-my-Ding-Dong-in-her-Ho-Ho-'cuz-True-Love-Waits, home-schooled, there-was-*sooo*-nothing-gay-about-my-boy-parts-getting-tingly-when-I-practiced-mouth-to-mouth-on-Billy-for-my-merit-badge freak cheered.

"I wanted you all to know," continued Dad, "that I just got off the phone with my opponent, John Fisk. We had a friendly conversation, and"—Dad, total Easter ham that he is, paused to take a sip of water. You could practically hear the room mouthing, *And? And?*

"And I graciously accepted his concession. He also told me that he'll resign as assistant state's attorney by the end of the year to take a job in private practice."

People cheered, cheap champagne was popped, some geriatric made a pathetic attempt to toss confetti. Everybody was in a festive mood, but for some reason, I couldn't help thinking about Fisk. How much would it suck to have to call up the guy who just beat you, say, "Hi, I'm a loser," and pretend to be the bigger man when all you really wanted to do was crawl into bed, pull the covers over your head, and cry yourself to sleep listening to Cure albums?

Friday, November 9

Since Dad's big win, I've been wondering what would happen to Mr. Hunt. I finally asked Dad while he had me out practicing my driving.

"We're working on a way to drop the case in a way that the office can still save face, but doesn't expose the county to any potential lawsuits. Ideally, we'd like to say that upon closer review, the evidence doesn't support the charges and that we now have no reason to believe that Mr. Hunt did anything wrong."

"That wouldn't be so bad, would it?" I asked as I put the car into park.

"That's what I'm hoping. Maybe once it's all over, your friend, Rob, will get along better with his dad."

Saturday, November 10

So I turned eighteen today. Big deal. I don't feel any older. Don't look it either. I've still got only three pubic hairs, and it's not looking great for one of 'em. I'd tried tugging it the other day so that it'd grow out some more and I think I pulled it loose.

The Ps got me a computer for college. Yeah, they still won't let go of that bone. The thing is, they won't let me keep it in my room. They say it's so I don't lock myself away playing games on it, but it's not like I don't know the real reason it's staying downstairs in the family room. They're convinced I'm only going to use the thing to watch barely legal boys doing each other on lawn chairs, staircases, car hoods, bar stools, trampolines, wherever.

Who am I kidding? They're right.

Sunday, November 11

Rob and I actually talked at church today. And here's a shocker—our conversation didn't involve Rob tearing off my limbs and beating me to death with my own arms.

The whole morning was absolutely bizarre. When the service was over, Pastor Taylor locked himself in his office to watch the Bears-Falcons game, which absolutely pissed off the coffee klatch set. It was like they wanted him to fawn over their strudel, telling each of them that theirs was the best and that, because of it, surely, Jesus wanted them for a sunbeam, but next week He'd prefer something low-cal. A spare tire wasn't going to make His time on the cross go by any easier.

Since people knew that Dad wouldn't be hitting them up for votes or campaign donations any time soon, it was almost like the Stewart family had shed its pariah status. Folks came up to talk to Dad and not out of the usual are-you-happy-now-Lord?-see-I'm-talking-to-him sense of Christian charity. Mom and Dad smiled, shook hands, and accepted congratulations. The way they kept yapping made me realize that you actually could die of boredom. I asked Mom if I could be excused. Before I left, I noticed Mr. Hunt getting up from the pew where he'd been sitting alone. He walked toward where Rob'd been sitting with his uncle. Rob backed away and his uncle, Chris, stepped between them.

"Rob," Mr. Hunt said.

"Give it time, Paul," Chris said. "He'll come around."

I ended up in Luther Hall, staring at my reflection in the Boy Scout trophy case. With the exception of the zit that was on the end of my nose, I didn't look too bad. If I tilted my head the right way, my ears didn't seem so damn big and, in the right light, it looked like I had a little bit of peach fuzz on my cheeks. I may have still looked like a kid, but I didn't feel like one. I felt all in-between, grown-up and scared; kinda cute, kinda awkward; maybe a little smarter, but still pretty damn dumb.

"I called you, you know. When you weren't in school."

I turned. Rob was in the doorway, hands in his pants pockets, looking at his feet. He looked older. I don't know why, but I hadn't expected Rob to talk to me. My chest tightened.

"The other day, after school, that was me. When your Dad answered, I freaked. I said I was Josh."

I leaned against the trophy case of Eagle Scout awards, wishing Mom'd let me wear the Ray-Bans. (*Oh, no, not in church with those things!*) I'd've killed to slip 'em on and act like I was too cool to care. Rob looked like he wanted more from me, but wasn't sure what. I nodded.

"And if I answered?"

Rob's cheeks burned pink. "I hope I'd've said I was sorry for everything."

I almost told him he could say it now. You know, say he'd do anything to get me back. I didn't. Something told me whatever Rob said wouldn't matter. Maybe I was just tired, maybe it was 'cuz my painkillers were wearing off or maybe it was just 'cuz I didn't care anymore.

"Look, Charlie," Rob said, grinding his shoe along the tiles like he was stubbing out a cigarette, "I'm sorry for going off on you about not saying anything about the pills, about my mom. It wasn't your fault."

I nodded and sucked in my lower lip. It was blubbering.

"My dad and Uncle Chris are still trying to convince me the overdose was an accident. I keep telling myself I've got to believe it."

"How come?" I asked.

"Because, I don't see how you could do something so shitty to someone you love."

When I didn't say anything and Rob realized I was probably thinking about all the shitty things he'd done to me, he mumbled that there wasn't any school tomorrow—Veterans Day—and said, "Maybe we could hang out."

"Maybe," I said. I could tell he knew I didn't mean it.

"Guess I'll see ya," I said.

"Yeah," Rob said. He rubbed a knuckle across an eye, then shook his shoulders, his shirt cuffs popping from his suit coat.

Rob walked away, but when he was gone, I didn't feel better. I don't know why, but I had it in my head that if I made Rob feel like shit, then I'd feel this rush or something. I didn't. I felt empty, like there was this warm hollow in my chest. I dunno. Maybe that's the way it is with love. Maybe it's about wanting something even when it's gone.

Wednesday, November 14

I can't believe it. I actually made it through the entire day without jerking the gherkin while thinking about Rob once. Now if I could only stop molesting the Binkmeyer boys in my imagination. Fat chance. They're too hot.

Rob called today. We didn't talk long, mostly 'cuz having to talk to him or be around him is still too weird for me. He thinks we can still be friends, but I'm not so sure. I like the guy and all, but . . .

Rob says he and his dad are in family therapy to try to work things out.

Saturday, November 17

Here we go again. I'm going to marry a punk rock boy from Central High School. I'm in love. Okay, it's *way* too soon for that. It's more like I'm in lust. Well, not the I'm-going-to-hide-in-the-bushes-with-a-pair-of-binoculars-and-watch-you-undress-so-please-do-some-naked-pull-ups creepy kind of lust. More of the humina-humina-go-ahead-and-lick-my-neck kind.

Last week, Bink basically ditched me on my eighteenth—get this, he actually chose dumping baby-batter in Dana over hanging out with me and the Ps and pretending that the bone-dry Duncan Hines cake decorated with little plastic soccer players was cool. To make it up to me, he decided he was taking me to see The Lawrence Arms at the Metro last night. We ended up taking the train into Chicago 'cuz, even though it was an all-ages show, Bink stupidly thought the fake ID he bought online would help him score some booze. If you ask me, he wasted a hundred bucks.

Anyhow, the train car we were in was mostly empty, so Bink and I flipped one of the seatbacks around and spread out. Between swigs from a bottle of Grape Crush that was really camouflaging the Mogen David he'd lifted from Mrs. B's pantry, Bink wouldn't shut up and kept yammering about how the show was gonna be awesome, how their latest album was brilliant—*frickin' brilliant*—how after the show we should go to Uptown to see the building where the band got its name. Up until he said something about Dana doing this kinky thing with her throat that made missing my birthday worth it (*there's an image I wish I could sandpaper off my brain*), I hadn't been paying too much attention to him. I'd been staring at this guy sitting toward the front of the train car with his back to us.

He seemed to be about our age—messy, dishwater-blond hair, skinny neck, brown hoodie. I figured he had to go to Central. Trust me, I'm such a perv that I don't think there's a guy at South who I couldn't recognize by the back of his head. And from behind this guy seemed like a total hottie.

I must've been drooling or Bink suddenly inherited his mother's "amazing" powers of perception (*Charlie, you will not die alone. Look at Montgomery Clift—he was a big Hollywood sex symbol before Elizabeth Taylor had to fish two of his teeth from his throat after a car accident, and he was*

253

with his partner until he died. Then again, he's probably not the best example. By the end he was completely washed-up.) 'cuz when Bink saw me staring at the guy, he shook his head.

"We need to get you a boyfriend," Bink said, a purple circle staining his lips.

The guy in front of us turned around and had a totally sweet, kinda scruffy face, greenish eyes, and one of those grins English teachers like to call "puckish"—all you-can't-prove-it-was-me mischief. I blushed, feeling my ears burn. He smiled wider. I slid down in the seat and wished that I could disappear.

We ended up playing eye-tag the rest of the train ride. In the window's reflection, he'd catch me looking at him, smile a bit, and then turn around to look at me. I'd look away, and thirty seconds later it'd start up again.

"Enough with the flirting, Charlie," Bink said, kicking my foot and groaning. "Go talk to him already."

"He's probably not into guys."

"Trust me, dude. He's into guys." Bink rolled his eyes, then shouted, "My friend thinks you're hot." Embarrassed, I slid low in my seat so I couldn't see him or his reflection.

When we pulled into the station, I made sure I got the hell off the train first. There was no way I was gonna risk Bink "accidentally" forcing me to bump into Mr. Totally Sweet Face or worse, offer to get us a hotel room somewhere.

"You're such a total wuss," Bink said as he lit a cigarette while we waited for a cab to take us to Wrigleyville.

I was about to tell him that I wasn't a wuss, it's just that my idea of a good time didn't involve hitting on strangers on a train, when Mr. Totally Sweet Face came up to us and

254

asked Bink if he could bum a square. Bink gave me a see-I-told-you-so wink that made me want to slug him. As soon as Mr. Totally Sweet Face lit the cigarette and took a puff, he started hacking like he was coughing up both lungs and his entire ribcage.

"I don't really smoke," he said, letting the Marlboro fall to the curb. Bink body-checked me with his hip. I was about ready to kill him. "So you guys are going to see the Larry Arms, too? I heard you on the train."

"Yeah," Bink said, "wanna share a cab with us?"

"Cool."

I got stuck in the middle, mostly 'cuz it gave Bink the chance to spread out and push me into Mr. Totally Sweet Face, whose real name was Ben. When my thigh touched his, he didn't move away. He smiled and eased his against mine. Ben and Bink did most of the talking. I was too busy trying to keep Mr. Five-Incher from deciding to interrupt the conversation by making an appearance. Ben was a senior at Central, he'd been to all the all-ages Lawrence Arms shows in Chicago, even the guitarist's solo show last summer. He wasn't into labels, he said, but he was into *me*. Cheesy, I know, but I still loved it.

The show was good, but the best part was the train ride back to Crystal Lake. Ben sat with us and he ended up falling asleep with his head resting on my shoulder. That had to make Bink gag.

Ben and I traded numbers. Thank God he had some paper, 'cuz I was gonna have him write his digits on my palm, which wouldn't have done me any good—especially after all the hand-to-glans combat in the bathroom. We're supposed to hang out sometime this week.

Sunday, November 18

Ben called. I'm supposed to meet him at Colonial tonight. I was too embarrassed to tell him that I don't have my driver's license yet and there's no way I'm asking Mom or Dad to drive me to a date. Guess that means I'll be biking across town and it's frickin' freezing out.

I *sooo* need to get my license.

Friday, November 23

I've caved. It's the day after Thanksgiving and I've been working on a personal essay for my college application. I'm only doing it 'cuz the Ps say they won't take me for my driver's test—even Dad thinks I'll pass this time—unless I promise to "at least try to get into college."

So here it is:

My name is Charles James Stewart, II. Charles the Second. My friends call me Charlie . . . but this isn't about them. This is supposed to be about me telling you how wonderful I am, what a great addition to your student body I'll be, and how some day I'll be this famous alumni who you can brag about in your brochures and hit up for cash.

And we both know I'm writing this (read: lying through my teeth) to convince you I'm a cross between Mother Teresa and JFK. You're supposed to be impressed that during my summer vacation junior year, I organized and presided over a new organization, Wet Nurses for Bangladesh, for which I personally convinced pregnant unwed teens to spare their families from shame and embarrassment by putting their own bastard children up for adoption and then arranging for them to breastfeed third-world orphans. I was a member of choir, speech, student government, boys and girls swimming, football, baseball, girls lacrosse, Students Against Drunk Drivers, Students Against Young Christian Athletes, and National Honor Society.

I was also the writer-slash-director-slash-executive producer of Nutcracker!: Mongoloids in Tutus, *which featured a cast of elementary schoolchildren with Down Syndrome whose plucky, can-do spirit more than made up for the drool on their leotards. The critics raved, saying that the performance was a triumph of the human spirit in the face of adversity and ill-fitting costumes. Even* The Chicago Reader—*and they hate everything—wrote, "Under Stewart's masterful direction, this reviewer couldn't help but be moved—if only to stifle his own impolite and uncomfortable laughter."*

Then, of course, I'm supposed to write about how I couldn't have done any of this if it weren't for 1) my strong faith in God; 2) a tough-love teacher who

took the needle out of my arm and inspired me to
stop shooting heroin and read Wordsworth and Keats;
*3) the support of my dirt-farming parents (*Yes, they
actually farmed dirt until one night a horrible tornado
blew away the whole season's crop.*); or 4) my own*
battle with masturbation, which I'm hoping your col-
lege's men's gymnastics or wrestling teams can cure
me of. I plan on being a big athletic supporter.

But before I write anymore, let me ask you some-
thing: What's the point of this, really? We both know
none of it's the real me—or true. Isn't it a bit ridicu-
lous to think an eighteen-year-old kid's got any an-
swers, any real sense of who he is? Isn't that why I'm
supposed to be coming to you? To figure it all out? I
mean, what'd be the point otherwise?

I do know this: There's stuff I'm not proud of, but
I think I'm better for what I've been through. And, yeah,
maybe I haven't had to overcome anything whackin'
big like polio, a wicked overbite, a prison sentence of
two years' hard labor, court-ordered testosterone in-
jections, or filial cannibalism. The best I've got for you
is that after the last few months I know more about
me than I did before. And let's face it, that's a pretty
big accomplishment.

Yep, it needs work.

What do I think my chances are? My fingers aren't crossed
and I'm not holding my breath. But I'm actually kinda happy
for once.

Christ, what am I supposed to do now?

THE SCREWED-UP LIFE OF CHARLIE THE SECOND

DREW FERGUSON

ABOUT THIS GUIDE

The suggested questions are included to enhance your group's reading of Drew Ferguson's *The Screwed-Up Life of Charlie the Second.*

Discussion Questions

1) As a novel, *The Screwed-Up Life of Charlie the Second* is told entirely through Charlie's journal. Does the journal form allow Charlie to reveal more than first-person narrators in other books? What are some examples of the things that Charlie reveals or discusses that main characters in other books avoid? Are there any moments in the book in which Charlie censors himself? Are there moments when he exaggerates?

2) Throughout the book, Charlie writes explicitly about his sexual fantasies and experiences. Do you think he's ever too explicit? Why or why not? What do Charlie's graphic descriptions of his sexual fantasies and activities reveal about him? When Charlie writes about losing his virginity, he details the wide range of emotions that he experiences. What are they and do they seem authentic?

3) At the beginning of the book, Charlie writes that his father, whom he's still calling First at the time, often refers to Charlie as "smartass." Is Charlie truly a smartass all the time? Are there moments when his sarcasm might be a defense mechanism? At what moments in the novel does Charlie stop being sarcastic and reveal his true feelings?

4) Since the novel is in the form of Charlie's journal, we only get to see the people in Charlie's life through his eyes. Are his opinions of his friends and family fair or unfair? Are his opinions about the people in his life 100 percent reliable?

5) Charlie and First have a difficult relationship for much of the book. When, if ever, is Charlie too hard on First? How does their relationship change over the course of the novel?

How is Charlie's relationship with First different from and similar to Charlie's relationship with his mother?

6) It's been said that there are only two types of stories— "a man goes on a quest" and "a stranger comes to town." In the first chapter, Charlie meets Rob Hunt, whose family has just moved to Charlie's hometown of Crystal Lake; and Rob, in many respects, changes the direction of Charlie's life. At the same time, Charlie is on his own quest for self-discovery. In what ways is *The Screwed-Up Life of Charlie the Second* a "stranger comes to town" story? A "man goes on a quest" story? Can it be both?

7) In many of his journal entries, Charlie compares and contrasts the romantic relationships of the people in his life. What do you think he learns about the various types of love from them? Does he apply these lessons to his relationship with Rob or ignore them? Charlie says in his journal that he's in love with Rob, but also writes that he loves his best friend Bink, and he is frequently jealous of Bink's girlfriend Dana? Does he love Rob and Bink differently? What type of partner do you think would be better for Charlie—one like Rob or Bink? Why?

8) At one point in the book, Charlie expresses the desire to be "human wallpaper." Is he being truthful? Does Charlie really want to blend in or does he want to stand out while being accepted for who he is?

9) Charlie mocks just about everyone he comes in contact with—stoners at school, sensitive goth girl poets, rural rednecks, lesbians until graduation and closet-case varsity jocks, his parents, the old, the mentally handicapped, give-peace-a-chance flower children "gone to seed," ROTC Nazi gun nuts, and even himself. How many of his views are affected by his age? His personality? His own experience with being mocked?

10) By the end of the book, most of the characters have made their own decisions as to whether Mr. Hunt, Rob's dad, played a role in his wife's death, but there's no definitive evidence introduced in the book to show whether her death was an accidental overdose or an assisted suicide. How do each of the characters come to his or her own conclusion about Paul Hunt's innocence or guilt? Do you believe Paul Hunt intentionally killed Rob's mother? Why or why not?

11) The book begins and ends with the personal essay Charlie is writing for his college applications. What do the two versions of the essay show about Charlie? What about his life is or isn't screwed up at the end of the book?